GENDERED BODY

TECHNOLOGIES
OF THE
GENDERED BODY

Reading Cyborg Women

Anne Balsamo

Duke University Press

Durham and London

Third printing, 1999
© 1996 Duke University Press
Printed in the United States of America on acid-free paper ∞
Typeset in Sabon by Keystone Typesetting, Inc.
Library of Congress Cataloging-in-Publication Data
appear on the last printed page of this book.

CONTENTS

※

FIGURES

✳

ACKNOWLEDGMENTS

✸

This project, begun as a dissertation in 1988, benefited from the insight and encouragement of many friends and teachers at the University of Illinois at Champaign-Urbana and elsewhere. My gratitude to Larry Grossberg, Norm Denzin, and Cary Nelson is far ranging. They each were instrumental in helping me keep my focus on the project during times of anxiety and uncertainty. Norm first suggested the topic; Larry guided the development of my theoretical framework. Cary Nelson served as a role model of a passionate scholar. Visits to U of I from Ruth Bleier, Donna Haraway, and Catherine Hall offered me the opportunity to discuss my work with other feminist scholars and teachers interested in similar topics. Many others were helpful at various moments along the way: Jan Radway, Jim Berlin, Andrew Ross, and Cheryl Cole. Karen Ford, Brad Wegrich, and Lana Rakow were there in the beginning. Midway through I received generous intellectual support from friends and colleagues at Illinois State University: Jeffrey Deshell, Victoria Harris, Ron Strickland, Deborah Wilson, and Curtis White. Since 1991, I have enjoyed the intellectual camaraderie of my colleagues at Georgia Tech: Richard Grusin, Alan Rauch, Stuart Moulthrop, Philip Auslander, Jay Bolter, Carol Colatrella, Ken Knoespel, Terry Harpold, and Rebecca Merrens. In unusual ways, my work has improved within the emotionally "charged" atmosphere we work in at Tech. My thanks also to those who helped me to finish: Libby Cates-Robinson, Robinette Kennedy, Kim Loudermilk, Mary Hocks, and especially my husband, David White.

There were several people involved during the entire process to whom I owe a great deal of gratitude for their words of wisdom, intellectual and critical insight, and unflagging emotional support: Keya Ganguly, Georgeanne Runblad, Angela Wall, Carolyne White, Charles Acland, and

John Erni. Finally, but not least, I want to thank the two people most centrally involved with my thinking, writing, and emotional processing during the development of this project: Paula Treichler and Michael Greer. Paula lent her support, intellectually and emotionally, at a critical point in my graduate education, opening the door to feminism and feminist theory at exactly the right time; she kept me from dropping out of graduate school in the face of overt harassment. Her scholarly work is a cherished source of intellectual inspiration. Even more, her friendship and encouragement have been life-sustaining. Michael Greer was involved in this book's production from the inside at the very beginning. Although it wasn't always easy going, I owe him a great deal of appreciation for his abiding belief in my work and my talents. He nurtured my embryonic sense of the project and discussed every aspect of it with care and critical insight. I thank him for his thoughtfulness and support.

Sections of this book have been published elsewhere: an earlier version of chapter 1 was published as "Reading Cyborgs Writing Feminism," *Communication* 10 (1988) 331–344. Excerpts from chapter 2 were published in "Feminist Bodybuilding," *Women, Sport, and Culture,* ed. Susan Birrill and Cheryl Cole (Champaign, IL: Human Kinetics Pub., 1994) 341–352. I would like to thank Susan Greendorfer and John Loy for their comments on a very early draft of chapter 2; Kim Sharp provided valuable insider information about female bodybuilding. Chapter 3 was originally published as "On the Cutting Edge: Cosmetic Surgery and the Technological Production of the Gendered Body," *Camera Obscura* 28 (1992): 207–237; Lisa Cartwright offered several helpful comments on this piece. Chapter 5, "The Virtual Body in Cyberspace," was published in the *Journal of Research in Technology and Philosophy* 13 (1993): 119–139. Joan Rothschild offered insightful editorial advice, and several colleagues responded to an early draft; Glenn Barry offered valuable insider information about Internet and UNIX operations. Chapter 6, "Feminism for the Incurably Informed," was published in a special issue of *South Atlantic Quarterly* called "The Discourse of Cyberculture," 92.4 (Fall 1993): 681–712. I thank Mark Dery, guest editor for that issue, for his feedback and encouragement.

For help with the production of the book, I would like to thank Heather Kelley for constructing the index, Pam Morrison for her careful editing, and Reynolds Smith for his continued support and encouragement.

TECHNOLOGIES
OF THE
GENDERED BODY

INTRODUCTION

✺

In a special preview of the year 2000 and beyond, the February 1989 issue of *LIFE* magazine (figure 1) featured an article called "Visions of Tomorrow," which includes a report on the replacement body parts that are already available in the 1990s — such as pacemakers, elbow and wrist joints, and tendons and ligaments — and those we can expect in the future.[1] We are told how succeeding generations of artificial "devices" will be even more complex than the ones we have today, aided by research in microelectronics and tissue engineering. For example, glass eyes will be replaced with electronic retinas, pacemakers with bionic hearts, and use of the already high-tech insulin dispenser will soon become obsolete in favor of an organically grown biohybrid system that could serve as an artificial pancreas. The artificial reconstruction of the human body in parts and pieces has spawned numerous business ventures. Robert Jarvik, the "father" of the Jarvik 7 artificial heart, is president of a company called Symbion — a name combining "symbiosis" and "bionic" — which supports research projects and products that work on the interface of the body and technology. Jarvik's artificial heart was developed as part of his research with the Humana Foundation, a nonprofit organization that in 1987 reported revenues in excess of $3 billion.[2]

Bodybuilding, colored contact lenses, liposuction, and other technological innovations have subtly altered the dimensions and markers of what counts as a "natural" body. Even as techno-science provides the realistic possibility of replacement body parts, it also enables a fantastic dream of immortality and control over life and death. And yet, such beliefs about the technological future "life" of the body are complemented

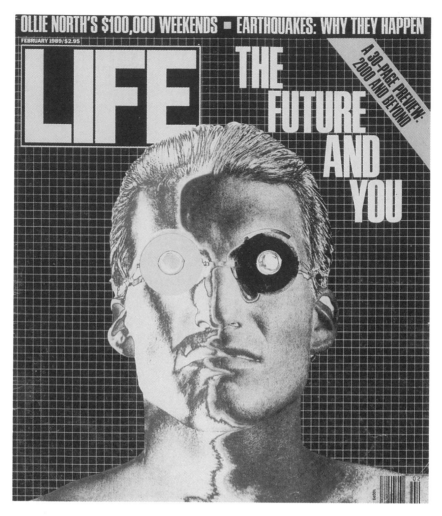

Figure 1. *LIFE* magazine cover featuring the special report "Visions of Tomorrow" (February 1989). Photograph by Duane Michals.

by a palpable fear of death and annihilation from uncontrollable and spectacular body threats: exotic new forms of viruses, radon contamination, flesh-eating bacteria. Although the popularization of new body technologies disseminates new hopes and dreams of corporeal reconstruction and physical immortality, it also represses and obfuscates our awareness of new strains on and threats to the material body.

This book describes a contemporary cultural conjuncture in which the body and technology are conjoined in a literal sense, where machines assume organic functions and the body is materially redesigned through the application of newly developed technologies. The events I examine here are parts of programs and strategies of inscription and rationalization that operate on the flesh of human bodies. As such, they are examples of the exercise of scientific biopower and are part of the network of relations that Donna Haraway identifies as the "informatics of domination." That is, these events signal the way in which the body is produced, inscribed, replicated, and often disciplined in postmodernity.

In one sense, my intent is to contribute to the development of a "thick perception" of the body in contemporary culture from a feminist standpoint.[3] For Michel Feher this process of perception involves analyzing the "different modes of construction of the human body." In "Of Bodies and Technologies," he asserts that the history of the body is

> neither a history of scientific knowledge about the body nor a history of the ideologies that (mis)represent the body. Rather it is a history of "body building," of the different modes of construction of the human body. The body perceived in this way is not a reality to be uncovered in a positivistic description of an organism nor is it a transhistorical set of needs and desires to be freed from an equally transhistorical form of repression. This body is instead a reality constantly produced, an effect of techniques promoting specific gestures and postures, sensations and feelings. Only in tracing these modes of its construction can one arrive at a thick perception of the present "state of the body." (159)

Accordingly, "thick perception" is a Foucauldian technique for understanding the ways in which the body is conceptualized and articulated within different cultural discourses. To think of the body as a social construction and not as a natural object provokes a deceptively simple question: how is the body, as a "thing of nature," transformed into a "sign of culture"? The works I examine in this book begin with the assumption that "the body" is a social, cultural, and historical production: "production" here means both product and process. As a *product,* it is the material embodiment of ethnic, racial, and gender identities, as well as a staged performance of personal identity, of beauty, of health (among other things). As a *process,* it is a way of knowing and marking the world, as well as a way of knowing and marking a "self."

More specifically, through a combination of close readings (of science fiction, films, and other popular media, as well as other texts of everyday life) and institutional analyses, I examine representations of the gendered body in U.S. culture during the 1980s and into the early 1990s. The process of elaborating an informed "perception" of the body in contemporary culture must simultaneously abstract a discourse of the body and construct an interpretation of it. "Reading" as a cultural and interpretive practice is the central mechanism of my discursive production. But what I read are not simply textual or media *representations* of the gendered body, but more specifically cultural *practices* of "making the body gendered."[4]

I begin with the understanding that the fundamental unity connecting distinct types of texts is not an empirical "fact" to be proven, but rather a code to be elaborated. Furthermore, such master codes are not transcendental "meanings," but rather are constructed, historically specific systems of understanding — that is, what I understand as culturally determined reading practices. Elaboration of the code involves a process of mediation or, as Fredric Jameson describes it, "the process of transcoding," through which the relationships between types of objects or texts are articulated. Any given text within a discursive system is a symbolic enactment of the cultural preoccupations of a particular historical conjunction. The relation of texts to one another is dialectical in that the intelligibility of any isolated work or text is always dependent upon the discourse within which it "makes sense" at the same time that the text in part constructs that very discourse. The act of reading as "making a discourse apparent" is meant to suggest an active practice of perception that has been determined in specific ways; I have been unconsciously trained, more consciously taught, cajoled, and ambushed in my efforts to decipher the cultural construction of the gendered body in various textual forms. This is to say that although this project is thoroughly grounded in contemporary body scholarship, it is not a reading that springs fully formed from the current moment as if there existed a singularly unified discourse to read or, relatedly, a singular body to write.[5]

Instead, I focus on a continuum of discourses, which includes the popular cultures of the body as well as scholarly works of body theory. In doing so, I read as a student trained in theories of interpretation as well as a subject addressed by these discourses. By the end, I offer a situated reading of these discourses of the body and technology in contemporary culture, a reading that is marked by my history as a working-class subject — who read to escape — and my present as a feminist scholar and white, middle-class academic — who reads because she's "incurably informed" (see chapter 6).

The examples I discuss, taken from the media of everyday life (newspapers, advertisements, television programs, magazines), signal ways in which the "natural" body has been dramatically refashioned through the application of new technologies of corporeality. These media examples announce the collapse of the temporal distance between the present and a science fictional future in which bionic bodies are commonplace. Although some scholars believe that biotechnology is actually an ancient practice, others identify it as emerging during the past half century, dating it from 1953 and the discovery of the DNA structure.[6] What is less contestable, though, is the fact that by the end of the 1980s the idea of the merger of the biological with the technological has infiltrated the imagination of Western culture, where the "technological human" has become a familiar figuration of the subject of postmodernity. For whatever else it might imply, this merger relies on a reconceptualization of the human body as a "techno-body," a boundary figure belonging simultaneously to at least two previously incompatible systems of meaning — "the organic/ natural" and "the technological/cultural." At the point at which the body is reconceptualized not as a fixed part of nature, but as a boundary concept, we witness an ideological tug-of-war between competing systems of meaning, which include and in part define the material struggles of physical bodies.

Techno-bodies are healthy, enhanced, and fully functional — more real than real. New body technologies are often promoted and rationalized as life-enhancing and even lifesaving. Often obscured are the disciplining and surveillant consequences of these technologies — in short, the biopolitics of technological formations. In our hypermediated technoculture, body awareness is technologically amplified such that we know not only what we do, but also how, why, and with what consequences. Modern medical discourse encourages us to monitor consumption of, among other things, sugar, caffeine, salt, fat, cholesterol, nicotine, alcohol, steroids, sunlight, narcotics, barbiturates, and over-the-counter medications such as aspirin. Consumption is monitored technologically through the use of such devices as electronic scales, sugar-diabetes tests, blood pressure machines, fat calipers. A range of new visualization techniques contribute to the fragmentation of the body into organs, fluids, and gene codes, which in turn promotes a self-conscious self-surveillance, whereby the body becomes an object of intense vigilance and control. This "know your body" obsession manifests itself in different ways in contemporary U.S. culture — for example, in the cultlike observance of practices of personal hygiene, manic fears of death through contamination, and diseases of body image.[7] Such obsessions are part of a cultural apparatus of body surveillance that also includes practices of random urine testing among high school teenagers and adult workers, covert blood testing for HIV, and genetic fingerprinting.[8] Aided by a host of new tests and devices, anonymous "health" guardians (often appointed by the state) monitor intrauterine fetal blood composition to determine the possibility of cocaine-addicted infants. Fractured body parts are taken up as elements in the construction of cultural identities—agent of infection, cocaine mother, drug user—so that, as unknowing subjects of a disembodied technological gaze, our bodies betray us. Nowhere to hide from our bodies ourselves, we have no other choice but to comply and live cleanly; docile creatures practice safe sex or self-destruct.

Technologies of the Gendered Body

When the human body is fractured into organs, fluids, and genetic codes, what happens to gender identity? When the body is fractured into functional parts and molecular codes, where is gender located? What is the relationship between reconstructed body parts and gender identity? Images such as the *LIFE* magazine illustration of the "future body" show how male and female bodies are constructed differently with respect to their reproductive and sexual functions.[9] The replaceable body pictured in the *LIFE* article is gendered through the inclusion of photographs of plastic penile implants and the plastic nonfunctional testicle (figure 2). It is certainly ironic that although the article speculates about a future when "a Sears catalogue of body options" will be widely available, the one body prosthesis *currently* available through the Sears catalogue is not pictured—the female breast form (figure 3).[10] Although its symbolic and ultimately hegemonic function has been sharply criticized, this nonfunctional prosthesis is widely used by women who have had radical mastectomies.[11] Since the *LIFE* photograph includes other body prostheses that are neither implanted (an arm-hand device, for example) nor functional (the plastic testicle), the exclusion of the artificial breast form, which is also not implanted and nonfunctional, subtly reveals the intended gender of the future body. Obliquely referred to in the article but not pictured in the *LIFE* photograph, the female body is signified through a reference to the development of an artificial uterus. This association between the female body and the uterus or the womb signals the dominant cultural

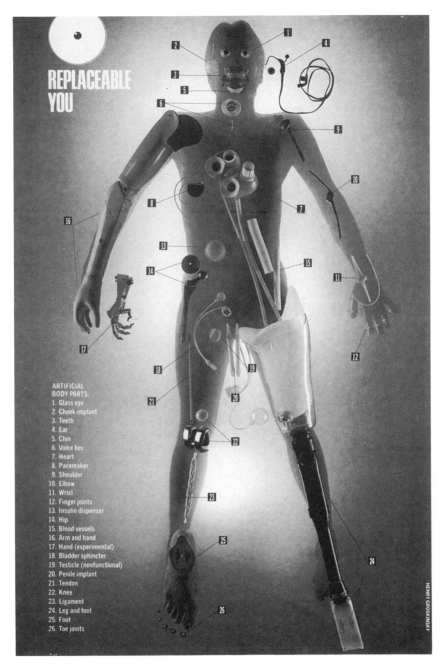

Figure 2. "Replaceable You," a miscellany of replacement body parts. From *LIFE* magazine's special report "Visions of Tomorrow" (February 1989). Photograph by Henry Groskinsky.

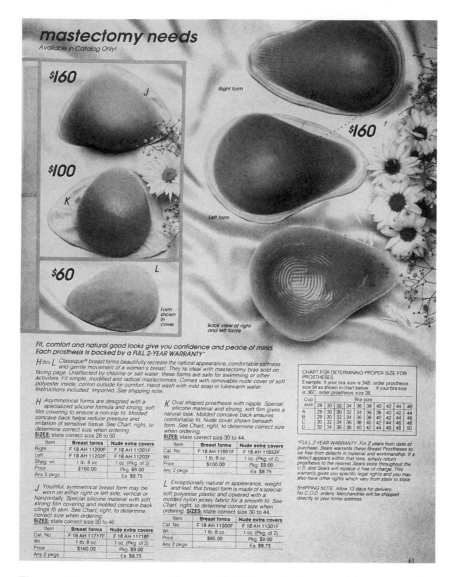

Figure 3. Postmastectomy products available from the Sears Health Care Specialog "Health Care Merchandise" (Sears, Roebuck and Co., 1988), p. 61.

definition of the female body as primarily a reproductive body. Such a metonymic relationship is far from innocent, though. In this future vision, the male body is marked by the sign of a full-bodied person whereas the female body is marked only by an artificial uterus; such significations offer an ominous warning about the imaginary place of women in the technological future. The question becomes, though, how do we interpret the meaning of such cultural projections?

Gender, like the body, is a boundary concept. It is at once related to physiological sexual characteristics of the human body (the natural order of the body) and to the cultural context within which that body "makes sense."[12] The widespread technological refashioning of the "natural" human body suggests that gender too would be ripe for reconstruction. Advances in reproductive technology already decouple the act of procreation from the act of sexual intercourse. Laparoscopy has played a critical role in the assessment of fetal development, with the attendant consequence that the "fetal body" has been metaphorically (and sometimes literally) severed from its natural association with the female body and is now proclaimed to be the new and primary obstetric patient. What effects do these technological developments have on cultural enactments of gender? As is often the case when seemingly stable boundaries are displaced by technological innovation (human/artificial, life/death, nature/culture), other boundaries are more vigilantly guarded. Indeed, the gendered boundary between male and female is one border that remains heavily guarded despite new technologized ways to rewrite the physical body in the flesh. So it appears that while the body has been recoded within discourses of biotechnology and medicine as belonging to an order of culture rather than of nature, gender remains a naturalized marker of human identity.

Despite the technological possibilities of body reconstruction, in the discourses of biotechnology the female body is persistently coded as the cultural sign of the "natural," the "sexual," and the "reproductive," so that the womb, for example, continues to signify female gender in a way that reinforces an essentialist identity for the female body as the maternal body. In this sense, an apparatus of gender organizes the power relations manifest in the various engagements between bodies and technologies. I offer the phrase "technologies of the gendered body" as a way of describing such interactions between bodies and technologies.[13] Gender, in this schema, is *both* a determining cultural condition and a social consequence of technological deployment. The following chapters illuminate the ways in which contemporary discourses of technology rely on a logic of binary gender-identity as an underlying organizational framework. This underlying structure both enables and constrains our engagement with new technologies. In many cases, the *primary* effect of this technological engagement is the reproduction of a traditional logic of binary gender-identity which significantly limits the revisionary potential of new technologies.

The construction of a boundary between nature and culture serves several ideological purposes. Most notably, it provides a rhetorical framework for the establishment of a hierarchy of culture over nature. This socially constructed hierarchy functions to reassure a technologically overstimulated imagination that culture/man will prevail in his encounters with nature. The role of the gendered body in this boundary setting process is significant; it serves as the site where anxieties about the "proper order of things" erupt and are eventually managed ideologically. Investigating the interaction between material bodies and new technologies illuminates the work of ideology-in-progress, where new technologies are invested with cultural significance in ways that augment dominant cultural narratives. The meaning of these new technologies is produced by a complex arrangement or articulation of texts, narratives, institutional structures, economic forces, bodily practices, and other material effects.[14] These effects, in turn, establish a set of possibilities for the further development and deployment of new technologies. Possibilities shape ongoing ideological struggles.

As Judy Wajcman reminds us in *Feminism Confronts Technology*: "technology is more than a set of physical objects or artefacts. It also fundamentally embodies a culture or set of social relations made up of certain sorts of knowledge, beliefs, desires, and practices."[15] My aim here is to describe how certain technologies are, to borrow Wajcman's phrase, ideologically shaped by the operation of gender interests and, consequently, how they serve to reinforce traditional gendered patterns of power and authority. When Judith Butler describes the gendered body as "a set of repeated acts within a highly rigid regulatory frame that congeal over time to produce the appearance of substance," she also suggests a way to understand the process whereby "naturalized" gender identities are socially and culturally reproduced as part of new technological formations.[16] This is to say that in investigating the gendered aspects of new technological formations, I have tried to specify the forms of institutionalization that support the use of these technologies and the system of differentiation that structures a person's participation, rights, and responsibilities vis-à-vis such technologies. Written as stand-alone essays, the following chapters each describe a different technology that functions culturally as the frame or—as seen most clearly in the case of virtual reality applications—as the *stage* for the enactment of gender.

Chapter 1: Reading Cyborgs, Writing Feminism

This chapter begins with a review of famous cyborgs in popular culture. The cyborg image can be read in two ways: as a coupling between a human being and an electronic or mechanical apparatus, or as the identity of organisms embedded in a cybernetic information system. In the first sense, the coupling between human and machine is located within the body itself—the boundary between the material body and the artificial machine is surgically redrawn. In the second sense, however, the boundary between the body and technology is socially inscribed, at once indistinct and arbitrary, but no less functional. A cyborg body, as Gregory Bateson might argue, "is not bounded by the skin but includes all external pathways along which information can travel."[17] Cyborgs are hybrid entities that are neither wholly technological nor completely organic, which means that the cyborg has the potential not only to disrupt persistent dualisms that set the natural body in opposition to the technologically recrafted body, but also to refashion our thinking about the theoretical construction of the body as both a material entity and a discursive process. These bodies are multiply constituted parts of cybernetic systems—what we now recognize as social and informational networks. Cyborg bodies are definitionally transgressive of a dominant culture order, not so much because of their "constructed" nature, but rather because of the indeterminacy of their hybrid design. The cyborg provides a framework for studying gender identity as it is technologically crafted simultaneously from the matter of material bodies and cultural fictions.

By rereading Michel Foucault through various feminist studies of the historical construction of the gendered body, and revisiting Mary Douglas's treatment of the material body as a generative symbolic system, I seek to elaborate the foundational axioms of what Elizabeth Grosz has referred to as a new "corporeal feminism."[18] This newly emergent critical framework draws its methods and interpretive practices from feminist cultural studies more broadly, to suggest that (1) the body is a central symbolic resource for cultural work; (2) the discursive, symbolic body and the material body are mutually determining; and, (3) gender is often a submerged discourse within many studies of the body and culture. In setting the stage for an analysis of the way in which *technologies* construct gendered bodies, the second part of this chapter implicitly draws on Norbert Wiener's theory of cybernetics and Marshall McLuhan's media analysis to discuss more explicitly the role of the female body in one well-known account of the postmodern body. I take issue with the view that the material body has all but disappeared from postmodern theory. I conclude with a discussion of a range of feminist scholarship on the body that establishes the importance of maintaining an emphasis on the notion of a material body within cultural theory by promoting a gendered body that has always been not simply material (i.e., natural) but rather a hybrid construction of materiality and discourse. To elaborate this argument, I discuss work by Donna Haraway, Ruth Bleier, and Paula Treichler, who in different ways investigate how the material female body is actually constructed by and within discourse.

Chapter 2: Feminist Bodybuilding

In analyzing the mechanical reconstruction of the gendered body, it is clear that women's bodies remain a privileged site for the cultural reinscription of the "natural." In this chapter I turn my attention to the subculture of female bodybuilding. Perfectly attuned to contemporary culture, the female bodybuilder is a machine dream of cyborg identity, the female form that works to recreate the female form, using the science of weights, resistance, and kinesthetic labor. Upon closer inspection, though, I find that the normalizing powers of media representation establish new ideals for the female body such that muscularity and physical development are heralded as women's "new sex appeal."[19] In this sense the popular culture of female bodybuilding can be seen to enjoy a licensed complicity with the very forms of gender identity it seeks to technologically disrupt. The subculture of female bodybuilding that developed during the 1980s is in part constructed within a historical discourse concerning women and sport, in which the athletic female body of the early 19th century was subjected to various forms of medical and moral discipline. More contemporary text-images of popular female athletes illuminate how the sporting female body is both objectified and eroticized in ways that promote its sexual desirability over its athletic capabilities. One of the favorite cult films of female bodybuilders, *Pumping Iron II: The Women,* features three female bodybuilders who embody competing definitions of femininity. In a close analysis of the film, I argue that it not only narrates the symbolic reproduction of dominant ideals of femininity, but also directs our attention to how deviant constructions of the female body are staged and disciplined.

Chapter 3: On the Cutting Edge

New visualization technologies exercise a new form of scientific biopower that effects, first, the objectification of the female body, and second, the subjection of that body to the surveillance of a normative gaze. In this chapter, I trace the way in which the medical gaze of the cosmetic surgeon has been transformed into a technological perspective, with the attendant consequence that the female body is itself transformed into a surface for the inscription of cultural ideals of Western beauty. Cosmetic surgery enacts a form of cultural signification where we can examine the literal and material reproduction of ideals of beauty. Where visualization technologies bring into focus isolated body parts and pieces, surgical procedures actually carve into the flesh to isolate parts to be manipulated and resculpted. In this way cosmetic surgery *literally* transforms the material body into a sign of culture. The *discourse* of cosmetic surgery offers provocative material for discussing the cultural construction of the gendered body because, on the one hand, women are often the intended and preferred subjects of such discourse, and on the other, men are often the bodies doing the surgery. Cosmetic surgery is not then simply a discursive site for the "construction of images of women" but is actually a material site at which the physical female body is surgically dissected, stretched, carved, and reconstructed according to cultural and eminently ideological standards of physical appearance.

Chapter 4: Public Pregnancies and
Cultural Narratives of Surveillance

In this chapter I discuss the politics of new reproductive technologies by examining media accounts of public pregnancies. One of the most highly regarded fictional narratives about the dystopic possibilities of the "politics of surrogacy" and the "spectacle of public pregnancy" to appear during the 1980s was Margaret Atwood's novel *The Handmaid's Tale*. Published at a time when the various spectacles of frozen embryos and cocaine mothers were just coming to public attention, it had the chilling impact of projecting a science fictional future that was just around the corner. I argue that the Atwood novel offers a framework to make sense of the situation of women in relation to the contemporary application of new reproductive technologies. In so doing, I explicitly frame this analysis in terms of one of the problematics at the heart of cultural studies: the relationship between cultural narratives and the material conditions of women's lives. The second part of the chapter seeks to illuminate the context of the Atwood novel by reviewing a range of current events that, although they serve as a springboard for fiction, are now becoming matters of the lived experience of women of child-bearing age. They include the use of laparoscopy, a visualization technique, in the service of *in vitro* fertilization. In an attempt to flesh out the way in which such technologies augment the development of a cultural logic of surveillance, I consider the conditions of possibility that emerge from the use of these technologies, which result in contested definitions of rights of privacy and invigorated debates about the relationship between women's bodies and public health. As these rights are negotiated and adjudicated, certain technologically inscribed identities are institutionalized. As such, an apparatus of surveillance processes gendered bodies in ways that redefine all female bodies as potentially maternal bodies and all pregnant bodies as inherently duplicitous and possibly threatening to public health.

Chapter 5: The Virtual Body in Cyberspace

In the development of virtual reality (VR) applications and hardware, the body is redefined as a machine interface. In efforts to colonize the electronic frontier — called cyberspace or the information matrix — the material body is repressed and divorced from the locus of knowledge. In one virtual reality application, for example, the material body of the user bears no relation to the disembodied, floating point of view (pov) of the cyberspace traveler except as a hat stand for the VR rig. In the development of virtual reality applications, the deconstruction of the "natural" body is now a completely naturalized phenomenon. As technological apparatuses replace sense organs as the media of knowledge, "the body" becomes a piece of obsolete meat — nothing more than excess baggage for the cyberspace traveler. In this chapter, I investigate the subculture that has developed around and within cyberspace, as it serves as the context for a discussion about the biopolitics of the virtual body. In traveling through various virtual cyberworlds, it no longer makes sense to ask whose reality or perspective is *represented* in cyberspace; rather we should ask what reality is created therein, and how this reality articulates relationships among technologies, bodies, and narratives. The body may disappear representationally in virtual worlds — indeed, we may go to great lengths to repress it and erase its referential traces — but it does not disappear materially, either in the interface with the VR apparatus or in systems of technological production. I suggest that studying the development of and popular engagement with virtual reality technologies allows us to investigate how myths about identity, nature, and the body are rearticulated with new technologies in ways that ensure that traditional (and occasionally revisionist) narratives about the gendered, race-marked body are socially and technologically reproduced.

Chapter 6: Feminism for the Incurably Informed

New communication technologies engender new realities for the material body. Scientific research draws on science fiction to specify the dimensions of new spaces for the staging of corporeal identity. This chapter develops a reading of Pat Cadigan's cyberpunk novel *Synners* to itemize the dominant forms of technological embodiment endemic to the Information Age. As a science fictional account of the various relationships that characters can have to the nonmaterial space of computer-mediated information exchange, *Synners* directs our attention to a neglected dimension of new information technologies: the status of the gender- and race-marked material body. Based on this reading of *Synners,* I elaborate the kinds of questions one could ask about the role of the material body in the cultural formation of what *Mondo 2000* calls "The New Edge." The questions I focus on include ones about the historical role that women have played in the development of computer technologies, the gendered distinctions between men's and women's computer communication practices, and the differential political consequences of the deployment of such technologies for women of different races. The point is to seriously challenge the dominant myth of cyberspace that celebrates it as a gender- and race-neutral space of disembodied, democratic exchange.

Epilogue: The Role of the Body in Feminist Cultural Studies of Science and Technology

In the epilogue, I outline the contributions that my approach offers to feminist cultural studies of science and technology. I consider the work of

Elizabeth Grosz on the notion of "corporeal feminism" in order to situate the readings in this book in relation to other feminist body projects. Borrowing Grosz's insight, that sexual difference is one form of "alterity" that is both primary and constantly displaced, I trace the ways in which various technological practices reproduce this "alterity" as a gender identity for material bodies. Although the readings in this book do not specifically discuss the sexual dimensions of the gendered body (as is the purpose of Grosz's project), I hope they make a significant contribution to the emerging discussion on "corporeal feminism."

In studying the interactions between bodies and technologies, I take on the task of analyzing an emergent cultural formation that manifests itself in dissimilar (discursive) forms. In doing so, my analysis relies on a broadened notion of discourse borrowed, in part, from Ernesto Laclau and Chantal Mouffe that includes readings of narratives and material practices, relations of power and mass-mediated representations.[20] I offer interpretations not only of texts and stories, but also of social relations, institutional arrangements, popular cultural images, and systems of logic. These are all part of the cultural apparatus that constructs gendered bodies. The final point is to demonstrate how a discursive framework of analysis can elaborate the historically specific production of material bodies. On this note, I implicitly address an ongoing project of feminist scholars and activists more broadly: that of developing a framework for the analysis of the relationship between discursive studies of cultural forms and the material conditions of women's lives.

CHAPTER ONE

Reading Cyborgs, Writing Feminism:
Reading the Body in Contemporary Culture

Well I stopped in at the body shop
I said to the guy, I want stereo FM
installed in my teeth.
And take this mole off my back
and put it on my cheek.
And while I'm here,
why don't you give me
some of those
high-heeled feet?
—Laurie Anderson, "Monkey's Paw"[1]

From Mary Shelley's *Frankenstein,* published in 1818, to Maria, the robot in *Metropolis* (Lang, 1927), to *Frankenhooker* (a film released on video in 1989), the possibilities of human hybrids have fired our cultural imagination as the Western world has developed through the industrial revolution into the age of high technology (figure 4). But the decade of the 1980s stands out as the historical moment when a high-tech human hybrid moved off the pages of science fiction novels into everyday life: it was in many ways the decade of the cyborg. In 1986, Max Headroom stuttered his way onto American television and the cover of *Newsweek* (figure 5). That same year Elektra Assassin, Frank Miller's celebrated antihero, challenged the revitalized comic book industry's vision of a proper heroine (figure 6). By Christmas 1990, it was clear that Transformers™ were the toy of the decade, edging out sales of plastic figures of other popular cyborgs such as RoboCop, Terminator, and Captain Picard's Borg. During the 1993 Christmas season, The Mighty Morphins PowerRangers™ flew off the shelves of U.S.-based *Toys R Us* discount stores; some parent went

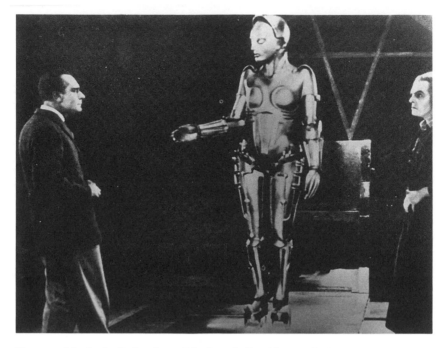

Figure 4. Maria the Robot from Fritz Lang's film *Metropolis* (1926).

so far as to bribe toy store workers to find Mighty Morphins™ for their videogame-weary children.

Cyborg, a shorthand term for "cybernetic organism," usually describes a human-machine coupling, most often a *man*-machine hybrid. Cyborgs are alternately labeled "androids," "replicants," or "bionic humans." Whatever label they attract, the cyborg serves not only as the focal figure of the mass-mediated popular culture of American techno-science, but also as the figuration of posthuman identity in postmodernity. From children's plastic action figures to cyberpunk mirrorshades, cyborgian artifacts will endure as relics of an age obsessed with the limits of human mortality and the possibilities of technological replication. In this chapter, I discuss how our technological imagination imbues cyborgs with ancient anxieties about human difference. But first a long detour is in order. I want to revisit the issue of "reading the body" as a way of constructing a framework for "reading cyborgs." This requires a discussion of certain developments within cultural theory, by Michel Foucault, Mary Douglas, and Donna Haraway, as well as other feminists, all of whom contribute to a framework for interpreting the body as a cultural text. This detour is

Figure 5. *Newsweek* magazine cover featuring video persona Max Headroom (April 20, 1987). Figure 6. *Elektra Assassin*, Marvel Comics (vol. 1, no. 1, August 1986). Story by Frank Miller, illustrated by Bill Sienkiewicz.

necessary for a second reason. It shows how the female body historically was constructed as a hybrid case, thus making it compatible with notions of cyborg identity promulgated by more recent cultural theorists.

Reading the Body

When the body is said to be "inscribed," "painted," or "written," it makes sense to write of the "discourse of the body," meaning the patterned ways that the body is represented according to broader cultural determinations and also the way that the body becomes a bearer of signs and cultural meaning. Following the work of Michel Foucault, several scholars — including Bryan Turner, Catherine Gallagher and Thomas Laqueur, and Emily Martin, among others — address the relationship between the body, culture, and society to enumerate the ways in which the body is put into discourse.[2] Using a variety of strategies, these scholars study modes of representation of the body: its iconography, its aesthetic and symbolic functions, or its discursive repression. Although they propose different body projects — Turner, for example, is concerned about reconstructing the problem of order as a problem of the government of the body, while Martin presents an ethnographic investigation of women's experiences with reproduction and menstruation — each scholar enacts a reading process that supports the theoretical understanding of the body as a sign-bearing (textual) form. To claim that the body is a discursive construction, and therefore can be read, already effects a deconstruction of its natural posture. Such is the first act of thick perception.

Michel Foucault is not so much interested in the truth of the body as he is in elaborating the apparatus that produces truth effects at the level of the body. His concern is to describe the discursive systems that produce serious truth claims about bodies. Thus, in his genealogical projects he annotates the intelligibility of the body in terms of the discursive, social, and political practices that construct it as an object/subject with meaning. For example, in *The History of Sexuality,* he describes the four central apparatuses of control that mark the transition between a traditional order and one constituted by "scientific biopower": (1) the hysterization of the female body; (2) the construction of homosexuality; (3) the creation of distinctions among infant, child, and adolescent sexualities; and (4) the establishment of a discourse of perversion. These "apparatuses" organize the deployment of power; control is established through the cultural transformation of the meaning of body practices and bodily markers of identity. In short, these apparatuses identify a "conjunction," or what I understand as an "articulation of discursive practices" that produce body knowledges.

Foucault goes on to delineate the *means* by which power is exercised. Central to his work is the assertion that the *means* of the production of discourse include a more ambiguous process of the construction of knowledge claims. For example, the hysterization of the female body, as one way in which scientific biopower is organized and reified, was accomplished through the exercise of new discursive practices (of science, of psychoanalysis), institutionalized social relations (the family under capitalism), and knowledge claims (the medicalization of the female body). This is to say that the meaning of the female body as a "hysterical entity" — a corporeal being susceptible to hysteria — was a meaning constructed through discursive practices, i.e., not only in the discourses of science and medicine, but also through the establishment of social institutions. These institutions, in turn, reproduce specific knowledge claims through the practices established by the profession and as part of the education and socialization of practitioners. Foucault suggests the term "apparatus" and later "technology" to name the process of connection between discursive practices, institutional relations, and material effects that, working together, produce a meaning or a "truth effect" for the human body.

In this sense, an apparatus or "technology" articulates power relations, systems of communication, and productive activities or practices; "articulate" here is used both in the sense of "expressing" that which is already given or operative and in the sense of conjoining or connecting. So, following Foucault's logic, the notion of "technology" describes the workings of a collection of practices that produce specific cultural effects. Technology names the process whereby discursive practices work interdependently with other cultural forces to produce effects at the level of the body. These effects, in turn, become part of an apparatus of control. Foucault goes on to argue that the notion of technology allows for the analysis of power in terms of a number of concrete relations: (1) systems of differentiation, (2) types of objectives, (3) means of bringing power relations into being, (4) forms of institutionalization, and (5) degrees of rationalization — all of which are *rooted* in social networks, language use, and the human body.[3] I find this notion of a technology and his enumeration of concrete relations particularly useful as a framework for investigating the way in which certain taken-for-granted "truths" are, in fact, culturally constructed and eventually institutionalized. This is of course the theory behind his notion of the "technologies of the self" as well as Teresa de Lauretis's notion of the "technologies of gender." It is also, as I noted in the introduction, the basis for my notion of "technologies of the gendered body."

From a feminist point of view, certainly one of the most obvious "truth effects" of the human body in Foucault's analysis is the gendered identity of what he often identifies simply as "docile bodies." As many feminists have argued, Foucault evades direct consideration of gender as an "effect" produced at the level of the body.[4] His broad-sweeping account of the disciplinary practices that produce subjugated bodies neglects to consider gender as an underlying organizing framework for deciphering the disciplined body. Thus, although he can identify the "hysterization of the female body" as one of the apparatuses of control of the body, his grid of analysis fails to consider gender itself as an organized, institutionalized, system of differences that constitutes the individual body and renders it meaningful. In a way that contradicts his analytical intentions to consider the system of differentiations that make the body meaningful, gender often functions for him as a natural given.

If Foucault's project is to deconstruct (in his own fashion) the most commonsensical, taken-for-granted "truths" about the workings of power, it is clear that he runs into problems with his elision of gender. This fact has provoked several feminists to reevaluate the history he offers.[5] For example, in Diamond and Quinby's *Feminism and Foucault* Francis Bartkowski argues quite directly that "what Foucault has done is to reproduce and produce as history the patriarchal history of sexuality."[6] It is clear that throughout his project he treats the gender identity of the female body as a naturally occurring bodily characteristic instead of a "truth effect" produced by cultural discourses that constructs some bodies as active and disciplines others to be passive. Within his analysis, gender materializes as a key "dividing practice" that objectifies the human body and makes it intelligible to him, yet he fails to consider it a technology of power/knowledge in its own right. For all his concern to elaborate systems of power *and* resistance, Foucault ends up writing not so much from a site of resistance but from a site of power — male-centered discourse. Given this, perhaps it is unavoidable that the more radical promise of his project would not be realized by him. Several feminist scholars are doing what he could not — articulating a history of sexuality from a site of resistance by addressing the construction of the feminine, femininity, and Woman to describe how gender is, in Foucault's terms, a primary apparatus of scientific biopower that constructs the body as an intelligible object.

For example, in Susan Suleiman's collection of essays *The Female Body in Western Culture* several scholars implicitly rebuke Foucault's oversight by showing how gender is one of the primary effects of the discursive construction of the human body.[7] Suleiman herself poses the question of the female body this way: "what place has the female body occupied in the Western imagination, and in the symbolic productions of Western culture over the past two thousand years?" (1). Foucault would have us believe that "she" was hardly present, marginal and uninteresting at best. The authors in Suleiman's collection collectively argue the contrary; they examine the many different sites of the ideological inscription of sexual difference by looking at representations of the female body in different cultural texts. The essays are organized thematically rather than historically, on the topics of eros, death, mothers, illness, images, and difference. The primary purpose of Suleiman's collection is to argue that the female body is not an essentially unchanging, given-in-nature, biological entity, but rather is symbolically constructed within different cultural discourses situated within different historical conjunctions.

Following Foucault, Suleiman underscores the importance of reading the body as a symbolic *discursive* construction:

> The cultural significance of the female body is not only (not even first and foremost) that of a flesh-and-blood entity, but that of a *symbolic construct*. Everything we know about the body — certainly as regards the past, and even, it could be argued, as regards the present — exists for us in some form of discourse: and discourse, whether verbal or visual, fictive or historical or speculative, is never unmediated, never free of interpretation, never innocent. (2)

The analyses offered in Suleiman's book are textually grounded and politically motivated; taken together, they articulate an understanding of how the relation between the body and culture is mediated through discourse such that the body is transformed into an epistemological issue — knowledge about the body becomes a matter of *representation* of the body. The critical point Suleiman stresses is that there is no "natural" approach to the female body that is rooted in an essentialist female nature. All understandings of the body are mediated through representations which, in turn, are constructed through interpretive frameworks. This approach, like Foucault's, keeps the body contained within discourse and subject(ed) to determinate systems of power and knowledge. But in many respects, this collection skirts the dangerous line of suggesting that knowledge of the body is *only* discursive. Or, put another way, when Suleiman writes that the "cultural significance" of the body is a matter of its symbolic construction, not its "natural femininity," she comes close to asserting that this is the singular definition of the female body. This approach *inadvertently* ends up invoking a dualistic logic, that the female body is either a "flesh and blood entity" or a symbolic construct. I stress the term "inadvertently" to remind readers of the historical situation of the production of this approach to the study of the female body. It was an approach that sought to correct the overreliance on an essentialist definition of the female body as a biological or "natural" entity. Since that time, feminist discussions of the constitution of the female body have been often sidelined by *debates* about the effectivity of essentialist versus anti-essentialist perspectives. I would like to sidestep this debate by focusing attention on the ways in which nature and culture are mutually determining systems of understanding. While it is true, as Suleiman says, that "everything we know about the body ... exists for us in some form of discourse," this discourse is not entirely divorced from the material manifestation of the "flesh and blood" entity.

The Material Body as a Symbolic Cultural Resource

Building on the work of Marcel Mauss, cultural anthropologist Mary Douglas describes the relationship between symbolic systems, social structures, and the body by analyzing the way cultural systems rely on the body's expressive resources to formulate social relations.[8] In her book *Natural Symbols,* Douglas asserts that social perceptions of the human body are never free from determining cultural influences; the body is always comprehended as an interaction between the materiality of what is given in a particular body and the symbolic constructions of the "body" embedded within a given culture. But the most important point she makes is that although the meaning of the *physical body* is itself structured by the symbolic representation of the body, it is at the same time an experiential resource for the construction of such representations:

> The social body constrains the way the physical body is perceived. The physical experience of the body, always modified by the social categories through which it is known, sustains a particular view of society. There is a continual exchange of meanings between the two kinds of bodily experience so that each reinforces the categories of the other. (65)

In this statement, Douglas follows Mauss by asserting that the human body is *always* defined according to cultural beliefs about social relations. But even as Douglas asserts that "most symbolic behavior must work through the body" (vii), she argues that the *meaning* of the body, and thus the meaning of different systems of body symbols, is, in fact, constructed through "a continual exchange of meanings between *two* kinds of bodily experience" (65) — of the physical body and of the social (or symbolic) body. While I don't want to belabor the point, it is important to note that Douglas keeps the notion of the physical body at the heart of her account of the cultural construction of the symbolic body. Her broader point, of course, is to argue that although the physical body is in many ways a naturally occurring referent for symbolic systems, its meaning is not "naturally" determined (vii). In this sense, there are no natural symbols, although there are plentiful symbolic representations of nature and of the "natural body."

Douglas offers an important contribution to an understanding of the cultural construction of the gendered body. "There can be no natural way of considering the body," she writes, "that does not involve at the same time a social dimension."[9] This assertion denaturalizes both the body and gender and provides a basis for accomplishing what Brown and Adams identify as a critical feminist project — the deconstruction of the "natural" female body.[10] Following this, gender identity can be redefined as a body attribute that is assigned, organized, and acquired through the process of social perception; in short, it can no longer be considered a "natural fact" of the human body. Rather, we must consider how the human body is "gendered" through a series of social acts that often begin long before physical birth and are determined only partially by personal (self-decipherment) perception of physiological body parts (the genitals, for example). But the important issue here is not only that gender is "denaturalized" but that so too are definitions of gender that rely on appeals to the natural body. Behind the construction of representations of "natural bodies" and "natural" gender identities, Douglas claims are beliefs and anxieties about the social body.

In keeping with Douglas's line of analysis, Thomas Laqueur argues that the female body was at the center of a radical 18th-century reinterpretation of the patriarchal social hierarchy. Sexual difference was reconsidered such that the female body was no longer considered merely an inferior, underdeveloped, and infantile version of the male body (ovaries as underdeveloped testicles, for example); rather a complementary relation between the male and female body was established, such that

> [w]riters of all sorts were determined to base what they insisted were fundamental differences between male and female sexuality, and thus between man and woman, on discoverable biological distinctions. . . . Thus the old model, in which men and women were arrayed according to their degree of metaphysical perfection, their vital heat, along an axis whose telos was male, gave way by the late 18th century to a new model of difference, of biological divergence. An anatomy and physiology of incommensurability replaced a metaphysics of hierarchy in the representation of women in relation to men.[11]

Since Laqueur explicitly draws on Douglas in his analysis of the construction of the female body, it is not surprising that he situates this transformation of the cultural understanding of the "nature" of the female body within the changing constitution of the 18th-century social order, "when the basis for a new order of sex and gender became a critical issue of political theory and practice" (4). Laqueur points out that the new order (which replaced the divine right of kings, a similar point of analysis in Foucault's historical genealogy) was concerned to establish naturalized hierarchies among human bodies. He explains how such a cultural imperative and the use of metaphors (of heat, of oestrus) functioned to define the female body in terms of its reproductive biology. The hierarchical relation between the male body and the female body was not overturned; rather

> the political, economic and cultural transformations of the 18th century created the context in which the articulation of radical differences between the sexes became culturally imperative. In a world in which science was increasingly viewed as providing insight into the fundamental truths of creation, in which nature as manifested in the unassailable reality of bones and organs was taken to be the only foundation of the moral order, a biology of incommensurability became the means by which such differences could be authoritatively represented. (35)

Here Laqueur offers an account of the exercise of scientific biopower on the female body. The turn toward a biologically based definition of the complementarity of the female body raised new questions about the relationship between that body and social control. For if female bodies are fundamentally different from male bodies, not just an inferior version, the issue of control becomes more critical: how does one control a body that isn't entirely knowable?

In her examination of medical textbooks of the nineteenth century, Mary Poovey illuminates the historical construction of the female body as the object of medical attention and control. Moreover, she explicates how medical discourse constructed the female body as excessive and threatening to the epistemological boundaries of the prevailing social order. Specifically she focuses on the medical debates concerning forms of anesthesia to show how they function as a discursive site of the struggle for authority over the female body between obstetricians, midwives, and other medical practitioners. Not incidentally it is a site in which the female body is thoroughly silent/silenced:

> [t]he debate presented itself as an argument about the nature of women and medicine's proper relation to them. . . . First, does the woman in labor properly belong to the realm of nature, which is governed by God, or to culture, where nature submits to man? Second, how can a man know — so as to master — the female body, which is always other to his own?[12]

If the female body properly belonged to nature, the argument went, then midwives were better positioned to serve the laboring maternal body, being female bodies themselves and skilled in reading the natural labor signs of that body. If the female body could be secured as belonging to the cultural order, then, by extension, it was beholden to the cultural authority of medicine and medical discourse and would be properly served by the administration of chloroform during labor (one of the two forms of anesthesia being debated).

At this point, Poovey implies that the articulation among new technologies (forms of anesthesia), social debates about medical authority and the status of medicine as a scientifically rational practice, and a definition of the female body as governed by its reproductive capacity, establishes a definition of the female body as "always lacking and needing control":

> This set of assumptions—that woman's reproductive function defines her character, position, and value, that this function is only one sign of an innate periodicity, and that this biological periodicity influences and is influenced by an array of nervous disorders—mandates the medical profession's superintendence of women.... [quoting Dr. Issac Ray:] With women, it is but a step from extreme nervous susceptibility to downright hysteria, and from that to overt insanity.... Seen in this way, hysteria is simultaneously the norm of the female body taken to its logical extreme and a medical category that effectively defines this norm as inherently abnormal. (146–47)

Furthermore, Poovey explains:

> On the one hand, representing woman as an inherently unstable female body authorizes ceaseless medical monitoring and control. But on the other hand, this representation of woman as always requiring control produces her as always already exceeding the control that medicine can exercise. (147)

Consequently, the female body is defined as simultaneously belonging within the "proper" domain of medical discourse and yet always threatening its epistemological boundaries. Here we read the conflation between the political contest to establish the physiological facts of female nature, and the physiological consequences of symbolic representations of the female body.

The female body that is an effect of the construction of identity/ authority of obstetricians in nineteenth-century medical discourse is a hybrid creature formed through the articulations among social practices, the development of new knowledge, and changing patterns of power and authority. In this sense, the female body functions as a border case; it is at once defined as part of a natural order *and* as an intensely fascinating and yet threatening object of cultural control. Its excessiveness strains the cultural authority of medical knowledge. As such it is a site of potential transgression against the boundaries of social order, at once constituted within the dominant discourses of science and medicine but threatening to the epistemological certainty of that discourse.

Panic Postmodernism and the Disappearing Body

The story about the female body doesn't change much in more recent history, especially in cultural narratives of postmodern identity. In *Body Invaders,* a collection of essays on panic sex in America, editor Arthur Kroker also seeks to intervene in the reproduction of a dominant discourse of the body that would define it as an organic, natural entity.[13] Following Marshall McLuhan, Kroker argues that the "natural" body has disappeared, replaced by a technologically produced simulacrum.[14] Kroker reads the current list of "panic" *body* issues (AIDS, anorexia, addictions of all sorts) as signs of significant *social* anxieties concerning control and safety. The "panic body" marks "a declining culture where the body is revived, and given one last burst of hyper-subjectivity, as the inscribed text for all the stress and crisis-symptoms of the death of the social" (27). With this statement he reasserts Douglas's understanding that "cultures think themselves through the body." He sees the proliferation of rhetorics that work feverishly to invest the body with meaning as a symptom of a culture in decline — a culture where meaning has been banished. For Kroker the body is simply obsolete, replaced by numerous technological extensions of its senses. The prevalence of body rhetorics masks the disappearance of the natural body (now replaced by technological devices) which in turn, masks the disappearance of the social — the final death of social solidarity that comes from daily living with the apocalypse. Discourse, now objectified as communication technologies, literally replaces the material body with simulated body senses. Whereas Foucault's project was to explicate how the discourses of modernity redefined the body as machine, in postmodernity what we discover is that technology now transforms the body into nothing more than discourse.

With the disappearance of the material body in McLuhan's analysis of media culture and Kroker's reading of postmodernity, gender too presumably becomes ephemeral, or at best an artifact of an outdated rhetoric that seeks to invest the body with meaning. And yet, we can read in both McLuhan's and Kroker's analyses a submerged discourse of gender that continues to organize and make intelligible the discourses of the body in late capitalism. Even as he claims that the velocity of cultural change blurs the boundaries upon which identity is constructed, Kroker identifies the special status of the female body in postmodernity:

> Because now as ever, the play of power within and against the text of women's bodies is an early warning sign of a grisly power field that speaks the language of body invaders. As privileged objects of a domination that takes as its focus the inscription of the text of the body, women have always known the meaning of a relational power that works in the language of body invaders. This is not, though, the wager of an old patriarchal power that announces itself in the transcendent and externalized language of hierarchy, univocity, and logocentricity, but a power field that can be multiple, pleasurable, and indeed, fully embodied. . . . women's bodies have always been postmodern because they have always been targets of a power which, inscribing the text of the flesh, seeks to make of feminine identity something interpellated by ideology, constituted by language, and the site of a "dissociated ego." (24)

Kroker elaborates this language of body invaders as the conspicuous consumption of late capitalism, which turns all bodies into sign vehicles for fetishistic commodities. As a companion to McLuhan's "Mechanical Bride," "The Capezio Woman" figures as a final icon in Kroker's analysis. Whereas the Mechanical Bride (figure 7) symbolizes the female body of American media culture that is docile, traditional, and subjected to "the wager of old patriarchal power," the Capezio Woman (figure 8) symbolizes the female body that is stylish, pleasure-anointed, and happy to find a snappy pair of new shoes. Both images testify to the persistence (nonobsolescence) of gender in a postcorporeal world. Even when the body is reduced to a discursive effect, notes Kroker, the female body functions as the privileged sign of the "body debased, humiliated, and inscribed to excess by all the signs of consumer culture" (33).

Upon closer reading, the female body hasn't been transformed at all; it is still *constructed* as the message-bearing and silent form of the (eighteenth and nineteenth centuries') unruly body, produced through the

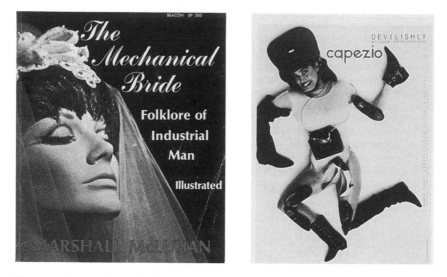

Figure 7. Cover of Marshall McLuhan's book *The Mechanical Bride* (1951; Boston: Beacon, 1967). Figure 8. "The Capezio Woman." Ad produced by Ross and Harasym, photograph by Shun Sasbuchio. Reproduced in Arthur and Marilouise Kroker, "Body Digest," *Canadian Journal of Political and Social Theory* 11, no. 1–2 (1987): xiv.

formation of the cultural imaginary; only now the cultural imaginary is expressed through the rhetoric of "panic" postmodernism. The female body continues to function as the sign of a gendered body opposed to a nonmarked (human) body that is said to be *now* (in late capitalism) subjugated to discursive systems of power and knowledge. If women have *always* been postmodern bodies, as Kroker asserts, then what is different about postmodern bodies that hasn't always been the condition of female bodies? The *compulsion* to theorize the condition of postmodern bodies as something new or even exhausted is due to the novelty the male body experiences coming under this totalizing system for the first time; understandably, panic results. In Kroker's analysis, female bodies continue to mark gender; thus they announce the deployment of a gendered opposition of bodies in postmodern theory. This is a gendered opposition, whereby the One (recently "invaded" body) is unmarked by gender and the Other (the always postmodern body) is female. Such is the fate of the female body in the postmodern cultural imaginary: an always silent/silenced conceptual placeholder in hysterical male discourse. As before, her excessiveness threatens the very order of the system.

Is it ironic that the body disappears in postmodern theory just as women and feminists have emerged as an intellectual force within the human disciplines?[15] A similar (ironic?) contradiction emerges with respect to the issue of the body. An organic body *marked* by certain biological characteristics provided a common identity for women to collectivize as feminists. But the bodily identity of woman proved unstable and unreliable as a source of collective empowerment. Diverse feminist action directs its attention to de-essentializing the biological identity of woman, thus working to deconstruct the organic foundation of feminist thought. After acknowledging the impossibility of biological essentialism as a foundation for the identity of "woman," feminist thinking proceeds to an analysis of the cultural construction of the body, and is immediately confronted with a discourse that gleefully joins it in deconstructing biological essentialism. In the process, feminists encounter unsolicited assistance in doing away with "the body," which served — at one point, if not now — as the necessary foundation of women's empowerment.

Faced with the prospect of being strategically eclipsed within the modern episteme once again, feminists have a political stake in constructing and critiquing theories of the body within postmodernism. As I have argued elsewhere, it is time for feminism to crash the postmodern party.[16] The final fate of "the body" should not be left entirely to the panic postmodernists — that is, Jean Baudrillard, Deleuze and Guattari, among others. Moreover, we cannot listen obediently while these very same postmodernists delineate for us "the special place of feminist theory today" and lay out for us the proper attitude that feminism should adopt toward the body.[17] But what is a feminist to do?

In her book *Gynesis: Configurations of Woman and Modernity,* Alice Jardine cautions feminist writers: "The attempt to analyze, to separate ideological and cultural determinations of the 'feminine' from the 'real woman' — seemingly the most logical path for a feminist to follow — may also be the most interminable process, one in which women become not only figuratively but also literally impossible."[18] Jardine describes the paradoxical situation of feminist criticism that on the one hand draws political strength from an essentialist identity of "woman," but on the other has been convinced of the necessity to interrogate such an identity for the differences it obscures:

While proceeding from a "belief" (in women's oppression), we are nevertheless, necessarily, caught up in a permanent whirlwind of reading practices within a universe of fiction and theory written, but for a few official exceptions, by men. Not believing in "Truth," we continue to be fascinated by (elaborate) fictions. This is the profound paradox of the feminist speaking in our contemporary culture: she proceeds from a *belief* in a world from which — even the philosophers admit — Truth has disappeared. This paradox, it seems to me, can lead to (at least) three possible scenarios: a renewed silence, a form of religion (from mysticism to political orthodoxy), or a continual attention — historical, ideological, and affective — to the place from which we speak. (31–32)

Another possible solution is to reconstruct our reading practices — which is ultimately what Jardine advocates. She suggests that feminists begin to write new fictions, written through "the continual attention — historical, ideological, and affective — to the place from which we speak" (32). This, to me, perfectly describes Donna Haraway's response to feminism's "profound paradox," and indeed, the founding imperative for her feminist manifesto; in elaborating a new fiction of feminist identity, her "ironic political myth" of cyborg citizenship, she enacts a new reading practice that takes the discursively constructed material body as its starting point and narrates a reconstructed fiction of gender identity.

Reading Cyborgs

According to Haraway, in "A Manifesto for Cyborgs," the only bodies that stand a chance in postmodern culture are cyborg bodies. Cyborg bodies are constructed by communication networks and other hybrid discourses such as biotechnology, biopolitics, and female bodybuilding.[19] Variously used as a symbol of antitechnological sentiments or of the possibilities of "better living through chemistry," cyborgs are a product of fears and desires that run deep within our cultural imaginary.[20] Through the use of technology as the means or context for human hybridization, cyborgs come to represent unfamiliar "otherness," one that challenges the denotative stability of human identity. Andreas Huyssen claims that the crisis of modernism pivots on the problematic of otherness.[21] In this way, cyborgs offer a particularly appropriate emblem of postmodern identity, since cyborg identity is predicated on transgressed boundaries. They fascinate us because they are not like us and yet are just like us. Formed through a radical disruption of otherness, cyborg identity foregrounds the constructedness of otherness. Cyborgs alert us to the way in which identity depends on notions of "the other" that are arbitrary, shifting, and ultimately unstable.

Every cyborg image constructs an implicit opposition between machine and human, at once repressing similarities and highlighting distinctions. In this way it defines the meaning of both the term "human" and the term "artificial." Signs of human-ness and, alternatively, signs of machineness function not only as markers of the "essences" of the dual natures of the hybrid, but also as signs of the inviolable opposition between humans and machines. But because the cyborg embodies both "natures" simultaneously, the resulting hybrid is neither purely human nor purely machine. The distribution of its dual dispositions is never simply symmetrical, and the proximity of each to the other and the combination of dissimilar parts produces a hybrid often unrecognizable as any familiar personage. By disrupting the stable meanings of the human/machine dualism, other reliable oppositions are also rendered unstable. The cyborg, for Haraway, has the potential to disrupt the persistent dualisms that have been "systemic to the logics and practices of domination of women, people of color, nature, workers, animals."[22] The most troublesome dualisms include some already mentioned in this chapter: culture/nature, human/artificial, male/female, as well as others such as reality/appearance, truth/illusion, theory/politics. Cyborg bodies, then, cannot be conceived as belonging wholly to either culture or nature; they are neither wholly technological nor completely organic. In a similar sense, cyborg bodies cannot be completely discursive. Cyborgs are a matter of fiction and a matter of lived experience. They not only subvert the certainty of what counts as nature, but, as Haraway lays out, they also subvert the certainty of the "textualization of everything" by pointing to the lived relations of domination that ground cultural reading(s).

By reasserting a material body, the cyborg rebukes the disappearance of the body within postmodernism. Yet it never contradicts the variety of discursive constructions of the female body. The cyborg connects a discursive body with a historically material body by taking account of the ways in which the body is constructed within different social and cultural formations. Ultimately, the cyborg challenges feminism to search for ways to study the body as it is at once both a cultural construction and a material fact of human life. The impact of this is decisive: understanding that the body is culturally, not "naturally," constructed means that the body is not solely a matter of materiality; nor can it be reductively a matter of discourse. Its "nature" is culturally determined even when this nature is said to be discursively constructed. To claim that the body is a discursive as well as material construction still leaves everything to say about the particular cultural design of that body within any given historical conjunction.

Haraway explicitly maps the identity of woman onto the image of the cyborg. This foregrounds the ambiguous constitution of the female body — predicated on the blurred boundaries between the individual and the collective, the material and the discursive, the fictive and the real. Both Woman and Cyborg are simultaneously symbolically and biologically produced and reproduced through social interactions. The "self" is one interactional product; the body is another. The cyborg further displaces the nature-versus-culture opposition since it is clear in this age of body technologies that the given-ness of the female body is a constructed artifact of various systems of meaning. Moreover, as Haraway reminds us, the search for a female "nature" is a utopian quest, which threatens to distract contemporary feminists from more important tasks, such as forming coalitions and alliances with other political groups based not on some natural gender identification, but on the necessity for shared political strategies. This tactical plan of action depends upon feminism's willingness to investigate how women live permanently partial identities, to discover what cultural meanings are taken up, how they are resisted, and in the process, ultimately transformed.

Writing Feminism

Recent feminist scholarship on the construction of cultural systems of power and knowledge question the *forms* of domination and control that operate in contemporary society. Feminist scholarship by Haraway, Sandra Harding, Ruth Bleier, and Paula Treichler (among others) describe how science, technology, and medicine — as institutionalized domains of socially constructed knowledge — enact practices of domination and oppression based on gender, race, and class distinctions.[23] Their discussion of issues relating to epistemology, gender, and identity elaborates how the material (gendered) body is discounted as a necessary condition and apparatus of knowledge. Science, medicine, and technology are defined as discursive, social, and symbolic systems in which the female body functions as an ideological marker of "natural sexuality" and "reproduction."

Taken together, these scholars argue that gender is a constructed effect produced at the level of the body.

"One important route for reconstructing socialist-feminist politics," Haraway argues, "is through theory and practice addressed to the social relations of science and technology, including crucially the systems of myth and meanings structuring our imaginations."[24] What this amounts to is the construction of a new reading strategy that is attendant to the historical legacy of the female body as (1) a conceptual placeholder, (2) discursively constructed, and (3) threatening to male systems of knowledge; but also attendant to the way the female body's constructedness organizes the perception of its materiality and the effects of this in women's lives. In this sense the female body is less a singular concept or discoverable unity and more an arrangement of texts, silences, laws, and lines of force. Perhaps the term "articulation" best describes this theoretical configuration of the female body: an articulation among reading effects, writing practices, relations of power, cultural stagings, material bodies, and socially constructed perceptions.

Ruth Bleier has orchestrated one such project, which addresses the shift from biology as clinical practice (a convention of an organic order) to biology as inscription (the reconstituted exercise as part of the informatics of domination). In her book *Science and Gender: A Critique of Biology and Its Theories on Women,* Bleier grounds her analysis of the relationship between gender and science in a consideration of biological determinism. She identifies the "nature versus nurture" debate as a false opposition:

> The underlying scientific issue in evaluating any theory of biological determinism is the feasibility of isolating biological from learned influences in the determination of physical characteristics, behaviors, social relationships, and social organization. The effort to separate genetic and environmental influences continues to plague thinking in many [scientific] fields. Yet it represents a false dichotomy that does not reflect biological processes, but like other dualisms . . . may serve reactionary social and political purposes. (7)

Bleier's particular area of interest is neuroanatomy, an increasingly significant area of scientific research in terms of artificial intelligence and the development of brain-imaging technology. The history of scientific research in craniology and neuroanatomy shows that in the early nineteenth century there was considerable interest in demonstrating that the differences between men and women "resided" in the different structures of the male and female brains. Bleier describes how craniology "went out of style" as a scientific field of study as the search for the physiological basis of women's inferiority yielded no significant conclusions.

In her analysis of the history of brain-related science, Bleier demonstrates how science as a specifically cultural institution participates in constructing naturalistic explanations of sexual differences. Bleier demythologizes science by arguing that "[it] is not the neutral, dispassionate, value-free pursuit of Truth; that scientists are not objective, disinterested, or culturally disengaged from the questions they ask of nature or the methods they use to frame their answers" (193). Furthermore, she argues, it is impossible for science or scientists to do otherwise, since science is a social activity and a cultural process created by persons who live in the world of science as well as in the societies that socialized them. In constructing this analysis, Bleier decouples "sexual difference" from the study of invariant biological processes by showing how the "meaning" of female physiology has been (and continues to be) constructed by the cultural and social practices of the biological sciences. This contributes to a denaturalizing of woman's subordination, which, as Mary Poovey describes, historically has been supported by biological theories of the female body as defined by its reproductive capacities. By exposing the position of the female body within neuroanatomy — as one form of scientific discourse — Bleier shows how particular physiological processes come to count as definitive emblems of sexual identity. In this way, Bleier takes a male construct, the female body, inscribed in one discourse, and reinscribes it within another textual/sexual system, one this time informed by feminism, which provides new codes and conventions for "reading" its meaning.

In Bleier's work we see how gender, like the body, is a hybrid construction, belonging both to the order of the material body and the social and discursive systems within which bodies are embedded. So when gender operates as a system of differentiation (in Foucault's terms), it must be considered as both a discursive and material system. As a discourse, gender includes representations, icons, symbols, utterances, signification, and codes. But this discourse is never separate from the bodies that are taken up within it or marked by it.

Paula Treichler's essay "AIDS, Homophobia, and Biomedical Discourse: An Epidemic of Signification" directly addresses the way in which discourse constructs the disease and makes it intelligible. Her reading of the biomedical discourse of AIDS demonstrates the ways in which words — more precisely, discourse — enact and re-inforce deeply entrenched, pervasive, and often conservative cultural "narratives" about gender; it is also about how words seek, ulti-mately, to contain and control women's unruly and uncontainable properties.[25]

She argues persuasively that a theoretically informed analysis of AIDS must not reduce it to a matter of attending to the "dual nature" of the body (of AIDS — as both a social and biological entity) but rather must appreciate the extent to which social constructions of the body orga-nize the very way of perceiving and knowing the body: "Our social con-structions of AIDS . . . are based not upon objective, scientifically deter-mined 'reality' but upon what we are told about this reality: that is, upon prior social constructions routinely produced within the discourses of biomedical science" (270). She goes on to describe the relationship be-tween popular and biomedical discourse as a *continuum,* not a *dichot-omy,* through which "reality" is constructed and its contradictions played out. This continuum also suggests that the relationship between science and popular discourse is an interaction, not a linear arrangement in which science dictates what popular thought is to think. Language is the arena within which this continuum manifests itself.

In a separate article, "AIDS, Gender, and Biomedical Discourse," Treichler demonstrates how gender continues to operate as a submerged discourse within contemporary medical discourse.[26] In her cultural studies of the AIDS body and her work on the epidemic of signification within the discourse on AIDS, she elaborates how the representation of the female body as inherently pathological and contaminated plays a complex role in the development of medical discourse about AIDS. Given the histori-cal association between the female body and disease, especially sexually transmitted ones, it is surprising to learn that women were explicitly ex-cluded as a targeted risk group of HIV infection for the first four years of the AIDS pandemic. The significance of this exclusion is sobering and illuminates a cultural narrative about the construction of the gendered body. As Treichler explains:

The construction of AIDS as essentially a male-only sexually trans-mitted disease depends upon the production and reproduction of gendered readings which often require reasoning so outlandish and speculative as to be dizzying. In turn this "knowledge" of AIDS infec-tion and who can "catch it" filters out counter-evidence in a variety of

ways, and creates a cycle of invisibility in which women do not believe themselves vulnerable and therefore do not seek medical care or
even anonymous testing. . . . The pie-shaped charts standardly include the classic 4-H "risk groups" — Homosexuals, Heroin addicts,
Hemophiliacs, and Haitians — plus their sex partners, gender often
unspecified — plus "others." (194)

By focusing on AIDS as something you get because of who you are, not
what you do, women were excluded from the list of populations believed
to be at risk. "As evidence of AIDS in women mounted," Treichler writes,
"speculations were put forward that linked AIDS to prostitutes, IV drug
users, and women in the third world (primarily Haiti and countries in
central Africa)" (197). So as the female body insisted on demonstrating its
susceptibility to the variety of afflictions associated with the AIDS syndrome, it became partially visible to the medical community, who used it
to mark an opposition between "sexually active males and promiscuous
females" (213).

Whereas in previous accounts of AIDS as "a male-only sexually
transmitted disease" the female body is literally invisible within medical
discourse, the definition of the female body advanced in the recent accounting for AIDS in women suggests that it is merely a container and
transmitter of the disease. In her discussion of the relatively recent attempt
to address the heterosexual transmission of the HIV virus, Treichler describes its problematic consideration of women:

> First, the women in the risk groups are given their "status" by virtue
> of their sexual partners — the men they're connected to — not by vir-
> tue of their own sexual activities. . . . And finally, above all, the
> purpose of studying women, we are told, is twofold: first, to use
> incidence in women as a general index to heterosexual spread of the
> virus, and second, to identify women at risk and prevent "primary"
> infection in them so that we can prevent the majority of cases of AIDS
> in children that would result from these maternal risk groups without
> our intervention. (215)

The female body of this AIDS discourse is identified by its reproductive
responsibilities and sexual connections to men. Now that it is established
that women can be infected, woman's legacy as an inherently pathological, unruly, uncontainable, but essentially passive vessel returns to haunt
her and render her again invisible within medical discourse.

Bleier's work in neuroanatomy and Treichler's on AIDS discourse both mark one of the transitions that Haraway identifies as an "informatics of domination": from an order concerned with organic sex role specialization to one that redefines biology as inscription. Central to this transition is the emergence of communication technologies as the premier technologies of culture. For Haraway, in "A Manifesto for Cyborgs,"

> [c]ommunication technologies and biotechnologies are the crucial tools recrafting our bodies. . . . Technologies and scientific discourses can be partially understood as formalizations, i.e., as the frozen moments, of the fluid social interactions constituting them, but they should also be viewed as instruments for enforcing meanings. . . . Furthermore, communication sciences and modern biologies are constructed by a common move—the translation of the world into a problem of coding, a search for a common language in which all resistance to instrumental control disappears and all heterogeneity can be submitted to disassembly, reassembly, investment, and exchange. (82–83)

The female body is at the center of this transformation of the social order. As a cyborg, simultaneously discursive and material, the female body is the site at which we can witness the struggle between systems of social order. In the process, new forms of gendered embodiment emerge which on the one hand may display inherited signs of traditional dichotomous gender identity, but which also reinvent gender identity in totally new ways. In postmodern social theory, as was demonstrated in various other historical moments, the female body has been constructed as uncontainable, unruly, and ultimately undecidable. Just as this is woman's legacy, so too is it her promise. Although the female body is subordinated within institutionalized systems of power and knowledge and crisscrossed by incompatible discourses, it is not fully determined by those systems of meaning; and although woman is technologically constructed, her excesses accumulate, assembling the resources/techniques to signify/construct herself as transgressive of, if not entirely resistant to, the discourses that seek to contain her.

Cyborg bodies pump iron—physically fit, yet unnaturally crafted, they are hyper-built. Cyborg bodies raise the issue of possible new form(s) of gendered embodiment. Their recrafted bodies defy the natural givenness of physical gender identity. The problem with postmodern body stories is that bodies are never nonmaterial, as these stories suggest. They are never outside history and concrete relations of power and domination. Just as women never speak, write, or act outside of their bodies, cyborgs never leave the meat behind. It is important that feminist approaches to "the body" resist the easy dissolution or dematerialization of the body offered by postmodernist theorists. The cyborg image works well to foreground the radical materiality of the body, which cannot be written out of any feminist account. Whatever its fate, "the body" in feminist theory has never been simply a blank slate (or screen) upon which or about which to write. From a feminist perspective, attempts to write about the relationship between the contemporary social order and the body are ill-fated endeavors if they do not begin with a consideration of gender, or more explicitly, with a consideration of the gendering of bodies. It seems, at times, that the more "the body" is subjected to theoretical scrutiny, the more resistant it becomes. Just as the disappearance of the body is announced in theory, the material body returns to thwart all attempts to repress it. It remains, for all of the various feminisms, a vital site for the working out of the intersections among feminist politics, theory, and practice in postmodernity.

CHAPTER TWO

Feminist Bodybuilding

As outlined in the introduction, I borrow Michel Feher's conceptualization of the modes of body construction as a framework for understanding the ways that the body is conceptualized in feminist discourse. The female body has been "built" within feminist discourse in several different ways; in the course of this essay I draw on three domains of feminist body work: (1) scholarship that investigates the *ideological* construction of the female body in the history of women's sport; (2) *semiotic* analyses of media representations of female athletes; and (3) a *cultural* interpretation of a filmic narrative about technologically reconstructed female bodies. More specifically, the first section reviews historical studies of women and sport to illustrate how the physiological body is culturally redefined according to dominant beliefs about women's proper and moral responsibilities for human reproduction. The second section focuses on media representations of prominent female athletes to examine how ideals about feminine beauty are being revised to include signs of muscularity and vigorous health. While these representations highlight the athletic capabilities and power of the female body, they also show the ways in which that power is symbolically recuperated to a dominant cultural order through the sexualization of the bodies of athletic "stars." The final section offers a reading of the film *Pumping Iron II: The Women*, which examines how it stages a symbolic contest about the proper definition of femininity; as a winner of the filmic bodybuilding contest is announced, so too is a preferred form of female embodiment. Each section addresses one form of feminist bodybuilding; they all illuminate the way in which the "naturally" female body is culturally reconstructed according to dominant codes of femininity and racial identity.

The Ideological Treatment of the Sporting Woman

Lynda Birke and Gail Vines, two feminist sport sociologists, identify both science and sport as cults of masculinity marked by a belief in the superiority of the male body.[1] Indeed, historical research on the cultural construction of the female body illuminates how sports experts continued the quest to locate woman's inferiority in her "physiological body" after the "science" of craniology failed to prove that her inferiority resided in her brain. In a similar line of analysis, Helen Lenskyj explains how reproduction became a defining characteristic of female athletes, regardless of whether or not an individual woman in fact menstruated or became pregnant. Her research documents how woman's gender identity became intimately tied to her reproductive physiology. The physiological "facts" of her reproductive system establish the biologically sexed female body as the "natural" emblem or guarantor of female identity. Quoting from medical textbooks of the early nineteenth century, Lenskyj describes how the medical profession emphasized the fact of "reproduction" when prescribing safe and appropriate sporting activities for women.

> Both women's unique anatomy and physiology and their special moral obligations disqualif[y] them from vigorous physical activity. Women have a moral duty to preserve their vital energy for childbearing and to cultivate personality traits suited to the wife-and-mother role. Sport wastes vital forces, strains female bodies and fosters traits unbecoming to "true womanhood."[2]

Encumbered as they were with the burdens of menstruation, pregnancy, lactation, and menopause, women were thus instructed to forgo athletic activity in favor of less strenuous pursuits. According to this passage, both a woman's physiology and her moral obligations tied to that physiology combine to disqualify her from vigorous sporting activity.

Patricia Vertinsky describes yet another way in which women were discouraged from participating in sports because of what we now understand to be culturally defined "facts" about the female body.[3] These facts asserted that women were "eternally wounded" because they bled during part of their reproductive (menstrual) cycle. This popular myth—again supported by medical knowledge of the time—defined women as chronically weak and as victims of a pathological physiology. Two things happen here: not only is the female body irrevocably tied to a culturally constructed obligation of reproduction, but also, through the association between femininity and "the wound," the female body is coded as inherently pathological. Limiting women's participation in sport and exercise functioned both to control women's unruly physiology and to protect them for the important job of species reproduction.

These historical studies illuminate the process whereby one set of beliefs (about female physiological inferiority) is articulated with another discursive system (concerning women's athletic practices). Through their feminist analyses of the historical discourse on women and sport, both Lenskyj and Vertinsky show how physiological characteristics come to count as definitive emblems of female identity. Their body scholarship involves "rereading" the female body as it is inscribed in one discourse from within another textual/sexual system. The textual system they use to read the female body "against the grain" is informed by feminist cultural theory and, as such, it provides a perspective from which to document the process of cultural recoding of the female body—first as a "gendered" body, and secondly, as one in need of special protection from the rigors of physical exertion. In this sense, their analyses provide a way of understanding the process of transcoding, where the "natural" female body is taken up as a cultural emblem of the reproductive body with the consequence that women were often discouraged from participating in athletic activities.

The Sexualization of the Transgressive Body

Lenskyj's and Vertinsky's analyses suggest that historically the properly feminine body was considered to be constitutionally weak and pathological. To be both female and strong implicitly violates traditional codes of feminine identity. Thus women who use bodybuilding technology to sculpt their bodies are doubly transgressive; first, because femininity and nature are so closely aligned, any attempt to *reconstruct* the body is transgressive against the "natural" identity of the female body. Second, when female athletes use technology to achieve physical muscularity—a male body prerogative—they transgress the "natural" order of gender identity. What we discover through an analysis of media images of female athletes is that representations of their bodies often highlight their transgressive nature.

For example, a recent *National Enquirer* article featured a photo of bodybuilder Tina Plackinger accompanied by a headline that reads: "Prizewinning Bodybuilder Quits Taking Steroids Because . . . Drugs were

Prizewinning Bodybuilder Quits Taking Steroids Because . . .

Once-beautiful Tina Plakinger was turning into a man — because the prizewinning bodybuilder had plunged into the nightmare world of steroid drugs.

Her voice became husky. She grew facial hair and bulging muscles. Her breasts virtually disappeared. And when she put on her prettiest dresses, she looked like a man in drag.

Tina was a winner — and a miserable loser.

"I went from being a soft creature to a raging bull," says the 29-year-old Encino, Calif., real estate agent — who is back to normal a year after "going clean" and kicking steroids.

About seven years ago, Tina — who'd been competing as an amateur bodybuilder for some time — decided to bolster her physique by taking steroids, which simulate the muscle-building properties of male hormones.

Drugs Were Turning Me Into a Man

MALE HORMONES helped create Tina's bulging muscles (right), but other side effects included shrunken breasts, facial hair and a powder keg temper that kept her itching for a fight.

"I felt steroids would get me to the top — and they did, indeed, make me a champ. I was stronger and bigger every day. My muscles were huge. I won contest after contest, including the top amateur bodybuilding contest in the world, the Ms. America contest.

"At the same time, I was ingesting 10 steroid pills daily and shooting up the drug once a week."

"The side effects were frightening. I looked like a smaller version of Arnold Schwarzenegger! My voice got so low that telephone operators called me 'sir.'"

Besides making her shockingly manlike, the drugs also turned Tina into a human powder keg.

"I became a raging fury, always itching for a fight. Once at a drive-through bank window, the woman in the car ahead of me seemed to be taking all day to complete her transaction. I became furious. I jumped out of my car, ran over to hers, yanked the poor woman out and began shaking her as I poured out verbal abuse. I had to be pulled off by others who came to her rescue!

"I used to keep a club in my car. If I didn't like the way someone was driving, I'd get out and threaten them at a red light.

"Once when my husband came home late for dinner, I was so enraged I threw him against the door and held him there while I let him have it. I hit him again and again until I finally calmed down.

"And I was strong — at my peak, I could lift 350 pounds! It took me years of using the drug to finally realize I was destroying myself. Steroids had made me depressed, terribly unhappy. I no longer wanted to live the hell that had become my daily existence. I decided to end the insanity before it ended me.

"I've been clean for a year, and I intend to stay that way. I still do bodybuilding for health and endurance. It helps me keep my stamina as a real estate agent.

"I'm happy with my feminine figure. I have curves again. I look attractive in clothes. Being off steroids has given me my life back. I'm thankful for every day I live free of the drug — and its horrible hold over me."   — PETER FENTON

FEMININE AGAIN: Tina in her real estate office (above) and lifting weights (right) one year after quitting the steroids that were ruining her life.

Figure 9. *National Enquirer* article about a prizewinning female bodybuilder (September 22, 1987), p. 4.

Turning Me Into a Man" (figure 9).[4] Here the juxtaposition of physical strength, represented in the photograph by Plackinger's well-defined "ripped" biceps, triceps, and chest muscles, with the markers of her female body (breasts, long curly hair) creates a gender "hybrid" that invokes corporeal codes of femininity as well as of masculinity. The reference to Plackinger's steroid use as part of her body reconstruction program fur-

Figure 10. *Newsweek* magazine cover featuring Florence Griffith-Joyner (September 19, 1988). Photograph by Mark Hanauer.

ther establishes the transgressive nature of her body. Plackinger's use of steroids to produce a grotesquely muscular body violates not only the "natural" order of health and fitness, but also of femininity and weakness. Of course, the specter of a transgressed gender boundary visually enhances the "spectacular" rhetoric of the *National Enquirer* article.

However, this also happens in less sensationalistic media treatment of professionally trained amateur athletes. For example, a close analysis of the newspaper accounts of Florence Griffith-Joyner's performances at the 1988 Olympic games reveals the process of sexualization at work. The week before the Seoul Olympics, glossy photographs of Griffith-Joyner graced the covers of *U.S. News and World Report, Time,* and *Newsweek* (figure 10). Most stories found a way to mention her body, not only in reference to its athletic capacity, but more obviously as it served as a mannequin for her flamboyant track outfits. One sportswriter began his account of her record-breaking performance by ironically calling attention to her running outfit:

Okay, let's get the important stuff out of the way first. Florence Griffith-Joyner wore a shocking pink one-legger with a white bikini bottom in the first round of the 200 meters in the U.S. Olympic trials Friday morning. She wore a fluorescent gold body suit with an orange print string bikini bottom in the quarterfinals Friday night. For both races, the fingernails on her left hand were painted cobalt blue and decorated with Hawaiian scenes, including palm trees, birds and the moon. The fingernails on her right hand were multicolored with a variety of rhinestone designs, including a cross. It took her three to five minutes to do each nail. By the way, it took her nowhere near that long to run the 200 meters Friday night. In fact, it took her less time than any American woman in history, (21.77 seconds, .04 sec. faster than the American record).[5]

The problem with such accounts is not that her flamboyant outfits discredit her athletic ability — she is widely recognized as a talented athlete — but rather that her appearance invokes the production of stereotypical comments about her sexual attractiveness. Given her own penchant for highly stylized athletic outfits and the fact that female athletes cannot easily escape the cultural fascination that objectifies the female body, "Flo-Jo" was recognized as much, if not more, for her sexual desirability as for her athletic ability. Tony Duffy, a sports photographer, had this to say about Griffith-Joyner's media popularity:

> She was one of the sexiest girls at the 1984 Olympics . . . She has this Polynesian look and an exotic feeling about her. I did a photo shoot of Florence eight weeks ago, in body suits and bathing suits on the beach, and I couldn't give the pictures away. In the past two days (after her Olympic trials record), my phone has been ringing off the hook. *Playboy, Sports Illustrated, People, Life* — everyone wants pictures of her.[6]

This quotation describes the construction of Flo-Jo as cultural icon of exotic otherness. Accompanying newspaper images of Flo-Jo foreground corporeal markers of erotic identity: long thick curly hair; lean arms and torso; thick, muscular legs; and dark skin. Without much coaching, we read in such newspaper images the construction of Flo-Jo as an idealized female body. But she is more than simply a body — she is identified as an attractive, *exotic,* female body. Her transgressive identity is as much a product of the color of her skin, "her Polynesian look," as it is of her athletic accomplishments. As such, these physical transgressions contribute to her construction as an object of desire. In contemporary U.S. culture, nonwhite racial and ethnic identities function as signs of cultural difference; skin color, hair texture, and facial features are among the more familiar physiological markers of the cultural construction of "otherness." Much in the way that the biological "facts" of a woman's reproductive system are used to define her as a gendered body, so too are certain body "facts" invoked to construct Griffith-Joyner as an eroticized "other." In this way we see how the athletic female body is also inscribed within other ideological systems of meaning, including those of race, ethnicity, and physical ability. This analysis describes the way in which the black female body is constructed as a sign of transgressive cultural difference and as a "natural" sexual object.[7]

The Technological Construction of the Ideal Feminine Body

Analysis of media representations of the female body shows quite clearly the way in which that body symbolizes cultural ideas of "natural" femininity and erotic beauty. But the *symbolic* transformation of the female body is only part of the story. Through the practices of bodybuilding, weight training, and powerlifting, many female bodies are *technologically* transformed into material embodiments of such ideals. Because the form and quality of the bodies of women who participate in bodybuilding activities directly contradict traditional beliefs about the inherent pathology of femininity, female bodybuilding appears to be one arena in which the culturally constructed "natural" attributes of femininity could be redesigned in a more empowering fashion. But upon closer examination, we see how technologically recrafted female bodies are delegitimated as cultural markers of proper femininity.

During the decade 1980–90, an entire subculture grew up around female bodybuilding. The annual Miss Olympia contest was first staged in 1980. By 1989 there were dozens of annual competitions, ranging from the World Professional Women's Bodybuilding Championships to amateur contests sponsored by local fitness centers. In 1989, the number of female competitors at the amateur level was estimated at 16,000, a significant increase from the 40 to 150 women who competed in 1980. The *Hardcore Bodybuilder's Source Book* lists several products specifically designed for female readers: training courses and routines, cookbooks, foods, jewelry, posing wear, posters, skin and hair care products, and bodybuilding horoscopes.[8] This subculture includes glossy magazines such as *Muscle and Fitness* as well as special workout books such as Rachel McLish's *Flex Appeal* (figure 11).

The film *Pumping Iron II: The Women* gained wide acclaim as a cult classic among female bodybuilders and gym participants. The film unfolds

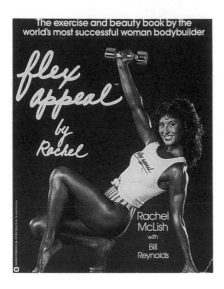

Figure 11. Cover of *Flex Appeal by Rachel* by Rachel McLish with Bill Reynolds (New York: Warner Communications, 1984).

a cultural narrative about the "natural" definition of femininity as it applies to the technologically reconstructed female body.[9] In an early scene, the head judge instructs other judges about the rules of competition and describes the ultimate purpose of the contest:

> We hope that this evening we can clear up the definite meaning—the analysis of the word femininity [by] determining what to look for [in these women competitors]. This is an official IFBB analysis of the meaning of that word.[10]

In an unambiguous address, the audience is told that the (film's) contest will determine with perfect clarity the "definite meaning" of the word "femininity." Apparently, the quality of feminine muscle definition is an ongoing concern for the judges of female bodybuilding contests. As reported in *The Hardcore Bodybuilder's Source Book,* judges are given the following instructions about judging female competitors:

> First and foremost, the judges must bear in mind that he or she is judging a woman's bodybuilding competition and is looking for an ideal feminine physique. Therefore, the most important aspect is shape, a feminine shape. Other aspects are similar to those described for assessing men, but in regard to muscular development, it must not be carried to excess where it resembles the *massive muscularity of the male physique.*[11] (emphasis added)

In fact, judges are instructed to look for certain faults in women that are not usually seen in men: stretch marks, operation scars, and cellulite; they are also directed to observe whether female competitors walk and move in a graceful manner, which seemingly is not a concern with male competitors.[12]

The film stages a contest between competing forms of female embodiment personified by two well-known female bodybuilders: Bev Frances, a muscular powerlifter, and Rachel McLish, a beauty-girl bodybuilder.[13] But members of the film's audience know that the film isn't a documentary at all; it is really a fictional account of a staged competition, the Caesar's Palace World Cup Championship. The film relies on several techniques and genre conventions to establish its documentary "look": the camera records spontaneously delivered (nonscripted) interactions between characters; contestants are interviewed by an offscreen voice; conversations are filmed up close. And although the film uses "real" bodybuilders, this pseudo-documentary lists them in "starring roles" to compete in a contest that was elaborately scripted.

The film records the reaction of judges and other women contestants to the embodied differences between the two stars. Symbolically, Bev represents the negative image of female bodybuilding: women who look like men. Rachel symbolizes the positive image of female bodybuilding: women with muscles who still look feminine (soft, curvy, and sexy when dressed in a bikini). Beginning with the sequences that introduce Rachel and Bev, the film visually constructs a system of differences between these two types of female bodies. Their differences concern not only the muscularity of their bodies, but also the type of clothes they wear, their local gyms, and their countries, cities, and families of origin. Narratively, the contest between Rachel and Bev structures the film's plot, so that at one level the film is about the competition between these two female bodies, but at another level, it is a film about ideologies of femininity.

The first shots of Rachel show her dressed in a black-and-white, zebra-print bikini, wearing a feather headdress and gold chains around her neck and belly. She is posing for a photo session for *Muscle & Fitness* magazine. Back in her home gym in Los Angeles, Rachel's posing coach wonders if her non-bodybuilding activities (commercials, posters, a beauty book project) diminish her status as a world-class bodybuilding champion. "Don't you think all this has made you a little soft, a little powder-puffish?" her coach inquires. "I've always considered myself a powder puff," drawls Rachel, "a really strong powder puff."

In contrast, Bev's introductory sequence opens with a shot of the rocky, rugged gray landscape of Melbourne, Australia. We meet Bev as she walks sideways up the walls of a hotel corridor. The next scene shows her competing in a power-lifting contest; she's just been introduced as a former ballet dancer who is now the strongest woman in the world. Bev, shown wearing a wrestling suit and sleeveless T-shirt, successfully dead-lifts 510 pounds. Relaxing after the contest, Bev talks with her family (and presumably the film's interviewer) about the upcoming competition in Las Vegas. She ponders the reaction she'll receive from an American audience who until now have seen only one type of female bodybuilder — skinny women with little muscles.

As the drama of the film unfolds, these two female bodies face off against one another. Side by side on stage, Bev and Rachel are the first pair of competitors judged in the first round of compulsory poses. While the other competitors pose, the audience is visually treated to several titillating shots of Rachel: the camera caressing her with a long, slow take that moves from her ankles to her thighs to her face. Bev is not treated so kindly by the camera, rather we witness her in the dressing room sitting hunched over, elbows on knees, talking with her trainer. "Did I look like a girl?" she asks sarcastically. "How was my feminine quality?"

At the end of the contest, Bev's name is announced first; she finishes last of eight finalists. Her last-place finish symbolizes the significance of her body transgressions when a judge explains: Women with "big grotesque muscles" violate the natural difference between men and women (figure 12). However, neither is Rachel's physique simply elevated as the ideal female form. Portrayed throughout the film as a petulant "bad girl," Rachel actually finishes third in the contest. When Carla Dunlap is announced as the winner, the film abruptly jags away from its narrative predictability (figure 13). Carla, a former Ms. Olympian, is clearly the best candidate in terms of overall athletic ability and bodybuilding sophistication. In terms of the film, however, her victory comes as a surprise because she is never constructed as a featured competitor in the way that Bev and Rachel are.[14] In fact, we learn very little about her personal body history or her philosophy about bodybuilding. Several times throughout the film she functions simply as a narrator, first to introduce Bev and the significance of Bev's participation in the contest, and later to interpret for the audience the meaning of the judges' struggle over competing definitions of femininity.

Yet Carla is an interesting selection as the winner. She is the only

featured competitor who is not associated with a male trainer/husband/
father. Instead, her "real life" companions are a sister and mother who
serve as a surrogate audience for her explanations about the significance
of Bev's and Rachel's participation in the contest. She is the only contestant to be shown doing non-bodybuilding physical activities: synchronized swimming and dancing. In choosing Carla, the film works hard to
achieve a compromise position on the issue of femininity versus muscularity. Carla has neither the massive muscle-bound physique of Bev
Francis nor the powder-puff figure of Rachel McLish.

But is Carla's winning a compromise or a cop-out? Carla is the only
black contestant. Although her racial identity is not discussed explicitly
within the film, by promoting her as the compromise between two technologically reconstructed forms of female embodiment, the film implicitly
engages a host of body issues that invoke different forms of body transgression. Carla's victory signals a transgressive body posture through the
identification of her as a black woman in a filmic world populated by
white women. The meaning of Carla's victory is subversively significant,
not with respect to the issue of muscularity versus femininity but with
respect to her racial identity. If this indeed was a contest to determine
the proper meaning of the word "femininity," how do we interpret the
answer we've been given? What can it mean that a black female body
is offered as a compromise between ideologies of muscularity and of
femininity?

For Annette Kuhn, the film *Pumping Iron II: The Women* raises
several issues regarding visual representation and feminist politics. Kuhn
argues that Carla's victory merely sidesteps the film's central question:

> The issue of the appropriate body for a female bodybuilder is not
> actually resolved: rather it is displaced on to a set of discourses center-
> ing on — but also skirting — race, femininity and the body, a complex
> of discourses which the film cannot acknowledge, let alone handle.
> Carla's body can be "read" only as a compromise: other major issues
> are left dangling.[15]

On the one hand, Carla's success as a bodybuilder is only one of many
athletic achievements of black women. She, along with Florence Griffith-
Joyner, are only the two most recent black female athletes to achieve
media popularity in U.S. culture. The reading that the film promotes suggests that it is not unusual (or noteworthy) for a black woman to succeed
as an accomplished athlete in U.S. sports; such a reading purports to be

Figure 12. Bodybuilder Bev Francis deadlifting 500 pounds. From *Pumping Iron II: The Unprecedented Woman* by Charles Gains and George Butler (New York: Simon and Schuster, 1984), p. 157.

Figure 13. Bodybuilders Bev Francis, Carla Dunlap, and Rachel McLish. From *The Hardcore Bodybuilder's Source Book* by Robert Kennedy and Vivian Mason (New York: Sterling, 1984), p. 161.

"color-blind" by purposefully forgoing any mention of her racial identity. On the other hand, Carla's victory suggests that racial distinctions are somehow less disturbing of a natural order than are the gender transgressions that Bev's body symbolizes.

But according to bell hooks, such an interpretation is constructed within a discourse of white racism:

> Racist stereotypes of the strong, superhuman black woman are operative myths in the minds of many white women, allowing them to ignore the extent to which black women are likely to be victimized in this society and the role white women play in the maintenance and perpetration of that victimization.[16]

Informed by hooks's analysis, we can look again at Carla's role in the film. Although she is never portrayed as a victim per se, she is constrained in many ways. We see her constructed as an interpreter and guide to help the audience make sense of the meaning of the contest between two white women's bodies. She, herself, is not featured as a competent, accomplished professional bodybuilder. She is not empowered to elaborate her own identity as a bodybuilder. In this sense, Carla's narrative, repressed throughout the film, emerges as an emblem of the film's sexist and racist agenda. In the end, the film sidesteps the issue of technologically constructed gender differences and opens onto the issue of racial difference, only to end without addressing either issue or the interaction between them. By denying Carla her own story, the film teaches us that the only stories that count are those about white bodies. Scripted in this way, Carla's victory enables the racist fiction that asserts that white bodies are the bodies that matter, even if black bodies win from time to time. But it also points out that when white female bodybuilders engage in transgressive body practices, they enjoy a greater range of possibilities for reconstructing their corporeal identity in opposition to a traditional notion of white femininity — defined as weak, pathological, and passive. Black transgressive bodies cannot as easily escape a "naturalized" race identity that codes the black body as "naturally" powerful. The efficacy of this power is recuperated as Carla is also shown to be "naturally" subservient to white bodies against whom she competes.

Thus, by sidelining Carla's story, the film sidesteps a much more potent challenge to the ideological contest playing out on the fictional stage of Caesar's Palace. What is much more interesting about Carla's story is that it is populated by supportive women and female relatives; men simply don't figure in Carla's narrative. In failing to offer a fuller account of her "woman-centered" athletic life, the film reveals how the debate that preoccupies most of the contestants, judges, and audience, about proper femininity and improper female masculinity, is constructed within a dualistic logic that privileges the ideal-type distinctions between masculinity and femininity as the most significant markers of cultural difference. The repressed elements of the film, Carla's racial identity and her connections to other women, suggest some of the other submerged discourses that also structure the organization of technological body practices, but which are rarely acknowledged in media accounts of technologically transgressive female bodies. In this case, we can begin to get a sense of other factors that influence the meaning of transgressive body practices — namely, those of racial identity and of homosocial relationships.

What I discover, not surprisingly, is that despite appearing as a form of resistance, these technological body transgressions rearticulate the power relations of a dominant social order. This is to say that when female bodies participate in bodybuilding activities or other athletic events that are traditionally understood to be the domain of male bodies, the meanings of those bodies are not simply recoded according to an oppositional or empowered set of gendered connotations. Although these bodies transgress gender boundaries, they are not reconstructed according to an opposite gender identity. They reveal, instead, how culture processes transgressive bodies in such a way as to keep each body in its place — that is, subjected to its "other." For white women, this other is the idealized "strong" male body; for black women, it is the white female body. A closer study of the popular culture of female bodybuilding reveals the *artificiality* of attributes of "natural" gender identity and the *malleability* of cultural ideals of gender identity, yet it also announces quite loudly the *persistence* with which gender and race hierarchies structure technological practices, thereby limiting the disruptive possibilities of technological transgressions.

CHAPTER THREE

On the Cutting Edge: Cosmetic Surgery
and New Imaging Technologies

Among the most intriguing new body technologies developed during the
1980s are techniques of visualization that redefine the range of human
perception.[1] New medical imaging technologies such as laparoscopy and
computer tomography (CT) make the body visible in such a way that its
internal status can be assessed before it is laid bare or opened up surgically.[2] Like the techniques that enable scientists to encode and "read"
genetic structures, these new visualization technologies transform the material body into a visual medium. In the process the body is fractured and
fragmented so that isolated parts can be examined visually: the parts can
be isolated by function, as in organs or neuron receptors, or by medium, as
in fluids, genes, or heat. At the same time, the material body comes to
embody the characteristics of technological images.[3] This chapter examines the discourse of cosmetic surgery as it relies upon new technologies of
visualization that function similarly to other visualization devices: to frag-
ment the body into isolated parts and pieces and to render it a visual
medium.

Carole Spitzack suggests that cosmetic surgery actually deploys three
overlapping mechanisms of cultural control: inscription, surveillance, and
confession.[4] According to Spitzack, the physician's clinical eye functions
like Foucault's medical gaze; it is a disciplinary gaze situated within apparatuses of power and knowledge that constructs the female figure as
pathological, excessive, unruly, and potentially threatening of the dominant order. This gaze disciplines the unruly female body by first fragment-
ing it into isolated parts — face, hair, legs, breasts — and then redefining
those parts as inherently flawed and pathological. When a woman inter-
nalizes a fragmented body image and accepts its "flawed" identity, each

part of the body then becomes a site for the "fixing" of her physical abnormality.[5] Spitzack characterizes this acceptance as a form of confession:

> In the scenario of the cosmetic surgeon's office, the transformation from illness to health is inscribed on the body of the patient. . . . The female patient is promised beauty and re-form in exchange for confession, which is predicated on an admission of a diseased appearance that points to a diseased (powerless) character. A failure to confess, in the clinical setting, is equated with a refusal of health; a preference for disease.[6]

But the cosmetic surgeon's gaze doesn't simply *medicalize* the female body, it actually redefines it as an object for technological reconstruction. In her reading of the women's films of the 1940s, Mary Ann Doane employs the concept of the "clinical eye" to describe how the technologies of looking represent and situate female film characters as the objects of medical discourse. In Doane's analysis, the medicalization of the female body relies on a surface/depth model of the body, whereby the physician assumes the right and responsibility of divining the truth of the female body — to make visible her invisible depths. The clinical gaze of the physician reveals the truth of the female body in his act of looking through her to see the "essence" of her illness. According to Doane, the clinical eye marks a shift in the signification of the female body, from a purely surface form of signification to a depth model of signification. She traces this shift through a reading of the difference between mainstream classical cinema and the woman's film of the 1940s.[7]

In examining the visualization technologies used in the practice of cosmetic surgery, we can witness the process whereby new imaging technologies are articulated with traditional and ideological beliefs about gender — an articulation that keeps the female body positioned as a privileged object of a normative gaze that is now not simply a medicalized gaze ("the clinical eye") but also a technologized view. In the application of new visualization technologies, the relationship between the female body and the cultural viewing apparatus has shifted again; in the process, the clinical eye gives way to the deployment of a technological gaze. This application of the gaze does not rely on a surface/depth model of the material body, whereby the body has some sort of structural integrity as a bounded physical object. In the encounter between women and cosmetic surgeons, it is not so much the inner or essential woman that is visualized; her interior story has no truth of its own. Both her surface and her interior-ity are flattened and dispersed. Cosmetic surgeons use technological imaging devices to reconstruct the female body as a signifier of ideal feminine beauty. In this sense, surgical techniques literally enact the logic of assembly-line beauty: "difference" is made over into sameness. The technological gaze refashions the material body to reconstruct it in keeping with culturally determined ideals of Western feminine beauty.

Cosmetic Surgery and the Inscription of Cultural Standards of Beauty

Cosmetic surgery enacts a form of cultural signification where we can examine the literal and material reproduction of ideals of beauty. Where visualization technologies bring into focus isolated body parts and pieces, surgical procedures actually carve into the flesh to isolate parts to be manipulated and resculpted. In this way cosmetic surgery *literally* transforms the material body into a sign of culture. The *discourse* of cosmetic surgery offers provocative material for discussing the cultural construction of the gendered body because women are often the intended and preferred subjects of such discourse and men are often the agents performing the surgery. Cosmetic surgery is not simply a discursive site for the "construction of images of women," but a material site at which the physical female body is surgically dissected, stretched, carved, and reconstructed according to cultural and eminently ideological standards of physical appearance.

There are two main fields of plastic surgery. Whereas *reconstructive* surgery works to repair catastrophic, congenital, or cancer-damage deformities, *cosmetic* or aesthetic surgery is often an entirely elective endeavor. And whereas reconstructive surgery is associated with the restoration of health, normalcy, and physical function, cosmetic surgery is said to improve self-esteem, social status, and sometimes even professional standing.

All plastic surgery implicitly involves aesthetic judgments of proportion, harmony, and symmetry. In fact, one medical textbook strongly encourages plastic surgeons to acquire some familiarity with classical art theory so that they are better prepared to "judge human form in three dimensions, evaluate all aspects of the deformity, visualize the finished product, and plan the approach that will produce an optimal result."[8] Codifying the aspects of such an "aesthetic sense" seems counterintuitive, but in fact there is a voluminous literature that reports the scientific measurement of facial proportions in an attempt to accomplish the scientific determination of aesthetic perfection. According to one surgeon, William Bass, most cosmetic surgeons have some familiarity with the anthropological fields of anthropometry and human osteology. Anthropometry — defined in one source as "a technique for the measurement of men, whether living or dead" — is actually a critically important science used by a variety of professional engineers and designers.[9] One example of practical anthropometry is the collection of measurements of infants and children's bodies for use in the design of automobile seat restraints.[10] Of course it makes a great deal of sense that measurement standards and scales of human proportions are a necessary resource for the design of products for human use; in order to achieve a "fit" with the range of human bodies that will eventually use and inhabit a range of products from office chairs to office buildings, designers must have access to a reliable and standardized set of body measurements.[11] But when the measurement project identifies the "object" being measured as the "American Negro" or the "ideal female face," it is less clear what practical use these measurements serve.[12]

If anthropometry is "a technique for the measurement of men," the fascination of plastic surgeons is the measurement of the ideal. One well-cited volume in a series published by the American Academy of Facial Plastic and Reconstructive Surgery, titled *Proportions of the Aesthetic Face* (by Nelson Powell and Brian Humphreys), proclaims that it is a "complete sourcebook of information on facial proportion and analysis."[13] In the preface the authors state:

> The face, by its nature, presents itself often for review. We unconsciously evaluate the overall effect each time an acquaintance is made. . . . This [impression] is generally related to some scale of beauty or balance. . . . The harmony and symmetry are compared to a mental, almost magical, ideal subject, which is our basic concept of beauty. Such a concept or complex we shall term the "ideal face."[14]

According to the authors, the purpose of their text is quite simple: to document, objectively, the guidelines for facial symmetry and proportion. Not inconsequentially, the "Ideal Face" depicted throughout this book — both in the form of line drawings and in photographs — is of a white woman whose face is perfectly symmetrical in line and profile (figure 14). The authors claim that although the "male's bone structure is sterner, bolder, and more prominent . . . the ideals of facial proportion and unified

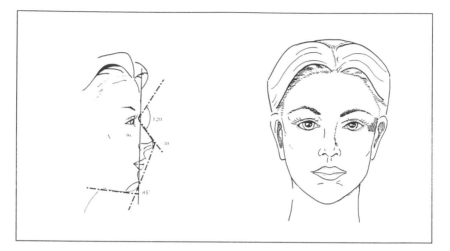

Figure 14. Line drawing from a cosmetic surgery text, illustrating the angles and proportions of the ideal female face. From the "Glossary of Terms" in *Proportions of the Aesthetic Face* by Nelson Powell, DDS, MD, and Brian Humphreys, MD (New York: Thieme-Stratton, 1984), p. 65.

interplay apply to either gender" (2). The only illustration of a male face is contained in the glossary (figure 15). As I discuss later, this focus on the female body is prevalent in all areas of cosmetic surgery — from the determination of ideal proportions to the marketing of specific cosmetic procedures. The source or history of these idealized drawings is never discussed. But once the facial proportions of these images are codified and measured, they are reproduced by surgeons as they make modifications to their patients' faces. Even though they work with faces that are individually distinct, surgeons use the codified measurements as guidelines for determining treatment goals in the attempt to bring the distinctive face in alignment with artistic ideals of symmetry and proportion.

The treatment of race in this book on "ideal proportions of the aesthetic face" reveals a preference for white, symmetrical faces that heal (apparently) without scarring. On the one hand the authors acknowledge that "bone structure is different in all racial identities" and that "surgeons must acknowledge that racial qualities are appreciated differently in various cultures," but in the end they argue that "the facial form [should be] able to confer harmony and aesthetic appeal regardless of race."[15] It appears that this appreciation for the aesthetic judgment "regardless of race" is not a widely shared assumption among cosmetic surgeons. Napoleon N.

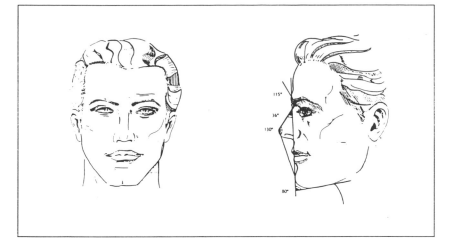

Figure 15. Line drawing from a cosmetic surgery text, illustrating the angles and proportions of the ideal male face. From the "Glossary of Terms" in *Proportions of the Aesthetic Face* by Nelson Powell, DDS, MD, and Brian Humphreys, MD (New York: Thieme-Stratton, 1984), p. 65.

Vaughn reports that many cosmetic surgeons, "mindful of keloid formation and hyperpigmented scarring, routinely reject black patients."[16] But the issue of scar tissue formation is entirely ignored in the discussion of the "proportions of the aesthetic face." Powell and Humphreys implicitly argue that black faces can be evaluated in terms of ideal proportions determined by the measurement of Caucasian faces, but they fail to address the issue of postsurgical risks that differentiate black patients from Caucasian ones.[17] Although it is true that black patients and patients with dark ruddy complexions have a greater propensity to form keloids or hypertrophic scars than do Caucasian patients, many physicians argue that black patients who are shown to be prone to keloid formation in the lower body are not necessarily prone to such formations in the facial area and upper body; therefore a racial propensity for keloid formation should not be a reason to reject a black patient's request for facial cosmetic surgery.[18] And according to Arthur Sumrall, even though "postoperative dyschromic changes and surgical incision lines are much more visible in many black patients and races of color than their Caucasian counterparts," these changes and incision lines greatly improve with time and corrective cosmetics.[19] As an abstraction, the "aesthetic face" is designed to assist surgeons in planning surgical goals; but as a cultural artifact, the "aesthetic face" symbolizes a desire for standardized ideals of Caucasian beauty.

It is clear that all plastic surgery invokes standards of physical appearance and functional definitions of the "normal" or "healthy" body. Upon closer investigation we can see how these standards and definitions are culturally determined. In the 1940s and 1950s, women reportedly wanted "pert, upturned noses," but according to one recent survey this shape has gone out of style: "the classic, more natural shape is the ultimate one with which to sniff these days."[20] The obvious question becomes, what condition does the adjective "natural" describe? In this case we can see how requests for cosmetic reconstructions show the waxing and waning of fashionable desires; in this sense, "fashion surgery" might be a more fitting label for the kind of surgery performed for nonfunctional reasons. But even as high fashion moves toward a multiculturalism in the employment of nontraditionally beautiful models,[21] it is striking to learn how great is the demand for cosmetic alterations that are based on Western markers of ideal beauty. In a *New York Times Magazine* feature, Ann Louise Bardach reports that Asian women often desire surgery to effect a more "Western"-shaped eye.[22] Indeed, in some medical articles this surgery is actually referred to as "upper lid westernization," and is reported to be "the most frequently performed cosmetic procedure in the Orient."[23] Surgeons Hall, Webster, and Dubrowski explain:

> An upper lid fold is considered a sign of sophistication and refinement to many Orientals across all social strata. It is not quite accurate to say that Orientals undergoing this surgery desire to look Western or American; rather, they desire a more refined Oriental eye. . . . An upper lid westernization blepharoplasty frequently is given to a young Korean woman on the occasion of her betrothal.[24]

Although other surgeons warn that it is "wise to discuss the Oriental and Occidental eye anatomy in terms of differences *not* defects,"[25] another medical article on this type of surgery was titled "Correction of the Oriental Eyelid."[26] In terms of eyelid shape and design, Hall and his colleagues do not comment on how the "natural" Oriental eye came to be described as having a "poorly defined orbital and periorbital appearance"; thus, when their Oriental patients request "larger, wider, less flat, more defined, more awake-appearing eyes and orbital surroundings," these surgeons offer an operative plan for the surgical achievement of what is commonly understood to be a more Westernized appearance.[27] In discussing the reasons for the increased demand for this form of blepharoplasty "among the Oriental," Marwali Harahap notes that this technique became popular after World War II; this leads some surgeons to speculate that such a desire for Westernized eyes "stem[s] from the influence of motion pictures and the increasing intermarriage of Asian women and Caucasian men."[28]

The Marketing of Youthfulness

When a young girl born with "hidden eyes" was scheduled to have massive face reconstruction surgery, surgeons hoped to construct eyelids for her where there were none.[29] The key objectives for her eye surgery were "normalcy" and "functionality," however a review of medical literature on reconstructive surgery reveals that blepharoplasty (eyelid operations) is a common technique of "youth surgery."[30] Because body tissue loses its elasticity in the process of aging, eyelids often begin to sag when a person reaches the early fifties. Bagginess is caused by fat deposits that build up around the eye and stretch the skin, producing wrinkling and sagging, and is most likely the result of a hernia — the weakening of the tissue around the eye — in which the fat deposits push outward and downward. Although eyestrain and fatigue can result from overworking the muscles around the eyes in an effort to keep eyes looking alert and open, eyelid surgery very rarely involves a "catastrophic" or "cure-based" medical rationale. Yet it is quite common, in both the popular and professional literature, for a plastic surgeon to refer to eye bags as a "deformity." This is a simple example of the way in which "natural" characteristics of the aging body are redefined as "symptoms," with the consequence that cosmetic surgery is rhetorically constructed as a medical procedure with the power to "cure" or "correct" such physical deformities.[31]

Several types of aesthetic surgery have been marketed explicitly for an aging baby-boomer population, with the promise that external symptoms of aging can be put off, taken off, or virtually eliminated. By the end of the 1980s, the most requested techniques of cosmetic surgery included face lifts, nose reconstructions, tummy tucks, liposuction, skin peels, and hair transplants — surgical techniques that are specifically designed to counteract the effects of gravity and natural body deterioration.[32] More than a few articles have reported that baby boomers are the preferred market for these new medical procedures; as a demographic group they (1) have more money than time to spend on body maintenance, and (2) are just beginning to experience the effects of aging en masse.[33] Given the size of the baby-boomer population, it is no surprise that as the first wave of baby boomers reach their late forties we should see an increase in advertisements for services such as dental bonding and implants, requests for "revolutionary" new drugs such as Retin-A, and articles about rejuvenation drugs manufactured in Europe from dried fetal extracts.[34] Even though the size of the target market for these produces will continue to increase during the next decade, the competition among plastic surgeons has so intensified that many of them are using image consultants to design advertising campaigns to attract clients. One campaign that drew a round of criticism from other surgeons displayed a surgically sculpted shapely female body draped over an expensive car. While this is hardly a new combination for U.S. beer advertisers, many cosmetic surgeons claimed that such advertising tarnishes the dignified image of their medical profession.[35]

Plastic surgeons are instructed to warn preoperative patients that "this is medicine and not the beauty parlor," but in the same breath, they are also taught that "in our society many cosmetic surgical procedures are not a luxury but are considered necessary."[36] Apparently this creates a bit of a tension for cosmetic surgeons who on the one hand are keenly aware of the fact that the service they provide is often an entirely elective endeavor, but on the other also realize the potentially serious physical consequences of their medical service. This tension is managed discursively when both physicians and patients construct "curative" justifications for the voluntary submission to surgical treatment.[37] G. Richard Holt and Jean Edwards Holt obliquely refer to the fact that most eyelid operations are done for purely cosmetic reasons and not to increase physical functioning:

> Although there are obvious cosmetic advantages to nearly every blepharoplasty, it must be remembered that functional indications are of primary importance. There are several alterations in function that can be improved by a blepharoplasty, and these should be identified preoperatively. They also serve as important diagnoses that are accepted by many third-party insurance carriers as sufficient to warrant payment for the procedure. *However, they should be reported as such only if they actually exist.*[38] (emphasis added)

Apparently, the use of "curative" justifications in a diagnosis not only functions discursively to manage an anxious patient, it also legitimates and authorizes the "elective" surgery for insurance coverage. In the cli-

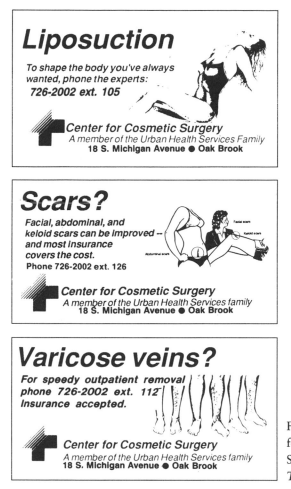

Figure 16. Advertisements for the Center for Cosmetic Surgery, Sunday *Chicago Tribune* (May 10, 1987).

mate of a recession, insurance reimbursement is vital to the continuing health of a medical specialty.[39] A more detailed discussion of the economics of medical diagnoses is beyond the scope of this essay, but it is likely that an investigation into the determining factors of medical reporting would find that economic forces influence the distinction between what can be identified as a "necessary" reconstructive procedure and procedures that are considered purely "elective."

Through the advertising channels of consumer culture, the practices of cosmetic surgery have been transformed into commodities themselves (figure 16). In one medical report, the surgeon-physicians blatantly claim, "Society's emphasis on a youthful appearance has created a demand for cosmetic plastic surgery."[40] Mary Ruth Wright, a clinical professor of psychology at Baylor University, explains:

> Today medicine encompasses far more than healing, saving, and serving. It has become a commodity, and consumer demands beyond reasonable expectations have emerged. Furthermore, today's concept of medical care goes beyond a physician-patient relationship; it involves society and the community as a whole. Perhaps medicine has overshot its marks; however, little is to be gained by looking back. We are here, practicing medicine in an age where the wonders of technology have put in the hands of physicians what used to be in the hands of fate. The elective surgeon, freed by an exemption from acute medical treatment, is especially affected by the changes that are occurring in the spectrum of modern medicine.[41]

Even though Wright raises the question of whether plastic surgeons are operating beyond the acceptable confines of a medical profession — by performing entirely elective procedures — she dismisses such concerns by refocusing on the biotechnological marvels that "the elective surgeon" can effect. Although her rhetoric sidesteps the question of agency when she states that "elective surgeons [are] freed from acute medical treatment," her statements implicitly argue that it is the mechanism of the marketplace that "frees" cosmetic surgeons from their duties to provide "acute medical treatment."

One of the consequences of the commodification and, correspondingly, the normalization of cosmetic surgery is that electing *not* to have cosmetic surgery is sometimes interpreted as a failure to deploy all available resources to maintain a youthful, and therefore socially acceptable and attractive, body appearance.[42] Kathryn Pauly Morgan, in an essay in a special issue of *Hypatia* on "Feminism and the Body," argues that the normalization of cosmetic surgery — "the inversion of the domains of the deviant and the pathological" — are "catalyzed by the technologizing of women's bodies."[43] From this point, Morgan goes on to discuss the more philosophical question of why "patients and cosmetic surgeons participate in committing one of the deepest of original philosophical sins, the choice of the apparent over the real" (28). The issue I'd like to consider, drawing on Morgan's analysis of the increasing "naturalization" of cosmetic alteration, is to elaborate the mechanism whereby the apparent is transformed into the real. How are women's bodies technologized? What is the role of cosmetic surgery in the technological reproduction of gendered bodies?

Cosmetic Surgery as a Technology of the Gendered Body

In recent years, more men are electing cosmetic surgery than in the past, but often in secret. As one article reports, "previously reluctant males are among the booming number of men surreptitiously doing what women have been doing for years: having their eyelids lifted, jowls removed, ears clipped, noses reduced, and chins tightened."[44] One cosmetic surgeon elaborates the reasons why men are beginning to seek elective cosmetic surgery:

> A middle-aged male patient — we'll call him Mr. Dropout — thinks he has a problem. He doesn't think he's too old for the lovely virgins he meets, but he wants to improve things. . . . When a man consults for aging, generally he is not compulsive about looking younger but he seeks relief from one or more specific defects incidental to aging: male pattern baldness . . . forehead wrinkling . . . turkey-gobbler neck. There are many things that can be done to help the aging man look younger or more virile.[45]

According to yet another cosmetic surgeon, the reason for some men's new concern about appearance is "linked to the increasing competition for top jobs they face at the peak of their careers from women and Baby Boomers."[46] Here the increase in male cosmetic surgery is explained as a shrewd business tactic: "looking good" connotes greater intelligence, competence, and desirability as a colleague. Charges of narcissism, vanity, and self-indulgence are put aside; a man's choice to have cosmetic surgery is explained by appeal to a rhetoric of career enhancement: a better looking body is better able to be promoted (figure 17). In this case, cosmetic surgery is redefined as a body management technique designed to reduce the stress of having to cope with a changing work environment, one that is being threatened by the presence of women and younger people.[47] While all of these explanations may be true — in the sense that this is how men justify their choice to elect cosmetic surgery — it is clear that other explanations are not even entertained. For example, what about the possibility that men and women are becoming more alike with respect to "the body

MEN AND PLASTIC SURGERY

It didn't take long for men to discover that they too can benefit from many of today's plastic surgery procedures.

And why not? It's just as easy for a man to be born with a nose that's too big or a chin that's too small. And sagging, wrinkled skin, puffy eyes and drooping jowls are just as unattractive on a man as they are on a woman.

The only difference is motivation.

A man's motivation to have plastic surgery is usually very different than a woman's. And it always seems to revolve around one issue.

Career advancement. Most men believe that their appearance has a direct impact on their careers. In today's extremely competitive business world, men wear their resume on their face. Being qualified isn't enough anymore. You have to look qualified, too.

Worn down, tired-looking executives who appear "over-the-hill" may get passed over for promotions and raises to younger-looking, healthier colleagues.

At least that's what many men believe. And this seemed to be confirmed in a recent nationwide study which had some interesting findings including:

84% of the men surveyed believed physical attractiveness was important for power and success on the job.

42% felt that improving one thing about their face would help their career.

32% agreed that if they had a more youthful appearance it would positively impact their job success.

22% agreed with the statement, "I use my personal appearance to my advantage in getting things accomplished on the job."

The message comes through loud and clear. The way you look can have a substantial impact on your job and your career. And this is the overwhelming reason why interest in plastic surgery amongst men has risen sharply over the last decade.

Favorite procedures for men include the facelift, forehead lift and eyelid surgery to eliminate that tired, worn-out, over-the-hill look.

Chin augmentation to project a more confident and powerful profile.

Surgery of the nose to reduce an oversized or poorly shaped nose. And liposuction to permanently get rid of "love handles," a double chin or to reduce the belly.

Of course, plastic surgery is no guarantee that you'll get a raise. A big promotion. Or that corner office you've been working for.

But, it can help.

It can help keep you looking young and physically fit.

It can help you let the boss know you're still ready for any challenge and up for any opportunity.

It can even boost your self-confidence and self-esteem.

The rest is up to you.

"In business today, men wear their resumes on their face. It's not enough to be qualified for the job — you have to look qualified, too."

Figure 17. Plastic surgery appeal aimed at a male audience. From *Everything You Always Wanted to Know about Plastic Surgery* (New York: Schell/Mullaney, 1991).

beautiful," that men are engaging more frequently in female body activities, or even simply that a concern with appearance isn't solely a characteristic of women? What about the possibility that the boundary between genders is eroding? How is it that men avoid the pejorative labels attached to female cosmetic surgery clients?[48]

In their ethnomethodological study of cosmetic surgery, Diana Dull and Candace West examine how surgeons and patients "account" for their decisions to elect cosmetic surgery. They argue that when surgeons divide the patient's body into component parts and pieces, it enables both "surgeons and patients together [to] establish the problematic status of the part in question and its 'objective' need of 'repair.' "[49] Dull and West go on to argue that this process of fragmentation occurs "in tandem with the accomplishment of gender" (67) which, in relying upon an essentialist view of the female body as always "needing repair," understands women's choice for cosmetic surgery as "natural" and "normal" and as a consequence of their (natural) preoccupation with appearance. However, because their "essential" natures are defined very differently, men must construct elaborate justifications for their decision to seek cosmetic alterations. This analysis illuminates one of the possible reasons why men and women construct different accounts of their decision to elect cosmetic surgery: the cultural meaning of their gendered bodies already determines the discursive rationale they can invoke to explain bodily practices. Although the bodies and faces of male farmers and construction workers, for example, are excessively "tanned" due to their constant exposure to the sun as part of their work conditions, their ruddy, leathery skin is not considered a liability or deformity of their male bodies. In contrast, white women who display wrinkled skin due to excessive tanning are sometimes diagnosed with "The Miami Beach Syndrome"; as one surgeon claims, "we find this type of overly tanned, wrinkled skin in women who not only go to Miami every year for three or four months, but lie on the beach with a sun reflector drawing additional rays to their faces."[50] It is no surprise then, that although any body can exhibit the "flaws" that supposedly justify cosmetic surgery, discussion and marketing of such procedures usually constructs the female as the typical patient. Such differential treatment of gendered bodies illustrates a by now familiar assertion of feminist studies of the body and appearance: the meaning of the presence or absence of any physical quality varies according to the gender of the body upon which it appears. Clearly an apparatus of gender organizes our seemingly most basic, natural, interpretation of human bodies, even when those bodies are technologically refashioned. Thus it appears that although technologies such as those used in cosmetic surgery can reconstruct the "natural" identity of the material body, they do little to disrupt naturalization of feminine corporeal identity.

Wendy Chapkis amplifies this point when she writes: "however much the particulars of the beauty package may change from decade to decade — curves in or out, skin delicate or ruddy, figures fragile or fit — the basic principles remain the same. The body beautiful is woman's responsibility and authority. She will be valued and rewarded on the basis of how close she comes to embodying the ideal" (figure 18).[51] In the *popular media* (newspapers, magazines), advertisements for surgical services are rarely, if ever, addressed specifically to men. When a man is portrayed as a prospective patient for cosmetic surgery (as in figure 17), he is often represented as a serious "business" person for whom a youthful appearance is a necessary business asset. In a 1988 advertising campaign for The Liposuction Institute in Chicago, each advertisement featured an illustration of a woman's (saddlebag) thighs as the "before" image of liposuction procedures (figure 19).[52] And of course, many cosmetic alterations are designed especially for women: tattooed eyeliner (marketed as "the ultimate cosmetic"), electrolysis removal of superfluous hair, and face creams.[53] An advertising representative for DuraSoft explains that the company has begun marketing its colored contact lenses specifically to black women ostensibly because DuraSoft believes that "black women have fewer cosmetic alternatives," but a more likely reason is that the company wants to create new markets for its cosmetic lenses.[54] The codes that structure cosmetic surgery advertising are gendered in stereotypical ways: being male requires a concern with virility and productivity, whereas being a real woman requires buying beauty products and services.[55]

And yet women who have too many cosmetic alterations are pejoratively labeled "scalpel slaves," to identify them with their obsession for surgical fixes.[56] Women in their late thirties and forties are the most likely candidates for repeat plastic surgery. According to *Psychology Today*, the typical "plastic surgery junkie" is a woman who uses cosmetic surgery as an opportunity to "indulge in unconscious wishes."[57] *Newsweek* diagnoses the image problems of "scalpel slaves":

Women in their 40s seem particularly vulnerable to the face-saving appeal of plastic surgery. Many scalpel slaves are older women who are recently divorced or widowed and forced to find jobs or date again. Others are suffering from the empty-nest syndrome. "They're re-entry women," says Dr. Susan Chobanian, a Beverly Hills cosmetic surgeon. "They get insecure about their appearance and show up every six months to get nips and tucks. . . . Plastic-surgery junkies are in many ways akin to the anorexic or bulimic," according to doctors. "It's a body-image disorder," says [one physician]. "Junkies don't know what they really look like." Some surgery junkies have a history of anorexia in the late teens, and now, in their late 30s and 40s, they're trying to alter their body image again.[58]

The naturalized identity of the female body as pathological and diseased is culturally reproduced in media discussions and representations of cosmetic surgery services. Moreover, the narrative obsessively recounted is that the female body is flawed in its distinctions and perfect when differences are transformed into sameness. However, in the case of cosmetic surgery the nature of the "sameness" is deceptive, because the promise is not total identity reconstruction — such that a patient could choose to look like the media star of her choice — but rather the more elusive pledge of "beauty enhancement." When cosmetic surgeons argue that the technological elimination of facial "deformities" will enhance a woman's "natural" beauty, we encounter one of the more persistent contradictions within the discourse of cosmetic surgery: namely, the use of technology to augment "nature."

Morphing and the Techno-Body

Surgeons are taught that the consultation process is actually an incredibly complex social exchange during which patients and surgeons must negotiate highly abstract goals. The accomplishment of goals is said to be directly related to patient satisfaction:

> [D]efining aesthetic goals with patients obviously involves the hazards of perception. . . . Any practitioner who has recommended and performed orthognathic surgery has most likely encountered patients with unrealistic aesthetic expectations. The surgical team most often accomplishes their functional and aesthetic goals, but, in this situation, the patient is disappointed. . . . Function, aesthetics, and shaping the patient's expectations into reality must all be addressed while keeping in mind the patient's best interests and desires.[59]

HOW MUCH DOES IT COST?

Less than you think.

After years of being perceived as something only for the rich and famous, plastic surgery is now priced for the middle class. People from all kinds of income brackets are undergoing surgery.

In fact, half of the patients who undergo plastic surgery make less than $25,000 a year. Breakthroughs in medicine and outpatient surgery have brought the price of plastic surgery down considerably over the years — even while the quality has gone up.

In addition to reasonable prices, financing is now readily available.

Your monthly payment will be determined by the amount of your down payment, the interest rate and the term of the loan. The examples below were based on an average price, no money down, a 36 month payback period and 17% APR financing. Even though every surgeon breaks down the various expenses (surgeon's fee, facility fee, anesthesia, medications, tests, etc.) in different ways, the prices outlined below are intended to include everything.

Your surgeon can tell you exactly how much your procedure will cost.

Plastic surgery has gotten so affordable that half the people who choose it make less than $25,000 a year.

	Low	HIGH	IF FINANCED...
Surgery of the Nose	$2000	$5000	$72-179 per month
Facelift	$3500	$10000	$125-357 per month
Forehead and Eyebrow Lift	$2000	$4500	$72-161 per month
Eyelid Surgery	$2000	$4500	$72-161 per month
Surgery of the Ear	$1500	$3500	$54-125 per month
Dermabrasion	$750	$3500	$27-125 per month
Chemical Peel	$1200	$4000	$43-143 per month
Cheek Augmentation	$750	$3000	$27-107 per month
Chin Augmentation	$1200	$2500	$43-90 per month
Lip Augmentation	$750	$2100	$27-75 per month
Scar Revision	$300	$4500	$11-161 per month
Breast Augmentation	$2300	$5300	$82-189 per month
Breast Lift	$3100	$6500	$111-232 per month
Breast Reduction	$3000	$7500	$107-268 per month
Breast Reconstruction	$3000	$10000	$107-357 per month
Liposuction	$750	$10000	$27-357 per month
Tummy Tuck	$4500	$12000	$161-428 per month

PLASTIC SURGERY THAT DOESN'T LEAVE YOU LOOKING PLASTIC

You can spot it in an instant.

Even from across the room. A facelift that looks plastic and unnatural.

A designer nose job that looks like it came off an assembly line.

Eyelid surgery that gives someone a slightly startled, surprised look.

We've all seen what bad plastic surgery can look like.

But have you ever seen it done well? You probably have — and didn't even

know it. Plastic surgery, when it's done well often goes unnoticed.

It should improve your looks without drawing attention to itself.

The ideal result always looks natural. Healthy. Beautiful.

This is the type of plastic surgery that delivers the best results and the happiest patients.

Plastic surgery, that doesn't leave you looking plastic.

Figure 18. Plastic surgery appeal aimed at a female audience. From *Everything You Always Wanted to Know about Plastic Surgery* (New York: Schell/Mullaney, 1991).

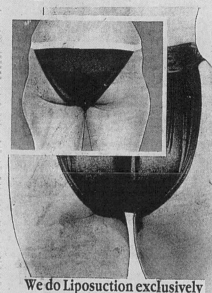
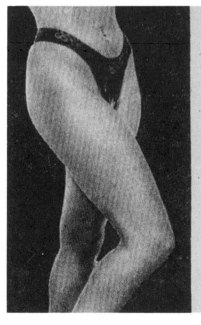
Figure 19. Advertisements for the Liposuction Institute and the Vein Specialists, Sunday *Chicago Tribune* (May 10, 1987).

The most commonly used methods of patient facial analysis are radiographic and photographic analysis, where the facial profile is rendered in a two-dimensional medium.[60] The use of photographs and grease pencils is perhaps the simplest method of the surgeon-patient consultation where the task at hand is to suggest the possible benefits of cosmetic surgery at the same time that the patient must be made aware of the surgical plan. Using a Polaroid camera to produce an instantaneous photograph, surgeons often draw lines with markers to indicate the locations of incisions or stretch lines. "Photograph surgery" is a communication method to negotiate between a patient's expectations and likely surgical outcomes; the reality of those black grease-pencil lines invoke the use of surgical procedures that literally cut into the face and reconstruct it, rendering whatever features nature created obsolete and irrecoverable.[61]

The various two-dimensional consultation methods were developed to effect an "objective method of facial analysis," which is understood to be a necessary part of adequate preoperative planning and postoperative evaluation.[62] Since 1989, however, some cosmetic surgeons have been employing new visualization techniques that render the patient's face in three dimensions. The use of video imaging replaces the use of grease-pencil lines and photographic surgery, which some surgeons found to be an inadequate system of consultation because "even when adjustments have been 'drawn on' by the surgeon, it is difficult for most patients to imagine what they might look like postoperatively."[63] Using video imaging, the surgeon can manipulate an actual image of the client's face. Although the cost and skill requirements of these computerized imaging systems represents a sizable investment, using this method of consultation is promoted as a way to manage patient expectations because it provides more information about the results that surgery can accomplish. More information, in this case, is said to lead to greater patient reassurance. Indeed, one recent study reports that the use of video imaging was well accepted by patients and that most felt that "video imaging improved communication between patient and surgeon, increased confidence in surgery and surgeon, and enhanced the patient-physician relationship."[64]

The video imaging consultation begins with a series of video shots that must be taken with great precision in terms of camera angle, lighting, face position, make-up, and hair display.[65] Preoperative photograph precision is necessary to ensure that postoperative photographs will objectively record surgical results and not camera special effects. The preoperative video shots are digitally scanned into a computer and then ma-

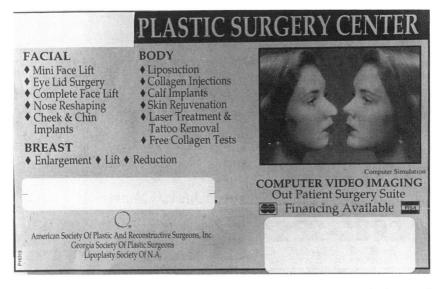

Figure 20. Yellow pages advertisement for cosmetic surgery, showing "before" and "after" images produced by video imaging program.

nipulated with the use of an imaging processing system. To begin the consultation, the cosmetic surgeon displays two images of the patient's face on the computer screen (figure 20). The left-hand image remains untouched and unmarked, serving as the prototypical "before" picture of the prospective cosmetic surgery client. The right-hand image is manipulated by the cosmetic surgeon, using a stylus and pressure-sensitive sketch pad. Using what is really a modified computer "painting" program, the surgeon can manipulate the image in several ways: (1) by picking up a line (a jaw line, for example) and moving it; (2) by reducing a part of the image with an eraser tool (thus eliminating a double chin, for example); or (3) by stretching a part of the face to show what heightened cheekbones might look like. Throughout the various manipulations, the right-hand image of the patient retains its visual integrity in that it continues to resemble the original, left-hand image save for the artistic manipulations performed by the surgeon. The surgeon can either display multiple procedures on one image or reproduce additional images that illustrate the effects of only one procedure at a time. With the use of a range of rendering tools, which are basically a set of artist's tools (spray can, pencil, eraser), the surgeon can redesign a client's face in the space of a 30-minute consultation.

In an interview with one surgeon who uses this method of patient consultation, he explained that when prospective patients seek surgery they have only a layperson's understanding of facial anatomy. For example, they might believe that in order to get rid of deep lines around the nose that all they need is to stretch the cheeks and tuck the extra skin behind the ear. But what they really need, he clarified, is to heighten the cheekbones with an implant and bob the nose, which will pull the skin taut over the new cheeks; consequently the lines and folds on either side of the nose will be eliminated and the size of the nose will stay proportionate to cheek width. In this example, the imaging device would enable the surgeon to educate the patient about the different methods for accomplishing surgical goals. In fact, this surgeon emphasized that the imaging device allows him to visually demonstrate the transformation of the patient's face that he could easily accomplish in surgery, something very difficult to demonstrate in a two-dimensional format. For him, the imaging system is a mechanism whereby his artistic skill can be previewed by prospective patients.

The imaging program can also be used as a surgical planning device. The program can calculate the distance, angle, or surface of the part of the right-hand image that has been modified. In this sense, a manipulated video image is more useful than a photograph in designing the actual surgery, because the comparison between the video image and the cephalometric radiograph "allows for computerized quantification of treatment goals."[66] Thus, if a nose profile line has been redrawn, the imaging program can measure the difference between the redrawn line of the right-hand image and the original line on the left-hand image to determine the degree to which the nose needs to be modified during surgery; the surgeon can then use that measurement to plan the surgical procedure.[67]

Some physicians believe that the only way to manage patients' expectations is to assure them of the competency of the physician's skill. Traditionally, physicians have done this by showing a prospective patient photographs of previous patients' surgical results. But more recently, the use of new high-tech imaging devices have been employed as a symbol of the quality of the physician's service.

A computer imaging system is a wonderful educational tool in terms of marketing to patients who may not be familiar with the treatments and materials available today. . . . Marketing the benefits of the system to patients is easy, according to [another physician], because the "high-tech" equipment lets patients know that they can receive "high-tech" treatment. It gives you the image and identity of being on the *cutting edge* of dentistry when you can offer the newest and best materials and techniques available.[68]

So in addition to using it as a counseling and planning device, the video imaging system can also be employed as a marketing tool. In this case, the expert manipulation of a video file using a computer painting program is translated into a marker of technological expertise in the operating room. But this use of the imaging system as marketing tool is denounced by some surgeons, who believe that its use borders on the unethical because it makes it easier to manipulate patients into having procedures that they do not need or want.

During interviews with surgeons who use or have used a video imaging system, I specifically asked about the controversy surrounding the new technology. The strongest claim for the use of video imaging is that it provides a realistic image of the aesthetic treatment objective that the patient can visualize. So while some surgeons dismiss it as a possibly unethical marketing device, other physicians argue that it produces "realistic images," "realistic expectations," and a better representation of reality itself. More telling is the fact that several cosmetic surgeons in the Atlanta metro area have stopped using video imaging as a consultation method because they found that it encouraged patients to form unrealistic expectations about the kind of transformations that can be accomplished through surgical procedures. They report that patients seemed to believe that if a modification could be demonstrated on the video screen, then it could be accomplished in the operating room — that the video transformation guaranteed the physical transformation. Apparently, the digital transformation of one's own face produces a magical, liquid simulation that is difficult to reject. What some patients fail to understand is that one of the significant difficulties with any kind of cosmetic surgery is that soft tissue changes are impossible to predict accurately. A surgical incision or implantation always disrupts layers of skin, fat, and muscle. How those incised tissues heal is a very idiosyncratic matter — a matter of the irreducible distinctiveness of the material body. After hearing from a number of disappointed patients, members of the American Society of Plastic and Reconstructive Surgeons designed an official "Electronic Imaging Disclaimer" to be used by physicians who employ computerized images in preoperative consultations. Among the release statements that the patient must sign is one that reads: "I understand that because of the significant

differences in how living tissue heals, there may be no relationship between the electronic images and my final surgical result."[69] Where advertising executives play with the possibilities of morphing political candidates,[70] cosmetic surgeons offer patients the promise of permanently
"morphed" features. One of the key consequences that some surgeons
have discovered is that witnessing video morphing dramatically under-
mines a patient's ability to distinguish between the real, the possible, and
the likely in terms of surgical outcomes.

Through the application of techniques of inscription, surveillance,
and confession, cosmetic surgery serves as an ideological site for examining the technological reproduction of the gendered body. A primary effect
of these techniques is to produce a gendered identity for the body at hand,
techniques that work in different ways for male and female bodies. In its
encounters with the cosmetic surgeon and the discourse of cosmetic surgery, the female body becomes an object of heightened personal surveillance; this scrutiny results in an internalized image of a fractured, fragmented body. The body becomes the vehicle of confession; it is the site at
which women, consciously or not, accept the meanings that circulate in
popular culture about ideal beauty and, in comparison, devalue the material body. In other words, the female body comes to serve as a site of
inscription, a billboard for the dominant cultural meanings that the female body is to have in postmodernity.[71]

For some women, and for some feminist scholars, cosmetic surgery
illustrates a technological colonization of women's bodies; others see it as
a technology women can use for their own ends. Certainly, as I have
shown here, in spite of the promise cosmetic surgery offers women for the
technological reconstruction of their bodies, in actual application such
technologies produce bodies that are very traditionally gendered. Yet I
am reluctant to accept as a simple and obvious conclusion that cosmetic
surgery is simply one more site where women are passively victimized.
Whether as a form of oppression or a resource of empowerment, it is clear
to me that cosmetic surgery is a practice whereby women consciously act
to make their bodies mean something to themselves and to others. A
different way of looking at this technology might be to take seriously the
notion I suggested earlier: to think of cosmetic surgery as "fashion surgery." Like women who get pierced-nose rings, tattoos, and hair sculp-
tures, women who elect cosmetic surgery could be seen to be using their
bodies as a vehicle for staging cultural identities. Even though I have
argued that cosmetic surgeons demonstrate an unshakable belief in a

Westernized notion of "natural" beauty, and that the discourse of cosmetic surgery is implicated in reproducing such idealization and manipulation of "the natural," other domains of contemporary fashion cannot be so idealized. The anti-aesthetics of cyberpunk and grunge fashion, for example, suggest that feminists, too, might wish to abandon our romantic conceptions of the "natural" body — conceptions that lead us to claim that a surgically refashioned face inevitably marks an oppressed subjectivity. As body piercing and other forms of prosthesis become more common — here I am thinking of Molly Million's implanted mirrorshades and Jael's nail daggers — we may need to adopt a perspective on the bodily performance of gender identity that is not so dogged by neoromantic wistfulness about the natural, unmarked body.

CHAPTER FOUR

Public Pregnancies and Cultural Narratives
of Surveillance

Pregnant women, as the material sign of the Reproductive Woman, cannot easily avoid the scrutiny of a fascinated gaze. A recent article in *SELF* magazine unselfconsciously gushes that "in the office, on the street, it's everybody's baby":

> A woman who is pregnant immediately knows that her body is no longer her own. She has a tenant with a nine-month lease; and should he spend every night kicking or hiccuping . . . there is nothing she can do. Sharing one's body with a small being is so thoroughly wondrous, though, that one can generally overlook the disadvantages. The real problem is sharing one's pregnant body with the rest of the world.[1]

Here we can read the three key features of our culturally determined "magical thinking" about reproduction: (1) a pregnant woman is divested of ownership of her body, as if to reassert in some primitive way her functional service to the species — she ceases to be an individual defined through recourse to rights of privacy, and becomes a biological spectacle. In many cases she also becomes an eroticized spectacle, the visual emblem of the sexual woman; (2) the entity growing in her, off of her, through her (referred to variously as a pre-embryo, embryo, fetus, baby, or child),[2] has some sort of ascendant right (to produce pain, to be nourished properly, to be born) that the maternal body is beholden to; (3) that the state of being pregnant is so "wondrous" — or, variously, thrilling, fulfilling, and soulfully satisfying — for a woman that she would endure any discomfort, humiliation, or hardship to experience this "blessed event."[3] This passage also demonstrates how easily the female body is "deconstructed" into its culturally significant parts and pieces: here the womb serves as a metonym for the entire family body. Not only does this fragmentation culturally reduce a woman to an objectified pregnant body, it also supports the naturalization of the scientific management of fertilization, implantation, and pregnancy more broadly.

To establish a context for a more detailed discussion of public pregnancies, I want to pose a question that will be familiar to those informed by the history of cultural studies: what is the relationship between cultural narratives and the social conditions of women? During the course of doing the research for this chapter, it became clear that the *question* of the relationship between literature and society, one of the abiding questions for scholars and students of cultural studies from the mid-1960s, has transformed into a much different concern about the relationship between mass-mediated cultural narratives, medical discourse, and material bodies. Although it is beyond the scope of this essay to rehearse the specific intellectual genealogy of this transformation — that is, the movement from a concern with literature and society, to one of language and materialism, to one of the material effects of cultural representations — I want to suggest that such questions are at the heart of what it means to me to do "cultural studies of science and technology." In this sense, the polemic of this chapter concerns the tensions and contradictions that emerge from a specific intellectual practice. Studying women and the deployment of new reproductive technologies involves asking questions that are theoretically interesting and intellectually gratifying to investigate, but which also illuminate cultural conditions that require immediate, critical political intervention. Is this not also the case for many other cultural studies of science and technology, whether or not they are framed by an explicit commitment to feminist politics? The question that grounds this chapter concerns the relationship between discourse and material bodies that preoccupies both feminist theory and feminist politics.

I begin with an extended discussion of Margaret Atwood's novel *The Handmaid's Tale,* which narrativizes current anxieties about reproduction in a technological age.[4] When the Handmaid Offred describes her public encounter with the pregnant Handmaid Ofwarren, we hear the echoes of *SELF* magazine: "She's a magic presence to us, an object of envy and desire, we covet her. She's a flag on a hilltop, showing us what can still be done: we too can be saved" (35). This reverence is also evident in medical discussions about new reproductive technologies. E. Peter Volpe, an expert in reproductive medicine, subtitles his 1987 book *Test-Tube Conception: A Blend of Love and Science* (figure 21). He too refers to the passage in *Genesis* (with Rachel, Jacob, and the maid) as the Ur-narrative of surro-

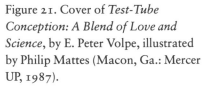

Figure 21. Cover of *Test-Tube Conception: A Blend of Love and Science*, by E. Peter Volpe, illustrated by Philip Mattes (Macon, Ga.: Mercer UP, 1987).

gate motherhood. The difference, though, between the surrogate story in *Genesis* and the ones we read about in Volpe's book and in our newspapers, is that in late capitalism "The surrogate performs the unusual service for a substantial fee."[5] Conceptualizing the relationship between a woman and her body as one between an individual and personal property offers some measure of liberty and economic freedom for women. "Be thankful," as Offred reminds us, "for small mercies" (127). But what is the quality of this mercy?

Reproductive technologies provide the means for exercising power relations on the flesh of the female body. These power relations are in turn institutionalized in several ways — not only through the development of medical centers that offer reproductive services, but also through the establishment of reconstructed legal rights and responsibilities of parents, donors, fetuses, and resulting children. Specific technological practices further augment such institutionalization; for example, the application of new visualization technologies — such as laparoscopy — literally bring new social "agents" into technological existence. In this way, the material applications of new technologies are implicated in, and in part productive of, a new *discourse* on maternal identity, parental responsibilities, and the authority of science.[6] At the heart of this discursive formation of reproduction are evocative cultural narratives about motherhood, the family, the role of techo-science, and the medicalized citizen. To illuminate the different levels at which a logic of surveillance informs the deployment of new reproductive technologies, I follow my discussion of Atwood's novel with an examination of the use of laparoscopy (a visualization device commonly used in egg retrieval and embryo implantation) as it belongs within a particular history of obstetrics. This technology has emerged at the same historical moment when the mass media (in the U.S. at least) have become preoccupied transforming "problem pregnancies" into public spectacles. This articulation of instruments, professional histories, and mediated discourses has created cultural conditions in which new reproductive technologies are used to discipline material, female bodies as if they were all potentially maternal bodies, and maternal bodies as if they were all potentially criminal.[7] The issue under consideration in this chapter is the relationship between fictional narratives, medical discourse, and the formulation of reproductive health policy that significantly impacts the material conditions of women's lives.

The Handmaid's Tale: *A Speculative Ethnography of the Present*

Published in 1985, Margaret Atwood's novel *The Handmaid's Tale* from early on was identified as a dystopian projection of some future society, in the tradition of Orwell's *1984* and Huxley's *Brave New World*.[8] The novel is set in the fascist Republic of Gilead, which succeeds contemporary U.S. society sometime in the late 1980s or early 1990s. The Gilead regime assigns every female to one of five classes of women: wives, econowives, aunts, marthas, and handmaids. The classes of wives and econowives include the spouses of free men. Wives are married to men with military rank, which allows them a measure of privilege, including the right to employ a handmaid and marthas; econowives are coupled with the younger men who form the rank and file of the military regime and who do not have enough status to obtain a handmaid or a martha. Aunts function as religious teachers and trainers of handmaids, and the marthas are a class of serving women — housekeepers, cooks, and nannies. Handmaids serve as surrogate wombs for infertile heterosexual (in identity but not necessarily in practice), privileged couples (wives and military leaders). Two other classes of women exist: "Jezebels," women who are used as unofficial prostitutes at the military club; and un-women, the women who resist their class assignment, are nonfunctional for the society, and/or are potentially or actively subversive of the regime.

Handmaids are socialized to perform their reproductive service for the state through an intense religious program of indoctrination, which begins with instruction by the aunts at the Rachel and Leah Center and is more widely supported by a system of social rituals. The central preoccupation of the Gileadean society is human reproduction, because most members are sterile or infertile due to the buildup of toxic wastes and nuclear fallout. All potentially fertile young women are forcibly drafted into service as handmaids or banished to the toxic waste "colonies" if they refuse. Thus, the central symbolic figure of the society is the potentially reproductive woman, the handmaid.

The point of Gileadean rituals is always the same for women — the complete destruction of individual identity and the social reproduction of collective identity. The most central ritual, called simply "The Ceremony," invokes a biblical passage in which Rachel offers to her husband Jacob her maid Bilhah to bear him the children that Rachel cannot. In a symbolic repetition of this offering of a fertile, surrogate womb from one woman to her husband, the handmaid lies between the legs of the wife as the husband penetrates the handmaid's exposed sex in an attempt to impregnate her. Any child born of a handmaid is given over to the wife as if it were her own. Other rituals reinforce the depersonalization of handmaids: "testifying" establishes women's primary guilt for licentious sexuality, "birth day" involves all handmaids in the collective Lamaze-like coaching of a handmaid in labor, "salvaging" requires handmaid participation in a collective execution of transgressive citizens.

The novel is organized in two parts; the first and longest part forms the bulk of the book and is divided into 15 chapters, which alternate between chapters titled "Night" or "Nap" and chapters that describe the focal rituals of the Gileadean society. The episodes are related from the point of view of a woman who was abducted by military guards as she, her husband, and daughter were trying to escape the country. In the first chapter, the narrator describes the gymnasium-turned-dormitory at the Rachel and Leah Center where she and other handmaids-in-training sleep on old military cots and are watched continuously by Aunts with cattle prods. The narrator reads the gymnasium as a palimpsest layered with the many histories of generations of teenagers who played and danced there. This opening chapter establishes the key tensions that will develop throughout the rest of the novel. Private moments of nostalgia for an earlier era, which at a distance seems somehow lonely and expectant, intertwine with an insatiable romantic fantasy of a future. The willful belief in their individuality and the fantasy of release provokes these handmaids-in-training to

> learn to whisper almost without sound. . . . [to] stretch out our arms, when the Aunts weren't looking, and touch each other's hands across space. We learned to lip-read, our heads flat on the beds, turned sideways, watching each other's mouths. In this way we exchanged names, from bed to bed. Alma. Janine. Dolores. Moira. June. (4)

Except for Moira, these subversive moments never quite congeal into an act of resistance, attesting to the totalitarian control effected by the Gilead regime. These internal dramas are counterpoised to more realistic descriptions of the public situation of women in the new regime: women watched, guarded, intimidated, and policed. Thus, in the opening section, we read a description of the structural tension between private rituals of individuality and public performances of collective identity that will organize the narrative to follow.

The second part, titled "Historical Notes on *The Handmaid's Tale*," formally stands as an epilogue or retrospective framing device in which the first part of the novel is revealed to be a "text" at the center of a future "symposium on Gileadean Studies held as part of the International Historical Association Convention, held at the University of Denay, Nunavit on June 25, 2195." The "Handmaid's Tale" is a historian's reconstruction of a collection of primary materials that come in the form of an (audio)taped account of a 33-year-old handmaid, who, we learn, is the narrator of the first part of the book. Ostensibly we know her only as "Offred," the handmaid in the service of a commander whose first name is "Fred."[9]

Offred's account gradually elaborates the repressive system of the republic of Gilead. The narrative she tells is limited to her severely restricted point of view, but as a picture of Gilead is pieced together through her description of rituals, the reader also witnesses the piece-by-piece assembly of the subjectivity of a handmaid. In these fragments, Offred offers readers a sense that the demoralization of handmaids is a well-orchestrated social phenomenon: accomplished both through *public* rituals, such as the mandatory monthly visit to the gynecologist to determine her fertility status, and in more *private* moments — in her clandestine visits to the commander to play Scrabble, and even during her subversive act of intercourse with the commander's chauffeur. A second series of events interrupts this account of her Gileadean life; these are scraps of personal memories and of cultural history — of her husband, her radical feminist mother, the origin of the Regime's takeover, and her early schooling with the Aunts at the Rachel and Leah Center.

Atwood inverts the contemporary associations between religion and ritual on the one side, and reproduction and technology on the other, so that in her novel religion is technologized (The Soul Scrolls) and reproduction is highly ritualized and radically detechnologized. This inversion sets the stage for two lines of critical analysis of contemporary society: one that addresses the quasi-religious belief in the benevolent power and application of technology, and a second that refers to a vehement denouncement of reproductive technologies, ostensibly by radical feminists of an earlier generation.

Although Atwood has consistently asserted that every indignity that the handmaids suffer in her novel has actual historical precedent (some during colonial New England, others in Europe during World War II), the importance of the novel lies not (solely) in its relation to those historical precedents nor in its offering of a dystopic projection of some *future* version of the United States, but rather in the fact that it helps narrate and make manifest the often obscured situation of reproductive-age women in contemporary U.S. culture. For some women, the regime of surveillance described in humiliating detail in the novel is less fiction than biography. In this sense, we could read it as ethnography rather than as science fiction. The novel focuses critical attention on the cultural rearticulation of the meaning of reproduction and provides a narrative frame through which to read the meaning of the interaction between the female body and new forms of reproductive technologies that are subtly but unmistakably being used as surveillance devices.

In Gilead, no less than in the United States during the 1980s and 1990s, women are defined primarily in terms of their reproductive facility. In the process, the female body is deconstructed into its functional reproductive parts. When Offred describes her first "Ceremony" ritual with the Commander and Serena Joy, she articulates the subjectivity of a fractured female body:

My red skirt is hitched up to my waist, though no higher. Below it the Commander is fucking. What he is fucking is the lower part of my body. I do not say making love, because this is not what he's doing.

Copulating too would be inaccurate, because it would imply two people and only one is involved. Nor does rape cover it: nothing is going on here that I haven't signed up for. There wasn't a lot of choice but there was some, and this is what I chose. (94)

As a womb with legs, Offred understands her importance for the society: "I am a national resource" (65), a "sacred vessel," an "ambulatory chalice" (136). She recalls that she used to think of her body as an instrument

of pleasure, or a means of transportation, or an implement for the accomplishment of my will. . . . But now . . . I am a cloud, congealed around a central object, the shape of a pear, which is hard and more real than I am and glows red within its translucent wrapping. Inside it is a space, huge as the sky at night and dark and curved like that, though black-red rather than black. Pinpoints of light swell, sparkle, burst and shrivel within it, countless as stars. Every month there is a moon, gigantic, round, heavy, an omen. It transits, pauses, continues on and passes out of sight, and I see despair coming toward me like famine. To feel that empty, again, again. (73–74)

But as a "national resource," she must be vigilant about taking vitamins and eating healthy food. Aunt Lydia instructs her: "You must be a worthy vessel. No coffee or tea though, no alcohol. Studies have been done" (65). Studies done, no doubt, earlier in her lifetime that resulted in policies requiring warning messages posted on cigarette packages, tavern cash registers, and computer monitors that read: "Warning to pregnant women — smoking, drinking, working may be hazardous to the health of your fetus."

A second line of critical analysis takes up the position of some feminist critics of reproductive technologies. These passages in the novel are in many ways the most frightening for a feminist to read, because in a different context, in our context, the beliefs seem so benign and so reasonable. But articulated to the system of repression institutionalized in Gileadean society, these beliefs form the links of the chains that bind handmaids to their reproductive service for the state. During her account of the "Birth Day," Offred remembers her mother's feminist convictions. We find out that machines have been banned from the birth room; the technologized birth situation that was controlled by male doctors and technicians — the source of some feminist outrage in the 1980s — is outlawed in Gilead. Although a fully equipped (with machines and men) Birthmobile stands ready in case of a handmaid birth emergency, most of the time the men aren't needed, and they certainly aren't wanted:

> It used to be different, they used to be in charge. A shame it was, said Aunt Lydia. Shameful. What she'd just showed us was a film, made in an olden-days hospital: a pregnant woman, wired up to a machine, electrodes coming out of her every which way so that she looked like a broken robot, an intravenous drip feeding into her arm. Some man with a searchlight looking up between her legs, where she's been shaved, a mere beardless girl, a trayful of sterilized knives, everyone with masks on. A cooperative patient. Once they drugged women, induced labor, cut them open, sewed them up. No more. No anesthetics, even. Aunt Elizabeth said it was better for the baby, but also: *I will greatly multiply thy sorrow and thy conception; in sorrow thou shalt bring forth thy conception; in sorrow thou shalt bring forth children.* (114)

But for the ritualistic return to the biblical passage on birth and sorrow, this scene describes a birth situation that sounds similar to the ones advocated by feminists and others who lobbied in the 1980s for "natural" birth methods.[10] Offred is ambushed by another memory, this time of the movies the handmaids were shown to reeducate them about the benefits of the new society. The movies might be ethnographic films of primitive women or old porno flicks

> from the seventies or the eighties . . . [that showed] women kneeling, sucking penises or guns, women tied up or chained or with dog collars around their necks, women hanging from trees, or upside-down, naked, with their legs held apart, women being raped, beaten up, killed. Consider the alternatives, said Aunt Lydia. You see what things used to be like? That was what they thought of women then. (118)

In one of the films, Offred sees her mother at a "Take Back the Night" march. She reiterates her mother's feminist convictions about "freedom to choose," a woman's right to control her body, and her expectations of younger women. As Offred is mentally brought back to the scene of the collective handmaid birthing, she offers the most damning recollection yet: "Mother, I think. . . . You wanted a women's culture. Well now there is one. It isn't what you meant, but it exists. Be thankful for small mercies" (127).

The key for understanding this line of criticism comes from Offred herself in another chapter. After she has met with the commander secretly to play games in his study, she wonders how to make sense of this all: "What I need is perspective. The illusion of depth, created by a frame, the arrangement of shapes on a flat surface. Perspective is necessary. Otherwise there are only two dimensions. Otherwise you live with your face squashed against a wall, everything a huge foreground, of details, close-ups. . . . Otherwise you live in the moment" (143). The perspective she seeks comes to her as a simple understanding. "Context is all," she thinks as she fits her Scrabble playing into a framework of the forbidden. "Context is all," we should remember as we read familiar feminist criticism rearticulated within a seemingly distant future when women are protected as reproductive machines and reviled as threatening subversives.

The Reign of Technology

Although there are several interested histories of the profession of obstetrics, most would agree, according to William Ray Arney (writing in 1982), that the most "recent period of obstetrical history was characterized by exponential advances in technology."[11] Arney suggests that the orientation of obstetrics shifted after World War II from intervention into the process of childbirth to the monitoring and surveillance of the obstetric patient. In his view, in the late 1940s the "organizing concept in obstetrics changed from 'confinement' to 'surveillance,' . . . the hospital became the center of a system [of] obstetrical surveillance that extended throughout the community" (123) and eventually into women's personal lives. In our contemporary world, he asserts, "every aspect of a woman's life is subject to the obstetrical gaze because every aspect of every individual is potentially important, obstetrically speaking" (153). Protection of the fetus is often offered as a commonsensical and, hence, ideological rationale for intervention into a woman's pregnancy, either through the actual application of invasive technologies or through the exercise of technologies of social monitoring and surveillance.[12]

Arney goes on to argue that the increased monitoring of childbirth not only has brought the maternal body and fetus into a broader system of surveillance, but it also functions to control and monitor the obstetricians themselves. Several control "devices" developed over the last 40 years are designed to enhance fetal monitoring: intrauterine pressure catheters that measure contractions, a subcutaneous electrode that reads fetal blood pH, and, ultrasonic devices that monitor fetal respiratory movement. With the deployment of these new technologies, a dominant, traditional definition of obstetrics as a specialized practice that involves the exercise of professional judgment comes into conflict with the redefinition of obstetrics as scientistic clinical and technological protocol. Obstetricians themselves claim that the scientific studies that describe what to monitor and when to intervene inhibit professional "subjective" judgment. It is important to remember here, as Paula Treichler elaborates, that this earlier definition of the proper, authoritative role of the obstetrician is itself the outcome of a historical struggle.[13] Whereas some of the obstetrician's scope of authority may be curtailed with the advent of new monitoring technologies, such that technological monitoring becomes a system of obstetric control that promotes, for example, institutional concerns for cost containment over the practice of clinical judgment, it does not fully dislodge the authority of the obstetrician that has been "historically" accomplished. Thus, although in one sense the new monitoring technologies contribute to the feeling that the sovereignty of the obstetrician is gone, replaced now by the notion of a technologically enhanced clinical practice, in another sense the range of the obstetrician's authority has been expanded to include responsibility for interpreting the output of monitoring devices.

Situated within another historical context, the use of such technologies in the obstetric field is just another stage in the incorporation of technology into all fields of medicine — a process that has been going on for well over four centuries.[14] In keeping with this narrative, the introduction of new monitoring technologies has the consequence of bringing *both* the obstetrician and the pregnant women into a system of normative surveillance — although, as noted above, the range of agency of the obstetrician remains culturally and institutionally broader.

An equally significant consequence is that these monitoring devices also construct new bodies to watch. The most obvious is the body of the fetus, which is visualized through new imaging technologies.[15] This leads some obstetricians to claim that the fetus is actually the *primary* obstetrics patient. Less obvious is the creation of new identities for the female body. As a *potentially* "maternal body" even when not pregnant, the female body is also evaluated in terms of its physiological and moral status as a potential container for the embryo or fetus.[16] Clearly the use of technology in the service of human reproduction and maternal health has political consequences for all participants. As demonstrated by those who argue on behalf of fetal rights, it also has the consequence of constructing entirely new participants, who now play a role in the obstetric encounter. And as Barbara Duden convincingly argues, "the public image of the fetus shapes the emotional and the bodily perception of the pregnant woman."[17]

In the 10 years since Louise Joy Brown, the first "test-tube" baby was born in Britain (25 July 1978), more than 88 in vitro fertilization (IVF) clinics have opened in the United States — and these represent only one of several kinds of organizations offering technological reproductive services. In 1987, the first anonymous egg donor program was established at the Cleveland Clinic (officially called the Oocyte Donation Program). Administrators of this program claim that they can match "human eggs to their future parents by hair and eye color, by body size and blood type, even by national origin."[18] In its first year, the clinic reported being deluged with offers from women who wanted to donate eggs; a deluge no doubt due in part to the fact that the clinic pays a woman $1,200 for each egg donation. The technologies that these services use, what are called the "new reproductive technologies" (NRT), enable a range of egg manipulation: (1) *unfertilized* eggs can be retrieved from fertile wombs and then either placed in an infertile womb to be "naturally" fertilized, or fertilized outside of any womb and then implanted in another; or (2) *fertilized* eggs or embryos can be transferred from fertile womb to infertile womb. In fact, the extended degree to which the physiological process of reproduction is medically and technologically managed has prompted people to begin thinking of birth as an industry in itself, where, according to some critics, fertility clinics are nothing more than "commercial babymaking services."[19] Indeed, the cost of such reproductive services is quite expensive for the average American: in 1989 for example, the going price of surrogacy was $10,000; IVF usually costs between $3,000 and $7,000 for one implanted viable embryo; and artificial insemination ranges in price from $500 to $5,000. Not surprisingly, these services are usually marketed to upper-middle-class (infertile) couples who can afford to spend more than $35,000 trying to conceive a child.[20]

The technological isolation of the womb from the rest of the female body promotes the rationalization of reproduction, such that the process of reproduction itself can be isolated into discrete stages: egg production, fertilization, implantation, feeding, and birthing. In this way, the new reproductive technologies include several biotechniques that literally enact the objectification and fragmentation of the female body by isolating and intervening in the physical processes of human reproduction that

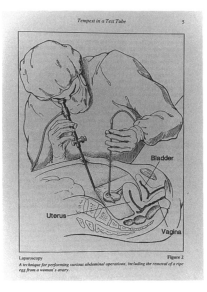

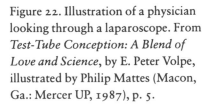

Figure 22. Illustration of a physician looking through a laparoscope. From *Test-Tube Conception: A Blend of Love and Science*, by E. Peter Volpe, illustrated by Philip Mattes (Macon, Ga.: Mercer UP, 1987), p. 5.

normally occur within the female body. These technologies may include the administration of ovulation-inducing drugs, artificial insemination, laparoscopy, in vitro fertilization, cryopreservation of embryos, ultrasound scans, and the use of instruments such as a specially designed catheter that can pass through the cervix into the cavity of the uterus, which is used to transport an ex vitro fertilized embryo.

Several of these procedures actually allow researchers and physicians to view the internal physiological state of the female body and the developing embryo/fetus. Patrick Steptoe and Robert G. Edwards, the two British scientists responsible for Louise Brown's "test-tube" conception, modified a surgical technique called laparoscopy to obtain ripe eggs from a woman's ovary (figure 22). E. Peter Volpe describes the procedure of egg retrieval in which a laparoscope is used as a visualization instrument:

A clear view of the ovary is obtained with a slender illuminated telescope-like instrument, or laparoscope, which is inserted through a small incision made in the navel. The viewing device illuminates the ovary, enabling the surgeon to examine the surface of the organ. The rounded follicle (containing the ripe egg) is readily detectable on the surface of the ovary as a thin-walled pink swelling. A specially designed hypodermic needle is then passed through a second incision in the abdomen, and the contents of the bulging follicle are aspirated.[21]

As the abdomen is pierced to insert the laparoscope, the technological gaze literally penetrates the female body to scrutinize the biological functioning of its reproductive organs. In the process the female "potentially maternal" body is objectified as a visual medium to look through.

After implantation of an IVF embryo is achieved using these sophisticated techniques, "the pregnancy" is carefully monitored. Given all the work, money, and physical discomfort involved in such conception, promoting a healthy developing embryo/fetus is of great concern:

> ... the pregnancy is monitored using all resources of the present state of the arts. The elaborate protocol includes continual office visits, hormonal analysis, ultrasound scans, serum alpha-fctoprotein testing (for spina bifida), amniocentesis (for prenatal biochemical and chromosomal analyses), routine obstetric laboratory tests, and two-hour postprandial glucose tests for signs of maternal diabetes.[22]

Some experts unabashedly agree that part of the new concern for the fetus is due to advances in visualization technologies and the promise of fetal medicine as a new medical specialty; a recent newspaper article quoted one physician as saying: "We can now view the fetus; we can determine its size and its sex. If it is ill, we can give it blood transfusions; nutrients can be offered in utero. And we now know that nutrition and lifestyle can harm the unborn."[23] Thus, the same technological advances that foster the objectification of the female body through the visualization of internal functioning also encourages the "personification" of the fetus.

Assessing the Political Consequences of New Reproductive Technologies

Many feminist-informed histories of the practice of obstetrics and gynecology see in the application and deployment of new reproductive technologies the continuation of an old campaign on behalf of the medical profession to consolidate its cultural authority by wresting control over the act of childbearing away from women. Although Margaret Mead long ago suggested that this desire is a result of "male jealousy of woman's ability to make a new life," others have argued more recently that men's participation in the development and application of new reproductive technologies represents an invigorated desire to control and conquer "nature." Following this, some feminists argue that birth control should be redefined as womb control. Gena Corea, for example, argues in her book

The Mother Machine: Reproductive Technologies from Artificial Insemination to Artificial Wombs that the current situation of the application of new reproductive technology extends far beyond mere concern with "unruly" and infertile wombs; in her words, "it is a war against wombs."[24] This leads other feminists to redefine birth as "reproductive engineering" in which the primary objective is *not* to assist the female body in its body business, but to eliminate paternal uncertainty.[25] Rebecca Albury describes how IVF programs already overtly test for the "fitness" of a woman who offers her body for such services.

> A woman must demonstrate her worthiness to become a part of a technological conception programme; she must fit the practitioner's notion of a "good mother." First she must be married. . . . in addition she must demonstrate the suitability of her skills and motives for parenting.[26]

In *The Mother Machine,* Corea informs us:

> The overwhelming majority of reproductive engineers are male. The overwhelming majority of persons on whose bodies these men experiment are female. The technology used emerges from a science developed by men according to their own values and sense of reality. . . . Reproductive technology is a product of the male reality. The values expressed in the technology — objectification, domination — are typical of male culture. The technology is male-generated and buttresses male power over women. (3–4)

Following this line of analysis, the patriarchal objectives served by the application of new reproductive technologies include the consolidation and maintenance of scientific authority, as well as paternal privilege, promotion of the institutions of heterosexual marriage and the traditional family structure, the continued accumulation of profit for medical institutions, and the reproduction of men's objectification of women's bodies for cultural and social gain. Women's objectives for birthing a healthy baby or for better birth management are subjugated goals often employed as rhetorical alibis for the application of new birth technologies, but rarely considered in their own right.[27]

As the new reproductive technologies developed during the decade of the 1980s, so too did the feminist response. In fact, certain positions have been staked out that are themselves being treated as important issues for debate among feminist scholars. For example, both Judy Wajcman and

Jana Sawicki summarize what they identify as the "FINRRAGE" position, as it is supported and directed by the writings of Gene Corea, Jalna Hamner, and others.[28] (FINRRAGE is the acronym for Feminist International Network of Resistance to Reproductive and Genetic Engineering.) Advocates of the FINRRAGE position criticize the development and use of reproductive technologies on several counts, but the central focus of their critique is that these technologies embody and institutionalize the patriarchal domination of women and of scientifically managed reproduction. As a gross simplification, the sign "FINRRAGE" often is invoked, at least semiotically, as the identity of the antitechnological feminist response. While there are no doubt differences even among FINRRAGE members about the role of women *in* science and technology, what is less contestable is that these feminists advocate the use of "women-centered" approaches to the development and application of scientific knowledge, especially as it concerns the issues of reproduction, maternity, and women's health. In line with this position, Patricia Spallone asserts:

> Feminist resistance to the new reproductive technologies is not a negative stance, but a positive one, where we can re-assert a women's power and knowledge and experience to ask our own questions about fertility, fertility problems, childbirth, childrearing, motherhood, abortion.[29]

Having said that, though, it is true that the strongest line of FINRRAGE analysis focuses on the way that reproductive technologies exploit women for men's gain. To this end, Corea advocates an interventionist strategy of resistance, where the plight of the few (the infertile) is not used to determine the wide-scale application of these technologies for the many. Fundamentally, she advocates the development of a new value system, where women "speak out against any injustice suffered by women, and in so doing contribute to the crystallization of women's well-being as a value" (322). This will happen when women break out of their culturally induced confusion about these new technologies and begin to assert their sense of dignity and worth.

   As both Wajcman and Sawicki note, there is feminist opposition to the FINRRAGE position. The crucial issue centers on whether or not reproductive technologies (and the scientific knowledge embodied by them) are inherently patriarchal and oppressive of women, as those associated with the FINRRAGE position assert. Opposed to this position are writings and research by other feminist scholars, most notably Michele Stanworth, who argue that the FINRRAGE position gets caught in an overly romantic view of "natural" reproduction and that FINRRAGE spokeswomen totalize the impact of reproductive technologies.[30] This position urges feminists to resist a version of technological determinism that suggests that technological knowledge somehow overdetermines human choices. As Stanworth counters, there are benefits for some women from the application of new reproductive technologies, which indicates that these technologies do not have the same impact on all women. Artificial conception and surrogate maternity offer hope to childless people (who are not always heterosexual couples) and to women who are physiologically incapable of having children.

Both Wajcman and Sawicki offer their own way out of the impasse generated by the debate between these seemingly incompatible feminist positions. Where Sawicki returns to her broader argument concerning the usefulness of what she calls Foucault's politics of difference, Wajcman writes a reasoned account of the crucial insights gleaned from both positions. In the end, both Sawicki and Wajcman offer a reasonable assessment of this debate: that although technologies and scientific knowledge are shaped by and indeed embody political and ultimately patriarchal interests, they are not monolithic structures that impose a singular reality or set of consequences on all women equally. When Wajcman asserts that in order to assess the political meaning of any technology, feminists should pay attention to both the social and economic forces that inextricably link certain technologies to "particular institutionalized patterns of power and authority" (63), she articulates the guiding impulse of this book.

Building on Wajcman's insight, I suggest that feminists think about technologies as *formations* in and of themselves—not as isolated processes or material artifacts. Furthermore, if we understand technological formations as *cultural* formations, we will be able to grasp the fact that an analysis of such a multidimensional cultural arrangement will require the work of many feminists who are likely to have divergent political aims. One consequence of this shift of understanding is that there will be less pressure to produce and defend a "bottom-line" evaluation of a given technology. It encourages feminists to think more complexly about the interrelations between technological devices, specialized knowledge, scientific practices, and a broader cultural context that is both historically determined in various ways and materially embodied. Perhaps a more critical concern for feminist scholars is how to gain access to the relevant information about technological use and development of reproductive technologies, how to disseminate such information to the women who are most likely to be the subjects of such expert knowledge, and how to enable people to make informed decisions about their own use of such technologies.

While I do not want to rehearse the various planks of these two emergent feminist positions, I do want to amplify what I consider to be of central importance here: the fact that feminists with various theoretical and political investments are "keeping watch" on the development and application of these new reproductive technologies. To the extent that reproductive technologies are articulated as part of a broad technological formation that takes shape in diverse geopolitical locations, there are many issues to track and monitor — issues related not only to ethical, legal, and policy debates, but also to issues of education, women's health, and the regulation of women's sexuality. In sidestepping a direct discussion of the issues of ethics and social policy, I am not suggesting that these are unimportant concerns for feminist analysis. On the contrary, several books by feminists and others have begun to dissect the issues regarding the ethics not only of reproductive technologies but also of genetic engineering more broadly.[31] Instead, I will discuss several examples taken from popular media, where the use of new reproductive technologies produce "cases" of public pregnancies that are transformed into media spectacles. I do this to suggest that one of the key cultural forces determining the meaning of these new reproductive technologies are the mass-mediated narratives about the relationship between women's bodies, technologies of surveillance, and threats to public health.

Maternal Surveillance and Public Health

Once an egg is fertilized, it becomes an embryo. But now that it is technologically possible for an egg to be obtained from one source, fertilized by sperm from another source, frozen for posterity, or implanted in a surrogate womb to produce a baby for an adoptive couple — who could have supplied either the egg, the sperm, the womb, or none of these — whose embryo is it? This is the issue at the heart of one well-publicized legal battle over custody rights.[32] Early in 1989, as part of her divorce proceedings, Mary Sue Davis sued for custody of seven fertilized and frozen embryos that she and her estranged husband had in cold storage at a Tennessee IVF clinic. In this celebrated embryo custody battle, Mary Sue Davis wanted custody so that she could fulfill her desire to have a child.

Her husband wanted custody so that he would not become a father. Although these are perfectly logical positions, both represent unnatural requests in many respects: Mary Sue Davis was suing for the right to determine her ex-husband's *future* reproductive effects, while her husband was suing for the right to determine what happens to the embryo *after* conception. Here is an example where the use of new technologies produce unprecedented "conditions of possibility." Mary Sue Davis's ex-husband testified that he "would feel raped of [his] reproductive rights" if the embryos were implanted without his consent, thus opening the door for a new precedent in the legal definition of the concept of rape. In fact, the case pivoted on the legal definition of the beginning of life: were the embryos children or not? The judge in the case ruled that human life begins at conception, therefore the embryos, as "little people," have the right to be implanted and carried to birth.[33] Thus custody was awarded to the mother. Although this judgment seemingly promoted a woman's right of ownership, it was transcoded and heralded by "pro-life" advocates as "a victory for unborn children."[34]

Although ownership of the embryo was awarded to the potentially maternal body in the *Davis vs. Davis* case, there is no guarantee that this judgment will establish an effective precedent for women's rights. In fact, it has already engendered a backlash of sorts. In May 1989, the Illinois State House of Representatives entertained a measure that would give a father the right to seek a court injunction to prevent a woman from terminating a pregnancy. One representative claimed, "We have recognized a woman's rights and ignored the father's rights. This amendment gives the father some rights." Rob Schofield, a representative of the American Civil Liberties Union of Illinois, urged lawmakers to oppose the amendment. As he argued, "Under this bill, a convicted rapist would have the right to ask that the rape victim's decision to seek an abortion be enjoined. You never know what a judge will do" (Rick Pearson and Jennifer Halperin, "Abortion Rights Gain for Fathers," *Chicago Tribune*, 5 May 1989, sec. 1, 7).

New reproductive technologies do not, in a singularly deterministic sense, construct these new social tensions. But they are implicated in the production of a new set of possibilities, wherein the rights of a pregnant woman are set against the "rights" of other people either to intervene in her pregnancy or to act on behalf of the unborn fetus.[35] Whereas the "fathers' rights" amendment was eventually defeated in Illinois, another measure approved by the state's House of Representatives gave the state more power to gain court-ordered custody of children who are born addicted to cocaine or other illegal drugs.

Of all the legal cases in the late 1980s that sought to establish a precedent for fetal legal rights, none received more media attention than the spectacle that came to be identified as the problem of "Cocaine Mothers and Crack Babies." In May 1989, a 24-year-old woman, Melanie Green of Rockford, Illinois, was charged with involuntary manslaughter and delivery of a controlled substance to a minor for allegedly taking cocaine shortly before her daughter was born.[36] The infant, Bianca Green, died two days after birth from fatal brain swelling due to oxygen deprivation before and during birth. Paul Logli, the Illinois state's attorney who filed the charges against Green, held a press conference to publicize his request for the development of tougher laws that would make it a crime to take illegal drugs while pregnant. As he explained, the voluntary ingestion of drugs by a mother results in the involuntary ingestion of substances by the fetus. From the very beginning, he framed the issue in terms of the rights of the fetus to state's protection.[37] It is not surprising then that the picture of Melanie Green accompanying her newspaper story looks like a police line-up photograph. She's black, pregnant, and addicted to cocaine. The Law, in the person of a state district attorney, intervenes to save her child from her, and failing that, to save society from her. In effect, Logli was mounting a "politics of surrogacy" that would grant rights to fetuses at the expense of maternal rights; as happened with the Green case, these politics are often enacted by anonymously appointed bureaucrats who function as public health guardians. The Green case has the trappings of what Anna Lowenhaupt Tsing calls, in her study of women charged with perinatal endangerment, a "Monster Story."[38] In terms similar to the ones elaborated by Valerie Hartouni in her analysis of the mass-mediated narrative context of a black woman who served as a surrogate mother for a white couple, Green is "a densely scripted figure, positioned in and by a crude, if commonplace, set of racial caricatures and cultural narratives about 'the way black women are.' "[39] The color of her skin activates certain cultural narratives about her questionable moral character. Her story was, in many respects, already written before she ever delivered her baby; the "welfare mother" is a mass-mediated controlling image, to use Patricia Hill Collins's term, of black mothers that elevates racist beliefs about black women and motherhood into an ideological narrative of mythic proportions.[40]

Indeed, in the words of Cynthia Daniels, a feminist scholar who studies the emergence of fetal rights:

> The very attempt to prosecute pregnant women for addiction has created a powerful social mythology about women. The power of this mythology may at times eclipse the power of law. Although women's rights may ultimately be upheld in the courts, a broader public culture may continue to endorse resentment toward women and more subtle forms of social coercion against those who transgress the boundaries of traditional motherhood. Social anxiety and resentment are most easily projected onto those women who are perceived as most distant from white, middle-class norms. Political power may ultimately rest not on the technical precedent of legal rights, but on the symbols, images, and narratives used to represent women in this larger public culture.[41]

Although all charges were dropped against Green, this case offers a warning about the scope of the campaign to establish the connection between maternal liability and fetal health—a campaign that is being waged not only in the courtroom but also in the dissemination of "official" statements about the dangers of maternal excesses.

Consider the following example: a governmental booklet published in 1990 by the U.S. Department of Health and Human Services (DHHS) lists the well-known hazards for "the unborn"— "alcohol, tobacco, marijuana, cocaine, heroine and other opioids or synthetic narcotics, phencyclidine, tranquilizers and barbiturates." It also lists those licit drugs known to have adverse effects on prenatal infants: antibiotics, anticonvulsants, hormones, and "salicylates including Bufferin, Anacin, Empirin, and other aspirin-containing medication."[42] In short, the point of the booklet is to educate public health officials and pregnant women about the dangers of maternal behavior. In the introduction to the booklet, authors Cook, Peterson, and Moore outline the "extent of the problem" of maternal influences on fetal health, which they see as a multidimensional problem related to the unreliability of information acquisition. They inform us that pregnant women are unreliable in reporting drug use, remembering the extent of drug use, and in truthfully admitting to illicit drug use. Although they point out that "urine testing is a more reliable method," they note that "it is not sufficient to track changing drug patterns throughout the pregnancy" (14), suggesting perhaps that if they could perform multiple urine tests throughout a woman's pregnancy they could circumvent her duplicity. This conceptual as well as technological separation of the woman from her body is certainly consistent with other cases of "urinal politics," where the material body is used against the "person," who is now understood to be an unreliable source of the truth. In the absence of reliable information about actual drug use in actually pregnant women, these authors suggest that "surveys of current drug-using behavior among women of childbearing age" are useful indicators of the "scope of the problem" of prenatal drug exposure. In a subtle move, the behavior of women of childbearing age is transformed into a sign of a "potential problem," and the female body of childbearing age is redefined as the "potentially pregnant" body. In a similar way, the pregnant woman is constructed as unreliable and duplicitous, while the pregnant female *body* is invoked as a guarantee of drug-use truth.

Historically this increasing interest in teratology, the study of causes of birth defects, is due in part to the high incidence of birth defects in babies born to women who had taken the drug thalidomide, a drug pre-scribed (routinely before 1960) to soothe the nausea of pregnant women. According to the DHHS booklet, this led to an increase in research efforts to determine the safety of fetal exposure to prescription medications, over-the-counter drugs, industrial chemicals, and pesticides. Another conse-quence of the public's growing concern with "thalidomide babies" was its interest in the impact of "social" drugs on developing fetuses. In the inter-vening 20 or so years, the booklet explains, the scope of teratology was expanded to include research into "more subtle behavioral and develop-mental abnormalities in offspring that only become apparent later in an infant's life" (6). Thus not only was the range of potentially dangerous substances targeted for research expanded, but so too was the range of time over which the behavior of the female body could be scrutinized for its influence on a developing fetus or eventual child.

In a telling absence, the behavior of fathers is rarely mentioned in the DHHS booklet. Other than a reference to a study in which the "male-to-female sex-ratio of offspring increased if *either* parent was a heavy mari-juana smoker" (25–26), the influence of drug use among fathers on result-ing fetuses or children is not discussed in any detail.[43] There is some evidence to suggest that interest in the possibility that paternal health conditions might have an impact on developing fetuses and resulting chil-dren is growing: studies of paternal drinking and of paternal-occupation/

cancer associations in workers in petroleum and chemical industries are examples of recent research in male-mediated teratogenesis and childhood cancers.[44]

One of the key differences in the cultural context of the reception of these medical studies of male-mediated defects is that there are few, if any, cultural narratives about paternal culpability. For example, in recent mass-mediated reports about "The Gulf War Syndrome" the responsibility for birth defects (manifesting in children born to male Gulf War veterans) is subtly transferred *from* the fathers who served in the Gulf to the military medical authorities who prepared them to serve. What emerges is a narrative about the destigmatization of male soldiers' (possible) contribution to a range of birth defects. In a complex rhetorical move, the U.S. military becomes the responsible agent of toxicity due to its failure—as one hypothesis suggests—to fully understand the consequences of the vaccinations it administered to Gulf-bound troops. In contrast to the portrayal of cocaine mothers, male soldiers and their afflicted offspring are cast as victims of the military's ignorance.

This new interest in paternal biological influences notwithstanding, it remains the case that the maternal body is overscrutinized in its relationship to the developing fetus. Having said that, though, it is important to remember that the issue of maternal health care has many sides. Many women who would like to get pregnant don't because of limited access or lack of access to prenatal care. Other women who do get pregnant and do not have access to prenatal care run the greatly increased risk of bearing low-birth-weight infants (less than 5.5 pounds). Low birth-weight is the single most predictive characteristic of infant mortality. As has been noted in the media many times, the United States ranks nineteenth among industrialized nations in terms of its infant mortality rate—9.7 deaths per 1,000. Black women in the United States have a higher incidence of bearing low-birth-weight babies than do white women; the infant mortality rate for black babies is almost double the national rate—18.0 deaths per 1,000.[45] Prenatal care is the single most important factor in preventing low-birth-weight babies; but while more than 82 percent of white women receive early pregnancy care, only 61 percent of Hispanic women and 60 percent of black women do.[46] These treatment rates are consistent with the history of maternal and child health (MCH) programs of the U.S. Public Health Service, which traditionally were designed to serve the needs of minority populations who are understood to be "medically underserved."[47] Indeed, as the range of minority populations has expanded in the United States to include groups from Asia and Central America, new grant programs target the health needs of these new underserved populations.[48]

Whereas the development of public health programs designed for the special needs of certain populations, especially minority women who are or would like to be pregnant, seem entirely beneficial and moral, there are unintended consequences of course. We are led to wonder about the consequences of the articulations among (1) medical research that establishes a broader list of substances and behaviors that endanger a fetus, (2) an expanded argument about the relationship between maternal behavior and fetal development, (3) new public health programs that seek to increase minority patient/client participation and institutional/clinic surveillance, and (4) the criminalization of certain forms of drug consumption in the invigorated "war on drugs." This articulation identifies and structures the set of possibilities for the technological management of the potentially pregnant female body.

In her article "The Body Invaded," which elaborates the political significance of "medical surveillance" practices for women of childbearing age, Jennifer Terry points out that the dual emergencies of AIDS and drug use "allow for the emergence of discourses and practices that place women of childbearing age in particular jeopardy."[49] The warning Terry illuminates is being tracked by other feminist scholars who are interested in different aspects of "maternalist" politics. For some, this means transforming "motherhood from women's private responsibility into public policy."[50] For others, this means investigating and analyzing social welfare activities that, in effect, criminalize pregnancy. Lisa Maher calls this an example of the "juridogenic power of law":

> The collusion between medical and legal discourse in relation to new reproductive technologies presents the potential for a more persistent intrusion into women's lives. As more areas of women's lives are colonized by medical interventions, they are also staked out as legal territory. . . . The interrelation between the current discourse surrounding crack pregnancies and historical attempts to regulate and control women's lives through their bodies serves to illustrate the "juridogenic" power of law.[51]

Maher thoroughly discusses the consequences of punishing and regulating drug-using mothers and concludes that "punishing pregnant women for the good of the foetus is not only paternalistic, but demonstrates how concerns such as public health can have a very punitive downside" (179). This confusion about how to treat the pregnant woman, as victim or criminal, lies at the heart of public health policy and accounts in part for the limited success in "treating" pregnant women who use drugs.

Early in 1994, several news sources reported that the Centers for Disease Control and Prevention (formerly the CDC) were going to take a new look at violence as a "critical health problem." As an extended example of how the logic of criminality conflicts with the logic of epidemiology — of public health — consider the following report by Teri Randall in the May 16, 1990 issue of the *Journal of the American Medical Association*. Randall quotes Linda Saltzman, the first and only criminologist hired by the CDC, who predicted that public health and the CDC must examine the problem of violence "or [they are] going to be avoiding one of the most significant health problems."[52] This is a case where the conjunction of two "logics" has important consequences for women. As Saltzman explained, whereas a criminal justice approach emphasizes the criminal, a public health approach focuses on the victim. Analyzing violence from an epidemiological perspective means asking certain questions about the incidence of violence: who is the population at risk? and what are the causes/ vectors of risk? Following this, "a public health model," according to Saltzman, "asks which women are most likely to be battered" (2612). Yet Saltzman was clear to assert that one would need to ask "additional questions . . . [as to] who are the batterers and what is the interaction between partners" (2614). These kinds of questions are implied by a criminal justice model. And yet, in a report on a study of the incidence of physical violence against women in the 12 months preceding childbirth, researchers failed to mention any study of the agents of the physical violence. Instead, the study focused on the relation between violence and maternal characteristics. Using data from a surveillance system called PRAMS (Pregnancy Risk Assessment Monitoring System), researchers suggested that a certain subgroup of pregnant women, those with fewer than 12 years of education, may be at increased risk for physical violence. As the editorial analysis of the report points out, one of the significant limitations of this study is that it cannot ascertain the specific vector of education level: level of education involves issues of race, economic status, and ethnic background. It was clear, in this case, that the issue of maternal health and physical violence was not conceptualized through a "maternalist" logic that would see the issue of violence against pregnant women as a social and systemic problem, tied closely to the characteristics of violent men, rather than an individual problem somehow tied to characteristics of the woman herself.[53]

Jennifer Terry also reminds feminists of the racial politics enacted in the articulation I described above, where medical research, public health initiatives, and surveillance practices have differential effects on women of color of a lower economic class than on white women more broadly. In "The Body Invaded," Terry writes:

> [T]he surveillance and punishment that potentially endangers all women is applied selectively to poor women and women of color. These women constitute the majority of patients in public clinics and are among the most likely to be brought into the criminal justice system of social welfare systems on grounds unrelated to their pregnancy. . . . In such instances it is impossible to distinguish the suspicion of certain women from the criminalization of poverty operating in the U.S. in the past decade. (21)

The real issue in the Melanie Green case, following Terry's analysis, is the "hidden" damage of drug abuse and the inadequate national resources for developing treatment programs, especially for pregnant women. Terry's note about the "suspicion of certain women" is evident in discussions about the racial disparity in the type of prenatal care advice women receive from health care providers. Although, as noted above, black women have a higher risk of bearing low-birth-weight infants, they are less likely to receive the same level of prenatal advice about their risk status as white women. Moreover, according to one study, they are less likely to receive specific advice about drinking and smoking.[54] Other factors confound the issue of the adequacy of prenatal care advice; for example,

> advice about two risk behaviors, smoking and drug use, was skewed towards poorer women, whereas advice about alcohol use and breast-feeding was skewed toward wealthier women. [In this case,] Health care providers may be giving advice based on their stereotypes of who is involved in what type of behaviors and not on a principal of equity.[55]

The sample population for this study showed significant differences between black women and white women: "Black women were more frequently single, less likely to be educated beyond high school, and had lower incomes." But the study indicates a set of complex findings. On the one hand, black women report receiving less advice overall about the dangers of smoking, alcohol, and illegal drug use, unless they had a lower income, in which case they received more advice about illegal drug use.[56] A lack of advice is ill-treatment; but when the advice is delivered about a specific risk behavior, it is likely to be based on "suspicion" and the stereotype of poor black women as illegal drug users. In any event, the study supports what feminists have long suspected, that black women do not receive the same level of prenatal care advice from public health providers as do white women. In this sense, more programs do not necessarily ensure better care for all women.

It is well documented that there are several barriers that prevent women from seeking prenatal care, especially if they are using illegal drugs. As Norma Finkelstein points out, although there are undoubtedly psychological issues at work — such as denial of the problem of substance abuse — it is also likely that the social stigma attached to drug use as well as the lack of gender-specific treatment services are equally prohibitive.[57] But if we look at the issue of cocaine use among pregnant women and at the documented effects of cocaine ingestion on the developing fetus, we find that the medical and scientific findings do not warrant the kind of surveillance that interferes with a pregnant woman's search for treatment. For example, several articles in a 1993 special issue of the journal *Neurotoxicology and Teratology* outline the difficulties in obtaining reliable information about the specific *toxicity* of cocaine on the developing fetus. Problems include the determination of toxic dosage, the unreliability of self-reported drug use, the wide lack of confirmation of catastrophic effects, and the methodological design of research studies. Noteworthy are several observations offered by medical researcher Donald E. Hutchings on the cultural context in which studies of cocaine "abuse" were conducted. In a discussion of recent research on humans and cocaine use, Hutchings reports on a study of the Society of Pediatric Research acceptance rate for medical research abstracts that discussed the effects of prenatal exposure to cocaine: "of the studies that reported adverse effects associated with cocaine, 58% were accepted, whereas only 11% of those that found no effects enjoyed a similar fate."[58] He argues that this indicates a selection bias on the part of medical journals and suggests that this selection bias is influenced by the wider media and political attention paid to the scandalous new drug menace. Throughout his detailed assessment of the methodological design and review of the findings, Hutchings is careful to assert that the toxicity of cocaine is a complex issue that is confounded by the fact that many users actually ingest a number of other potentially toxic substances, including alcohol, tobacco, and marijuana. He cautiously suggests that dosage level may be the more clearly determining factor of toxicity; at the same time he points out that in most studies, especially those that sample subjects from outpatient drug treatment programs, it is difficult to measure dosage level precisely.[59] It is far less possible, based on the current research, to formulate conclusions about the interactive effects of cocaine with other substances. Researchers simply have not made such studies.

Given this debate in the medical literature about the scientific facticity of cocaine toxicity, how are we to make sense of a study conducted in 1991 that tested for the presence of cocaine in the blood system of every infant born in Georgia's public hospitals? As reported by Adam Gelb on page 1 of the *Atlanta Journal Constitution:* "Every baby born in Georgia over a one-year period will be tested for cocaine in the most extensive study in the nation of the drug problem among pregnant women."[60] The article goes on to assert:

> The epidemic of "crack babies," the underdeveloped, quivering infants who have become a tragic symbol of addiction, is well known. But estimates of its scope range widely, from 100,000 born annually, the federal government's figure, to 375,000, the number cited by independent medical experts. "The bottom line is nobody really knows how common this is," said Dr. Paul M. Fernhoff, an Emory University pediatrics professor, who is director of the study. (A1)

This is an encapsulated version of the dominant narrative of maternal excess and fetal victimization. When Gelb cites the director of the study, Dr. Fernhoff, he commits the grave error of leading readers to make an erroneous inference about the gravity of the "problem." It is true, at some level, that no one knows the dimensions of the "problem," but it is also true, given the discussion among medical researchers summarized above that there is a great deal that researchers don't know about cocaine and its impact on fetal development. Although they have no official relationship to the study, researchers from the Centers for Disease Control and the Georgia Department of Human Resources say that they plan to use "the findings to develop education, intervention and treatment programs and boost prenatal care." It is this combination of journalistic sensationalism and public health rhetoric that makes the media treatment of "crack babies" so pernicious.[61] As Nancy L. Day and Gale A. Richardson ask in their essay "Cocaine Use and Crack Babies" (also published in the special issue of *Neurotoxicology and Teratology* discussed earlier), "how did it happen that an epidemic of such proportions was declared so quickly?" They go on to raise several other issues about the spectacular increase in the concern about cocaine dangers: namely, "What were the other forces within science and our society that propelled the early reports of cocaine effects to such prominence, and that still in large part continue to propagate the belief that cocaine is a terrible scourge visited on the unborn?"[62] They rightly point out, as do others in that special issue, that cocaine has enjoyed a special place in the history of American culture — from its alleged use in Coca-Cola (which remains a great unspoken secret in the official history of the company), to its use as an entertainment chemical by rich yuppies in the Reagan era, to its current demonized status as the drug of addicted, welfare mothers. They beseech scientists and medical researchers to "correct the damage that has been done. . . . [d]amage that has been done to women and to the 'crack babies' who have been given a label for which there is no cure and little hope" (293). They implore medical researchers to assume the responsibility to educate other professionals about the complexity of the issue of determining causality and to remember that "behaviors do not exist in isolation, but are part of and determined by the fabric of a woman's life" (293). But such an admonishment is likely to fall on deaf ears, in the sense that it really requires medical practitioners and researchers to rethink and retool their relationships to various social entities such as the press and other media that seize upon "first case" examples as signs of a crisis, and to journalists who are not equipped to discuss the subtle nuances of published medical findings. More importantly, this would also require medical professionals to reconsider women as a social class who are differently and complexly positioned at the nexus of broader social forces such as poverty, violence, and demoralization.

Among the other precipitating conditions for the wide-scale enactment of an apparatus of surveillance is the historical evolution of medicine as an agent of social control. In one of the few explicit discussions of this topic in the professional literature on public health policy, Stephenson and Wagner summarized the situation of reproductive rights and medical control in 1993:

Since 1987 there have been approximately 60 criminal cases in the U.S. (many involving physicians) against women who have either taken illegal drugs during pregnancy or have failed to obey doctor's orders. The charges have ranged from prenatal child abuse to manslaughter. Several women have been convicted. Others have been forced against their will into drug treatment programs or have been "detained" (a euphemism for imprisonment). . . . Advocates for fetal rights have proposed a reporting system where pregnant women would be identified and monitored by state officials. Women would be forced to attend their prenatal visits and obey doctor's orders; and women could be prosecuted and punished for smoking or using drugs and alcohol during pregnancy. While this does not reflect predominant medical opinion, one survey did indicate that 46% of the heads of obstetrical and perinatal training programs thought that women who refused medical advice and thereby endangered the life of the fetus should be taken into custody.[63]

Although they are not concerned to discuss specific physician culpability, Stephenson and Wagner point out that physician coercion of pregnant women is of a piece with the differential denial of reproductive health care to certain social groups — in their view these cases demand a return to the consideration of basic medical ethics. The coercion of pregnant women to undergo certain procedures on behalf of the fetus is unethical in the same way as would be forcing a father to undergo a bone marrow transplant to save a son; and they remind us that the international code of medical ethics expressly forbids such coercion of a patient. But they also argue that there is "little reason to believe that medicine, on its own accord, will relinquish its privilege to determine (ad hoc) reproductive policy" (180). When one considers that such ad hoc policy is being established by those in the position to make decisions at the scene — where the agents who establish this policy are predominantly white, middle-class and male — it is likely that the policy will reflect the "dominant culture's beliefs about morality and motherhood" (180). They call for the intervention of courts and legislatures to "begin the difficult but essential task of formulating explicit reproductive health policies" (180); to assist this project they suggest the guidance of several international human rights treaties.

In an article in *Trial* that discusses the criminal law implications of prosecuting pregnant women for fetal abuse, Dorothy Roberts itemizes how such action violates the rights of women; not only does it

> infringe on fundamental guarantees of reproductive choice and bodily autonomy . . . [but] applying drug-trafficking and child-abuse laws to conduct during pregnancy also violates the defendants' due-process

right to fair notice. Criminal penalties may not be imposed for conduct that is outside the plain contemplation of the penal code.[64]

More broadly, such prosecution establishes unequal treatment of women
in that there is no corresponding scrutiny of men and male body behavior.
In legally restricting women's agency while pregnant, a discriminatory
system of surveillance is established. One California woman was charged
with criminal neglect of her fetus because she engaged in sexual intercourse while pregnant (against her doctor's instructions); her husband,
who also knew about the doctor's orders, was not named as a collaborator
in the criminal act.[65] Prosecuting pregnant women for fetal negligence
compromises their fundamental reproductive choice and establishes the
precedent for the state to determine who has the right to bear children.

These events and discussions establish the fact that a foundation
has been set in place to de-individualize the notion of pregnancy and to
make women's reproductive health a matter of *public* health policy. Mass-
mediated narratives establish the pregnant woman as the agent of a new
public health crisis: the pregnant woman is both disempowered and held
responsible at the same time. As the guilty culprit, she requires additional
surveillance in order to protect her babies and society from her criminal excesses. So when a professor of obstetrics and gynecology writes,
"the active management of labor attempts to address a problem that is
of great public health relevance in North America," we witness the process whereby women are interpolated into a very convoluted narrative
that defines wombs as unruly, childbirth as inherently pathological, and
women of childbearing age as unreliably duplicitous and possibly dangerous.[66] This narrative foregoes the possibility that drug use by pregnant
women may be a consequence of other social forces. This situation requires a careful analysis — one that does not inadvertently delimit wom-
en's agency by reifying their identity as victims, and also does not bestow
upon them exaggerated powers of contamination and infection. Seeing
this issue through a "maternalist" logic would suggest the investigation of
the social forces that influence women's drug use, the conditions under
which drug *use* becomes abusive to self and other, and the institutional
arrangements that support women's stigmatized identity as public health
offenders. This reflects a deeper philosophy that seeks to establish a partnership between women and their health care providers in which the
objective is to increase the information women have about their choices
for self-care, fetal care, and birth, and where the care provider is treated as

a consultant for the mother, not an executive of the birth process and of public health morality.

Writing History, Telling Tales

In the 1990 DHHS booklet *Alcohol, Tobacco, and Other Drugs May Harm the Unborn,* a section on "Counseling Women about Childbearing and Childrearing Risks" repeats the recommendation of an expert panel on prenatal care:[67]

> Because healthy women are more likely to have healthy babies, assuring good health prior to conception simply makes good sense and should be standard care. Diagnosis and interventions to treat medical illness and psychosocial risks prior to conception will eliminate or reduce hazards to the mother and baby. Care is also likely to be more effective prior to conception because evaluation and treatment can be initiated without harm to the fetus. (50)

In the context of this booklet, in the chapter on counseling women about childbearing risks, this advice sounds caring and responsible to the interests of women. But in a slightly different context, like *The Handmaid's Tale,* or as part of an assessment interview for an insurance program, this advice takes on a much more ominous tone. And yet, as the booklet's authors summarize the situation for pregnant women in the 1990s, it is not always clear that women's interests are driving the development of public health policy: "Because of legal and social interest in protecting babies, a pregnant woman who continues to take drugs against medical advice risks losing custody of her baby after it is born. In some States, she also risks criminal prosecution" (57). Indeed, the booklet reports, the Centers for Disease Control and Prevention identify these goals as part of their priorities for women's health: "to prevent illness and death associated with reproductive occurrences, practices, and choices, and to promote adoption of healthy reproductive behaviors and environments, including work settings" (18). These goals are to be accomplished through various surveillance systems that identify causes of maternal death, infant mortality, and pregnancy complications:

> CDC serves as one of the primary federal resources for technical assistance in the epidemiology and surveillance of pregnancy and its outcomes. Working collaboratively with agencies and organiza-

tions at all levels, the agency evaluates the nation's pregnancy-related health problems, programs, and policies in an effort to improve the health of pregnant women and their infants. (20)[68]

In the vocabulary of epidemiology, the term "surveillance" carries no pejorative connotations. It is a technical term for the organized practice of observing the development of health-related phenomena. And yet, the semiotic context of a particular term is not so easily delimited. The technical use of this term in the epidemiological literature also invokes other connotations of discipline, normative evaluation, and moral judgment.

In the process of constructing an analysis of the "official" public health discourse on the surveillance of pregnant women, I learned to read between the lines by reading those statements through an interpretive framework provided by fictional accounts of the treatment of reproductive body. This is one of the contributions that science fiction literature in general makes to our understanding of contemporary situations. As works of fictions that generically extrapolate from the current moment to fictional futures (or pasts), these narratives offer readers a framework for understanding the preoccupations that infuse contemporary culture. In this sense, Atwood's novel provided a sharply focused lens through which to view the emerging situation of women of reproductive age in the U.S.

Interspersed within *The Handmaid's Tale* are fragments of yet another discourse, one that articulates Offred's self-reflexive thoughts on the act of storytelling, in which the reader is addressed directly. At one point Offred tells the reader that it is a pretense to believe that she is telling a story because that would imply that she has some measure of control over the ending. At another moment we are told "this is a reconstruction. All of it is a reconstruction." And indeed at different points in her tale, readers get different versions of the same events: a narrative technique that foregrounds the reconstructive act of narrative itself. Near the end of the novel, she "[wishes] this story were different. I wish it were more civilized" (267). And she apologizes to us, the readers:

I'm sorry there is so much pain in this story. I'm sorry it's in fragments, like a body caught in crossfire or pulled apart by force. But there is nothing I can do to change it . . . But I keep on going with this sad and hungry and sordid, this limping and mutilated story, because after all I want you to hear it, as I will hear yours too if I ever get the chance, if I meet you or if you escape, in the future or in heaven or in prison or underground, some other place. What they have in common is that they're not here. By telling you anything at all I'm at least believing in you. I believe you're there, I believe you into being. Because I'm telling you this story I will your existence. I tell, therefore you are. (267–68)

This passage must be juxtaposed with the concluding section titled "Historical Notes," because both of them foreground the impossibility of the narrative situation that we have just read. Here Offred's telling poses a similar narrative dilemma to the one of the narrator in Charlotte Perkins Gilman's short story "The Yellow Wallpaper."[69] How is it that we come to get the story of a woman forbidden to read or write? The explanation offered in the "Historical Notes" section solves some of the mystery: *The Handmaid's Tale* is a historian's reconstruction based on narrative material discovered on audiotapes. What we are never told, though, is how the tapes came to be made — that is, the relationship between the historical account of the discovery of the tapes and the historical reconstruction of the ending of *The Handmaid's Tale*. Are these tapes of Offred or someone else? Whose voice tells whose story?

In the final analysis, I want to suggest that the "Historical Notes" section offers the most interesting statement about the contemporary situation of reproductive-age women. Some readers have interpreted this section as a splendid send-up of an academic conference or, as one reviewer describes it, "a desperately needed and hilarious spoof of an academic convention in the year 2195, at which time Gilead is a defunct society, regarded by all as a trivial aberration in cultural history."[70] Ironic as it clearly is, it is also the most utopian part of the entire novel. Set against the more didactic warnings against feminist techno-criticism on the one hand and patriarchal technology lust on the other, this ending offers a false promise of hope and transcendence. It enacts a belief we hear in Offred's recollection of her mother's feminism: "history will absolve me." What it suggests is that something fundamental will change about people's willful acts of ignorance. Offred, herself, describes the fog we live within now, surrounded as we are by such seemingly isolated instances of technologically enhanced reproductive surveillance:

But we lived as usual. Everyone does, most of the time. Whatever is going on is as usual. Even this is as usual, now. We lived, as usual, by ignoring. Ignoring isn't the same as ignorance, you have to work at it. Nothing changes instantaneously: in a gradually heating bathtub you'd be boiled to death before you knew it. There were stories in the newspapers, of course. . . . The newspaper stories were like dreams to us, bad dreams dreamt by others. How awful, we would say, and they were, but they were awful without being believable. They were too melodramatic, they had a dimension that was not the dimension of our lives. We were the people who were not in the papers. We lived in the blank white spaces at the edges of the print. It gave us more freedom. We lived in the gaps between the stories. (56–57)

There are two messages in this passage. The first concerns our contemporary relationship to technology and the danger of an uncritical belief in technological progress. This we can understand as an act of "ignoring," rather than a quality of ignorance. Contemporary U.S. culture is completely saturated with technology; we must actively work to disregard the long-term consequences of such a saturation. In this case, Atwood's novel provides the perspective we need to understand the relation between seemingly isolated instances of technological surveillance. "Perspective is necessary," Offred tells us, "otherwise you live with your face squashed against a wall."

The second message addresses the place of women in cultural history. People who live on the margins, "in the gaps between the stories," women whose entire lives never make the news are not remembered. Their stories, the everydayness of their lives, are not the stuff of history. In this sense, the story we read in *The Handmaid's Tale* is a utopian vision of the development of a historical practice that would promote the importance of recording women's histories. This is not generally the trend within contemporary historical practice. It is, though, the project of feminist cultural studies. As I have argued elsewhere, ethnography can be reclaimed as a feminist practice in which we work to intervene in the production of the history of the present by writing the narratives of women's everyday lives.[71] In this light, I propose that we consider Atwood's novel as something generically different from a science fictional dystopia.[72] I want to read it "against the grain," perhaps as a speculative ethnographic account of our collective life in a technological era, where transcoded from one generic framework to another, it offers us a critical framework of analysis that will counteract our propensity to ignore the probable consequences for the female body of the application of the new technologies of reproductive surveillance. Such a reading requires that we forgo our willful acts of ignoring those "disturbing" newspaper stories as if they were inconsequential to our real work as scholars and critics.

My aim has been to investigate the narrative construction of reality accomplished through the articulation of cultural practices and cultural narratives. "Articulation" describes the process whereby meaning is constructed and assigned to a particular configuration of practices; it is a complex process in the sense that meaning is both an effect of practices and a determining condition of those practices. In this chapter I have described a select set of cultural stories about the maternal body that include scientific discourse about pregnancy and the development and application of medical protocols, as well as a fictional narrative of maternal surveillance. Throughout the analysis of these discursive sources, I have tried to elucidate the connection between these narratives and other social structures and institutional practices. I have also tried to examine the process of cultural analysis itself, whereby literary narratives are "interpreted" in the service of illuminating the meaning of other cultural discourses, which in turn are used to describe and critique the organization of social practices and material effects. As a map of the relationship between a particular configuration of discursive moments and a set of cultural practices, this chapter suggests not only the critical *issues* that I believe should be attended to by feminist cultural scholars, but also a critical *framework* for the analysis and intervention into such politically charged situations.

CHAPTER FIVE

The Virtual Body in Cyberspace

This chapter speculates about the body on the electronic frontier. In one sense, this frontier is an *imaginary* construction that identifies a horizon of contemporary cultural thought. But in another sense it is a real space on the fringe of mainstream culture: the "electronic frontier" names the space of information exchange that already exists in the flow of databases, telephone and fiber-optic networks, computer memory, and other parts of electronic networking services.[1] The frontier metaphor suggests the possibility of a vast, unexplored territory. Computer enthusiasts, also known as hackers, populate frontier villages; advance scouts/pilgrims include the by now infamous computer viruses, worms, and Trojan horses that were designed very simply to "map" the network into which they were released. In elaborating the Western frontier metaphor, John Perry Barlow explains that in the new small towns, "Main Street is a central minicomputer. . . . Town Meetings are continuous and discussions range on everything from sexual kinks to depreciation schedules."[2]

In a more material sense, the electronic frontier includes workstations, file servers, networks, and bulletin boards, as well as the code of application programs, information services such as Prodigy and CompuServe, and on-line databases.[3] This frontier functions as the infrastructure of the computer/information industry and, as such, structures the further development and dissemination of computer technologies and services. One of the most publicized computer applications of the last decade has been the construction of "virtual environments," now more widely known as "virtual reality."[4] Since 1987, virtual reality (VR) has further evolved into an industry in itself; it is also at the heart of an emergent (sub)culture that includes computer-generated realities, science fiction, fictional sciences, and powerfully evocative new visualization technologies.[5] My guiding question for this chapter concerns the role of the body in this formation.

To set the stage for a discussion of the body in cyberspace, I offer a reading of the cultural aspects of the virtual reality industry, including its embodiment in a cyberpunk subculture, its media spectacles, and commodities-on-offer. Reporting on a trip through cyberspace, I wonder how the repression of the body is accomplished so easily and about the consequences of this disembodiment. I conclude by posing several questions about the biopolitics of virtual reality.

Marketing Cyberspace

Virtual technologies use graphics programs to create a three-dimensional, computer-generated space that a user/participant interacts with and manipulates via wired peripherals. In contemporary science fiction, the 3-D, computer-generated space or virtual environment is referred to as "cyberspace," a term first used by William Gibson in his cyberpunk novel *Neuromancer* and now gaining acceptance among VR technicians to name the interior space of virtual reality programs.[6] In its fictional form, cyberspace is sometimes referred to as the matrix or "the Net," a shorthand name for the network constructed by the connections between fixed computer consoles and portable computer decks.[7] In cyberpunk novels, "real" geographic urban-suburban space is referred to as "the sprawl," and although hackers often have to hide out or navigate their way through it, the real "action" always occurs in the structured informational space of the matrix.

In its commercial form, cyberspace describes an electronic matrix or virtual environment. It is also listed as a trademark of Autodesk, one of the two better known companies that develop software tools for virtual realities. Standard cyberspace hardware includes a set of wired goggles that track head movement connected to a computer that runs VR software. In 1985, a computer musician named Jaron Lanier founded a company called VPL that prides itself on being a "pioneer in Virtual Reality (VR) and visual programming." Better known than his company's products, Lanier has become a cult figure in the virtual reality subculture, whose members include technological innovators, popular cultural icons, game designers, and computer entrepreneurs. Lanier is often quoted as saying "whatever the physical world has, virtual reality has as well."[8]

Mondo 2000, the preeminent hacker magazine of the 1990s, offers a

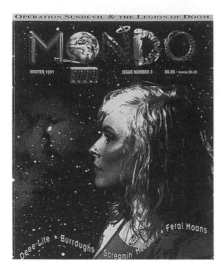

Figure 23. Cover of *Mondo 2000*
(vol. 3, Winter 1991), featuring
Debbie Harry.

glimpse into the subculture formed in and around the fictional world of
cyberspace (figure 23). Posing is certainly nothing new to popular sub-
cultures, and indeed, this is part of *Mondo*'s attraction for mainstream
readers: it lets us in to the in-crowd. Three features stand out: its glossy,
visually dense, techno-art layout; the regularly scheduled iconoclastic reports from the electronic frontier; and mediated interviews with the high
priests of street tech, notably William S. Burroughs and Timothy Leary. It
also promotes up-and-coming visionaries such as Lanier and John Perry
Barlow, as well as other cultural cybercritics (such as Kathy Acker, Avital
Ronell, and Ted Nelson) and various rock groups, performance artists,
smart drug advocates, and electronic industry movers and shakers. In
short, *Mondo 2000* publicizes the key features of the new subculture:
"founding fathers," mythic narratives of identity, a specialized language,
and a lot of new technology. In doing so, *Mondo 2000,* house organ for
the cyberpunk industry, popularizes the worldview of those addicted to
the possibilities of life in the microworld.

Topically, *Mondo 2000* picks up where McLuhan's *Mechanical Bride*
left off, without the rhetorical questions and, for the most part, without
the cultural criticism.[9] Where McLuhan fixated on magazine advertisements that hinted at the ominous fusion of sex and technology, *Mondo
2000* became the magazine to celebrate the fusion of sex and technology
in its advertisements for cyberpunk culture. And yet, in spite of its techno-
lust(er), *Mondo 2000* oddly evokes the countercultural rhetoric of the

1960s. In part this reflects the widespread 1990s nostalgia for 1960s fashions and fads; thus, an issue of *Mondo* might include retro-topics such as "on the road" stories, drug synthesis instructions, mod fashion icons, and reports from the underground. The difference is that in the 1990s the drugs are intended to make us "smart," hallucinogens are replaced with hallucino*genres,* the "Underground" is a band, and the best sex is virtual.[10] In a review of a show curated by Shalom Gorewitz, the *Village Voice* called the cyberspace artists and hackers "gonzo techno-hippies."[11] Indeed, the juxtaposition of countercultural rhetoric with technological elitism constructs an interesting stage for the promotion of virtual reality technologies. *Mondo 2000* makes no pretense of democracy and no attempt at accessibility, advising readers that unsolicited manuscripts are burned at the full moon and that "unsolicited art work will be electronically scanned and altered and appear uncredited in other magazines." Advertisements plug in-group products: Gibson and Sterling's new novel, reprints of Leary's work, Avital Ronell's *Telephone Book.* But the pleasure of recognition is high. Articles demonstrate the appropriate attitude to the "New World DisOrder" while they show you who/what you need to know/read/buy to be a member by imitation only. Even though electronically connected cyberpunks are dispersed from coast to coast, it's pretty obvious, according to *Mondo,* that the happening place to be is on the West Coast. So even though the real story about the development of virtual reality technologies takes shape all over the U.S. — and especially in Britain, Australia, and Italy (among other places) — in keeping with the frontier logic, the best (mythical) cyberspace events have all taken place in our own American wild, wild West.

Of course, the virtual reality industry includes much more than the subculture visualized by *Mondo 2000.* On the PR front, it includes conferences staged like media events — such as "Cyber Arts International," billed as "the world forum for emerging technologies in the arts, entertainment and education," and "Cyberthon" a multimedia virtual reality fair sponsored by the Whole Earth Institute.[12] Richard Kadrey describes the technology-saturated 24 hours of Cyberthon No. 1: "On October 6 and 7 [1990] . . . the Whole Earth Institute turned the sound stage of San Francisco's Colossal Pictures into the world's biggest virtual-reality fair. Almost four hundred people got the chance to see and experience a whole range of reality-bending technologies close up. Over three hundred lucky lottery winners got the chance to don goggles and gloves and actually enter virtual worlds created by teams from Autodesk, Sense8, and Jaron

Lanier's VPL."[13] Ironically, the conference announcements advertised in *Mondo* or disseminated through electronic bulletin boards often rely on a rhetoric of "reality" to attract conference participants.[14] For example, they offer to make available—for a price, of course—"real" VR programs and equipment. Registration for the 1991 CyberArts International cost $450 and allowed a participant to visit special exhibits such as the Cyber-Art Gallery and "Product Expo," where one could "experience" VR *live* by taking part in interactive music performances (where the audience directs the music) or by trying a "*live* exercise in producing integrated media." Cyberpunk night at CyberArt, sponsored by *Mondo 2000,* promised "an evening of elegant entertainment and high tech hallucinations," complete with master of ceremonies Timothy Leary and a "new kind of theatrical entertainment *experience.*" The exhortations to "experience it live"—the shows and the software systems on display—suggest more than an ironic subtext to the supermediated VR spectacles. They also draw our attention to the process whereby VR technologies are transformed into commodities, through the engagement between people and products.

For all the media hype, audience response to VR suggests that, at best, it is at the "Kitty Hawk" stage—more PR than VR, as one discussion list participant wrote. "Serious" VR research is another matter, though. It has been reported that some computer scientists do not like the term "virtual reality," originally coined by Jaron Lanier, the VPL maverick. "The term 'virtual environment' better fits a field of scientific research," claims a professor of computer graphics quoted in a 1991 *Chronicle of Higher Education* article. "Virtual reality is an unattainable goal, like artificial intelligence."[15]

Although no official history of VR has been drafted, computer science and computer graphics are its foundation; it draws on Norbert Wiener's work in the 1940s on the science of cybernetics as well as on the early history of calculating machinery.[16] Other historical contributions include research during the 1960s on two-dimensional and three-dimensional viewing, and work from the 1970s on "visually-coupled" systems. During the 1980s, VR-related research proliferated in the areas of interface design, telerobotics, optical sensors, simulation parameters, and image processing and display. Myron Krueger, sometimes referred to as the father of artificial reality, wrote a very interesting but brief essay on the history of the field, in which he explains that although it took awhile for "the notion of artificial reality to take hold"—due to some common constraints on technological research (few journals and scarce funding for new technologies) and several cultural constraints (such as Senator William Proxmire's Golden Fleece awards and geographical displacement) — "interactive computing is now the norm."[17] Implicitly he suggests that the biggest constraint inhibiting VR research was the lack of appreciation for its possible wide-scale market applications. Other than NASA's interest in head-mounted displays for reconnaissance and weapon delivery, no one had imagined the consumer market possibilities of human-machine interactive systems.

The scene has changed by the mid-1990s. Virtual reality applications in telecommunications, surgical simulation, and computer-aided design are of great interest to current industry planners. In the electronics industry, VR is touted as an attractive, albeit capital-intensive, business venue; it demands the development of a host of new products, including biotechnical apparatuses such as datagloves, wired bodysuits, head-mounted tracking devices, goggles, headphones, miniaturized LCD screens, and digitizing cameras.[18] These devices and programs are incredibly expensive, not only to develop, but also to purchase. A cyberspace system marketed by VPL, called "A Reality Built for Two" or RB2, retailed for $250,000 in 1991; it comes with two headsets, two sets of DataGloves, and a powerful minicomputer. One of the main purposes of the splashy VR demonstrations and conventions is to create investment interest as well as a market for VR applications. Members of the cyberpunk subculture — who are also the programmers, designers, and technicians — seem to take for granted the economic imperative to create a market for their products. In his description of the design of a cyberspace playhouse for sports and fitness, Randal Walser, then manager of the Autodesk Cyberspace Project, explains:

> The critical thing to realize about the design of cyberspaces for sports, is that sporting decks will generally have sophisticated props, like recombinant bicycles and inclined treadmills, and that sporting houses will make money by renting time on those decks. The purpose of a cyberspace for sports is not just to help people have fun and stay fit. It is also to help keep sporting houses in business, by keeping their decks full of players.[19]

Other industry futurists envision large-scale VR installations primarily for entertainment and leisure services and would love to attract the backing of Disney or Universal — who have theme parks that currently use robotics — to invest in the development of "Dream Parks" that are based on "interactive role-playing environments."[20] These speculations about the future of VR contribute to a "bottom-line" message about its potential: there is a lot of money to be made in the development and marketing of cyberspace.

In summary, the key features of this new subculture include popular cultural artifacts (e.g., *Mondo 2000* and the films *Lawnmower Man* and *Johnny Mnemonic*), a mythic set of founding fathers (Ted Nelson, Jaron Lanier), a specialized language that draws on the science of computer technology and computer programming, and the promise of new high-tech commodities. Oddly, at the same time that it promotes the sexiness of new technology and is unabashedly elitist, it also evokes a countercultural belief in the possibility of resistance within a corporate culture. Such juxtapositions — of technology and the counterculture, of "reality effects" and real demonstrations, of the science and the PR — suggest that cyberpunk subculture is actively engaged in the work of processing cultural meanings. As it plays itself out, the future of virtual reality is intimately tied to the capitalist structure of the information technology industry. Now that various cultural visionaries have turned their attention to the work of imagining the future of VR, they ensure that it will be fully articulated to a commodity structure. The staged subcultural events draw our attention to the process whereby technologies are transformed into technological commodities.

As "countercultural" as members of this subculture want to be, the virtual reality industry actually disseminates a certain mythology and a set of metaphors and concepts that cannot help but reproduce the anxieties and preoccupations of contemporary culture. As Jack Zipes claims, "the inevitable outcome of most mass-mediated fairy tales is a happy reconfirmation of the system which produces them."[21] More than once, the popular press have commented that simulated experiences "offer opportunities for safe activity in a risky world." Called "electronic LSD," or an "electronic out-of-body experience," VR in its celebrated media form seems little more than an escape from conventional reality, a way out for those who confront the severe limitations reality imposes in the form of corporate ideology, determining social structures, and the physical body itself.[22] A more traditional ideological critique of the VR industry probably would begin by elaborating its participation in postindustrial capitalist modes of production and would go on to expose the way that the "oppositional" subculture actually promotes bourgeois notions such as creative genius, hyperindividualism, and transcendent subjectivity. In his essay "Hacking Away at the Counterculture," Andrew Ross elaborates how the story "told by the critical left about new cultural technologies is that of monolithic, panoptical social control, effortlessly achieved through a smooth, endlessly interlocking system of networks of surveillance." But, as he goes on to write, this "is not always the best story to tell."[23]

I agree that this ideological critique may be too totalizing. When discussing new technologies, it is important to try to avoid the trap of technological determinism that argues that these technologies necessarily and unilaterally expand the hegemonic control by a techno-elite. Technologies have *limited* agency. Having said that though, it does appear that virtual reality technologies are implicated in the production of a certain set of cultural narratives that reproduce dominant relations of power. Perhaps a better approach for evaluating the meaning of these new technologies is to try to elaborate the ways in which such technologies and, more importantly, the *use* of such technologies, are determined by broader social and cultural forces.

One of the most often-repeated claims about virtual reality is that it provides the technological means to construct personal realities free from the determination of body-based ("real") identities. Whereas VR promoters have focused primarily on the subjective and expressive dimensions of VR in public relations campaigns for VR games, users are also told that the physical body is of no consequence in virtual worlds. Even though some games may soon allow players to design personal avatars or puppets — simulations of oneself — more frequently VR is promoted as a body-free environment, a place of escape from the corporeal embodiment of gender and race. Upon analyzing the "lived" experience of virtual reality, I discovered that this *conceptual* denial of the body is accomplished through the *material* repression of the physical body. The phenomenological experience of cyberspace depends upon and in fact requires the willful repression of the material body. In saying this, I am implicitly arguing that we need to extend the ideological critique of virtual reality technologies. From a feminist perspective it is clear that the repression of the material body belies a gender bias in the supposedly disembodied (and gender-free) world of virtual reality. In arguing that this repression is a technological phenomenon, I am not claiming that it is entirely determined by the technology. On the contrary, I will elaborate how VR technologies articulate cultural narratives about the techno-body so that these technologies have the effect of naturalizing a gendered body phenomenon.

A Trip through Cyberspace

In contrast to a 2-D database, VR applications allow users to interact with three-dimensional representations of information. So instead of searching a database for lexical indicators or parts of computer code, a VR patron can interact with a data storage environment and browse through information that is represented graphically. According to one article in *Industry Week,* with VR "you can imagine CAD models that, in effect, come alive. . . . You can enter them. You can make them any scale. They could be models of molecules, for example, and you could move about within these molecules with your whole body to examine their structures."[24] In this way, the cyberspacial matrix serves as an abstract environment within which computer patrons can navigate.

All VR systems involve the interface of the body and technology in the use of some kind of bio-apparatus; three of the more common ones are the Nintendo PowerGlove; a headmount that includes LCD screens; and a "hotsuit," which is a set of wired overalls.[25] Although my first trip through VR (with goggles and a track ball) was uneventful, I noticed the ease with which I made sense of the scene projected on small lenses mounted in the front of my helmet. The vision projected onto the small LCD screens was colored like a cartoon world, with yellow walls, orange floors, and brown tables. The point of contact with the interior spaces of VR — the way that this scene makes sense — is through an eye-level perspective that shifts as the user/patron turns her head; the changes in the scene projected on the small screens corresponds roughly with the real-time perspectival changes one would expect as one normally turns the head. Although other VR users have reported a noticeable time lag in the change of scene as the head turns, I notice no significant lag. The timing of the change of scene corresponded quite closely with the changes I would "normally" expect as I turn my head. The most disconcerting effect of my trip through VR was the inability to "right" my perspective after I would awkwardly move my "point of view" through the scene. Because the scenes still look like computer animations, there are few visual cues to use as markers of the right-side-up of the scene. Furthermore, in the program I used there is no gravity and therefore no way to orient oneself in the scene using the body as a kinesthetic point of reference.

In most VR programs, a user experiences VR through a disembodied gaze — a floating, moving "perspective" — that mimes the movement of a disembodied camera "eye." This is a familiar aspect of what may be called a filmic phenomenology, where the camera simulates the movement of perspective that rarely includes a self-referential visual inspection of the body as the vehicle of that perspective. The disembodiment of the eye is accomplished through the manipulation of the camera to approximate the height and angle of the point of view of an eye; the body of that eye is repressed, in that it is rarely shown (revealed) and never felt. The naturalization of the filmic gaze is one of the foundational planks of psychoanalytic film criticism and certainly not a new discovery. But what is of interest to me in my encounter with virtual reality is the way that the repression of the body is technologically naturalized. I think this happens because we have internalized the technological gaze to such an extent that "perspective" is a naturalized organizing locus of sense knowledge. As a consequence, the body, as a sense apparatus, is nothing more than excess baggage for the cyberspace traveler.

The Biopolitics of Virtual Bodies

What is becoming increasingly clear in encounters with virtual reality applications is that visualization technologies no longer simply mimic or *represent* reality — they virtually recreate it. But the difference between the reality constructed in VR worlds and the reality constructed in the everyday world is a matter of epistemology, not ontology.[26] They are both cultural as well as technological constructions, fully saturated by the media and other forms of everyday technologies. With respect to VR, it no longer makes sense to ask whose reality/perspective is represented in the various VR worlds, the industry, or the subculture; rather we should ask what reality is *created* therein, and how this reality *articulates relationships* between technologies, bodies, and cultural narratives. Where the first line of questioning assumes that "perspective" and "point of view" are the main channels of knowledge, the second line of questioning asserts that there is no singular reality to virtual reality, and that the "realities" constructed therein embody the desires of those who program them.[27]

Another critical framework, one informed by feminist epistemology, asks a slightly different set of questions about the realities of cyberspace; given this formation of an industry and now a subculture based on the use of virtual technologies, what are the biopolitics of virtual bodies in cyberspace? Which is to say, how do virtual reality technologies engage socially and culturally marked bodies? This set of questions begins with the material body and opens onto institutional and social issues. What is the relation of the material body to the "sensory" simulation provided by virtual technologies? What are the phenomenological dimensions of the technologically mediated body?[28] Does VR transform body-based subjectivities? How do various interfaces negotiate the split between the material body of the user and the locus of perception that either free-floats in a virtual world or is connected in some fashion to a virtual puppet? Demographically, what kinds of bodies reside in cyberspace: humanoid? More specifically, how is the disembodied technological gaze marked by the signs or logic of gender and race? What kind of "reality surplus" is produced? When virtual "realities" are bought and sold, who will profit? What kinds of bodies are cybernetically employed in the production of computer components? At one level, VR enables the willing suspension of disbelief whereby a participant adjusts the way that sensory information is processed; certain senses are realigned (vision without gravity) to process the simulated experience, while other registers of reality are repressed. The fact that a floating point of view is intelligible attests to the flexibility of embodied sense organs. So although the body may disappear representationally in virtual worlds — indeed, we may go to great lengths to repress it and erase its referential traces — it does not disappear materially in the interface with the VR apparatus or, for that matter, in the phenomenological frame of the user.

In VR discourse, where knowledge is operationalized as "data interconnectedness," there is little consensus on the main problematic of virtual reality, let alone on the particulars of a cultural critique of it. For Michael Spring, the major conceptual problem is developing a robust model to visualize data interconnectedness.[29] Virtual reality researchers, in reflecting on its significance, struggle to articulate an adequate understanding of the process of reality construction; almost intuitively, they understand the necessity of specifying the relationship between visual representations and meaning, but they often fall back on mechanistic models of the process of communication.[30] In delineating the difference between film and cyberspace, for example, Randal Walser writes: "whereas film depicts a reality to an audience, cyberspace grants a virtual body and a role, to everyone in the audience."[31] In this account Walser offers an extremely simplistic understanding of the relationships among film, representation, and the viewing situation. Although this is gradually changing as artists become involved in the design of virtual worlds, virtual reality applications for the most part show little understanding of the dynamics of visual representation, let alone spectatorship, subjectivity, or phenomenological embodiment. In the end, though, as Jaron Lanier reminds us, "whatever the physical world has, virtual reality has as well." So the question emerges, what exactly does it offer?

In short, what these VR encounters really provide is an illusion of control over reality, nature, and especially over the unruly, gender- and race-marked, essentially mortal body. It is not a coincidence that VR emerges in the 1980s, during a decade when the body is understood to be increasingly vulnerable (literally, as well as discursively) to infection as well as to gender, race, ethnicity, and ability critiques. With virtual reality we are offered the vision of a body-free universe. Despite the rhetorical disclaimers that this was *not* a Nintendo war, media coverage of the Persian Gulf spectacle provided numerous examples of the deployment of a disembodied technological gaze; the bomb's-eye view was perhaps the most fascinating and therefore most disturbing example of the seductive power of a disembodied gaze to mask the violence of reality.[32] The critical point here is that these new technological applications—VR, Nintendo, or bomb-cam—do not create disembodied citizens. Rather, they are themselves consequences of social changes already in place. If "the frontier" functions as a metaphor to describe the social and economic context for the development of new computer/information technologies, "cyberspace" functions metaphorically to describe the space of the disembodied "social" in a hypertechnological informational society. Cyberspace—as a popular cultural construct—shows us what can happen when popular culture "talks back" to cultural theory (to borrow a phrase from Fred Pfeil); cyberspace offers a way to think about the location of the social in postindustrial capitalism. Although this space is structured, it is impossible to map; there is no Archimedian point from which to construct a totalizing vision of the scene. At best you can wander through it, reading/writing as you walk, and maybe stumble upon something that was not programmed for you. Rich in information, if you know what you are looking for, the experience of cyberspace is always conjunctural: an effect of intersecting practices—economic, technological, bodily, political, and cultural.

In her *Esquire* article on virtual reality, Sallie Tisdale notes a "curious absence of narrative at Cyberthon, both in and out of the virtual worlds. It was an absence of plot—there is no story yet, no cosmology."[33] In part, this is true; virtual reality promoters are computer scientists and system hackers, not cultural critics, and, for the most part, they recognize this fact—which in part accounts for their willingness, and indeed, enthusiasm to engage the work of artists and other cultural visionaries. On the other hand, these new technologies are implicated in the reproduction of at least one very traditional cultural narrative: the possibility of transcendence, whereby the physical body and its social meanings can be technologically neutralized. If the applications that utilize a disembodied gaze as the locus of perspective do away with the body altogether, the applications that include a representation of the body project a utopian desire for control over the form of personal embodiment. The promises of VR-connected bodies are described by Scott Fisher in his article "Virtual Environments":

> The two users will participate and interact in a shared virtual environment but each will view it from their relative, spatially disparate viewpoint. The objective is to provide a collaborative worldspace in which remotely located participants can virtually interact with some of the nuances of face-to-face meetings while also having access to their personal dataspace facilities. . . . With full-body tracking capability, it will also be possible for each user to be represented in this space by his or her own life-size virtual representation in any chosen form—a kind of electronic persona. . . . these virtual forms might range from fantasy figures to inanimate objects or from different figures to different people.[34]

In the speculative discourse of VR, we are promised whatever body we want, which doesn't say anything about the body that I already have and the economy of meanings I already embody. What forms of embodiment would people choose if they could design their virtual bodies without the pain or cost of physical restructuring? If we look to those who are already participating in body reconstruction programs—for instance, cosmetic surgery and bodybuilding—we would find that their reconstructed bodies display very traditional gender and race markers of beauty, strength, and sexuality. There is plenty of evidence to suggest that a reconstructed body does not guarantee a reconstructed cultural identity. Nor does "freedom from a body," imply that people will exercise the "freedom to be" any other kind of body than the one they already enjoy or desire.

Fictional accounts of cyberspace play out the fantasy of casting off the body as an obsolete piece of meat, but, not surprisingly, these fictions do not eradicate body-based systems of differentiation and domination. In fact, Fred Pfeil demonstrates "several ways in which much of the new SF

written by men, for all the boundary erosions and breakdowns it drama-
tizes, remains stuck in a masculinist frame."[35] In the course of Gibson's
Neuromancer trilogy, for example, not only is the hero's body eventually
reconstructed from fragments of skin, so is his macho-male identity. It is
true that in cyberpunk narratives individual male and female bodies may
be coded slightly differently than they are in prevailing cultural norms. For
example, Gibson's main female character in *Neuromancer*, Molly, has
been technologically modified with implanted weaponry that on the one
hand makes her a powerful embodiment of female identity, no longer
constrained by norms of passivity and proper femininity. On the other
hand, Molly's body implants more fully literalize the characteristically
threatening nature of her female body. Early in his adventures, Gibson's
hero, Case, must negotiate a cyberspace invasion where he is plugged in to
Molly's body. Molly gets a rider, and Case gets to find out "just how tight
those jeans really are" (53).

> Then he keyed the new switch. The abrupt jolt into other flesh. . . .
> For a few minutes he fought helplessly to control her body. Then
> he willed himself into passivity, became the passenger behind her
> eyes. . . . Her body language was disorienting, her style foreign. She
> seemed continually on the verge of colliding with someone, but peo-
> ple melted out of her way, stepped sideways, made room. (56)

Once "inside" Molly, Case finds the "passivity of the situation irritating."
This passivity refers to his lack of control over Molly's body, so in a sense
Case does experience, with the help of VR technology, a bodily state more
traditionally feminine. But his simstim "experience" makes no lasting im-
pression. Nor does it provide the occasion for the development of some
insight into the politics of gendered bodies. His passivity is easily sexualized. To tease him, Molly reaches into her jacket, "a finger circling a
nipple under warm silk. The sensation made [Case] catch his breath" (56).
This cybernetic penetration, we discover, follows a sexual encounter between Case and Molly when he recalls "their mutual grunt of unity when
he'd entered her" (56). Inside of cyberspace, or out, the relations between
these cybernetically connected bodies often recreate traditional heterosexual gender identities.[36]

Probably no collection so effectively betrays the masculinist values of
the new cyberpunk writers as the science fiction anthology titled *Semi-
otext(e) SF*. In their attempt to "jolt" the commercial SF publishing industry, guest editors Rudy Rucker and Peter Lamborn Wilson invited contri-

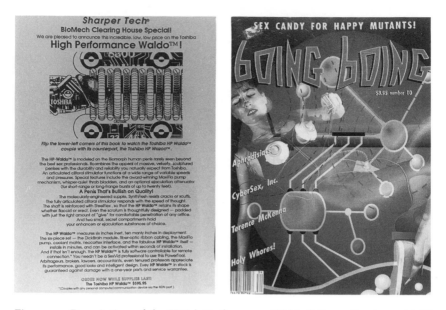

Figure 24. Description of the "High Performance Waldo." From *Semiotext(e) SF* (New York: Autonomedia, 1989), p. 15. Figure 25. Cover of *bOING bOING* (no. 10: special issue, "Sex Candy for Happy Mutants!").

butions that had been rejected by other, more mainstream magazines. As they explained, "we hoped to tap a deep and almost-inarticulate ground-swell of resentment against the ever-increasing stodginess, neoconserva-tism, big-bucks mania and wretched taste of most SF publishers" (12).[37] Although they clearly collected a range of formerly rejected material, they also produced a volume that loudly announces the gender conservatism of cyberpunk writers. Penetrating penises figure prominently on every page in the form of a flip-book illustration of the "High Performance Waldo" (figure 24), a penis that is modeled on "the Biomorph human penis rarely seen beyond the best sex professionals" (15). Indeed, the sexualization of the female body is a common theme in the various cyberpunk short sto-ries. On this point, Andrew Ross argues that cyberpunk fiction offers the "most fully delineated urban fantasies of white male folklore."[38] In saying this, he also describes the logic behind the techno-fantasies embodied in VR applications where chic French women are made available as flirting partners to help you, the ideal male audience member, perfect your French language skills. In contemporary cyberpunk narratives, as in VR applica-tions, cyberspace heroes are usually men, whose racial identity, although rarely described explicitly, is contextually white. Cyberspace playmates are usually beautiful, sexualized, albeit sometimes violently powerful women (figure 25). Cyberspace offers white men an enticing retreat from the burdens of their *cultural* identities. In this sense, it is apparent that although cyberspace seems to represent a territory free from the burdens of history, it will, in effect, serve as another site for the technological and no less conventional inscription of the gendered, race-marked body. So despite the fact that VR technologies offer a new stage for the construction and performance of body-based identities, it is likely that old identities will continue to be more comfortable, and thus more frequently reproduced.

The Rearticulation of Old Identities to New Technologies

The virtual body is neither simply a surface upon which are written the dominant narratives of Western culture, nor a *representation* of cultural ideals of beauty or of sexual desire. It has been transformed into the very medium of cultural expression itself, manipulated, digitalized, and technologically constructed in virtual environments. Enhanced visualization technologies make it difficult to continue to think about the material body as a bounded entity, or to continue to distinguish its inside from its outside, its surface from its depth, its aura from its projection. As the virtual body is deployed as a medium of information and of encryption, the structural integrity of the material body as a bounded physical object is technologically deconstructed. If we think of the body not as a product, but rather as a process — and embodiment as an effect — we can begin to ask questions about how the body is staged differently in different realities. Virtual environments offer a new arena for the staging of the body — what dramas will be played out in these virtual worlds?

Even though the fetishistic nature of such technological devices (especially of the splashy demo tapes) fuels the fantasies of VR technicians (for ultimate world control), the possibilities for realizing these fantasies are probably determined more by the socioeconomic context of corporate sponsorship than by the libidinal promise of virtually safe sex — which is to say that VR research and development cannot continue without commercial investment. But this isn't the whole story. Interspersed throughout the pages of *Mondo 2000* and conference announcements, a tension of sorts emerges in the attempt to discursively negotiate a corporate commodity system while upholding oppositional notions of countercultural iconoclasm, individual genius, and artistic creativity. The result is the formation of a postmodern schizo-culture that is unselfconsciously elitist and often disingenuous in offering its hacker's version of the American Dream.

As Donna Haraway argues, we must be able to get beyond the rhetoric produced by both the techno-advocates and the cultural critics, because both of them inadvertently construct a demonology of technology. The issues we need to investigate concern the way that VR technologies produce simultaneous effects that are not easily judged to be "good" or "bad," or moral or immoral. For example, virtual reality applications, in an ideal form, involve a network of individual-machine interfaces located at remote outposts. In this sense, VR promotes both technological access and decentralization. But then, does it promote the further instrumental rationalization of everyday life or a new epistemological pluralism? Even as VR technology promises a new form of intersubjectivity, it contributes to a heretofore unknown epidemic of cultural autism. Intimacy is now redefined as a quality of interaction between the human body and the machine.[39] What about notions of privacy and hygiene? Who will have access to virtual reality applications and, more broadly, to the networks that serve as the infrastructure of the emerging information society? Sensory processing is a fertile field for scientific research. In fact, we are fascinated by the possibility that we may be able to technologically monitor brain functioning. Several sophisticated new visualization technologies — such as PET (positron emission tomography), MRI (magnetic resonance imaging), and MEG (magnetoencephalogy) — offer ways to visualize brain activity. In the best light, this is done in hopes of constructing a map of brain processing patterns; but even as these technologies promise new vistas for scientific research, the possibility for establishing new "biologically based" standards of body functioning — for example, defining what is "normal" according to neural firing patterns — suggests that this is not a politically neutral technology. The fact that new imaging technologies produce "better" images of human anatomy does not guarantee that doctors are using the images to produce "better" diagnoses and/or treatment programs for patients.[40] By analogy, the fact that virtual realities offer new information environments does not guarantee that people will use the information in better ways. It is just as likely that these new technologies will be used primarily to tell old stories — stories that reproduce, in high-tech guise, traditional narratives about the gendered, race-marked body.

CHAPTER SIX

Feminism for the Incurably Informed

My mother was a computer, but she never learned to drive. Grandmother was an order clerk in a predominantly male warehouse; she did all the driving for the family, having learned to drive almost before she learned to speak English; her first car was a 1916 Model-T Ford equipped with a self-starter.[1] Both my mother and grandmother worked for Sears, Roebuck and Co. in the 1940s; mother entered orders on a log sheet, grandmother filled those orders in the warehouse.[2] When an opening in payroll came through, my mother enrolled in night school to learn to be a computer. Within two years she received a diploma from the Felt and Tarrant School of Comptometry, which certified her to operate a comptometer, one of the widely used electromechanical calculating machines that preceded electronic calculators.[3] She worked at Sears for two more years before she was replaced by a machine.

My sister and I both work for the techno-state — it seems only natural. In 1991, my sister was deployed to the borderland between northern Iraq and southwest Turkey as part of the U.S. military's humanitarian effort called "Operation Provide Comfort," to give medical attention to the Kurdistani refugees exiled during and after the technologically hallucinogenic Gulf War.[4] At about the same time, I was deployed to a technological institution to teach gender studies (their term) or feminism (mine). Situated within different histories, biographical as well as cultural, these technological encounters suggest several topics of investigation for feminist studies of science and technology.

These working-class histories will span 100 years before they're finished, and even that is an arbitrary span of time, determined more by the mangling of immigrant names than by any formal sense of narrative closure. I do not want to invoke an experiential framework for this essay; I

have no stories to tell here about the subjective experiences of a grandmother, mother, or sister using technology, displaced by it, or even cleaning up after it. Instead, I use these autobiographical notes as a platform
upon which to stage a feminist reading of the current (cyber)cultural moment. This scene — which novelist Pat Cadigan's main hacker-girl, Sam,
says is gripped by an "information frenzy" — is the present context for
those of us who pride ourselves on being plugged in, on-line, and living on
the New Edge.[5] Like the hackers and domestic exiles who populate Cadigan's cyberpunk novel *Synners,* we too definitely qualify as "incurably
informed."[6]

My opening remarks were about working-class histories, but Cadigan's second novel *Synners,* published in 1991, is much more about the
postindustrial present; as a particular kind of science fiction novel — a
cyberpunk narrative — it offers a techno-mythology of the future right
around the corner.[7] When *Synners* is discussed as a cyberpunk novel, it is
usually mentioned that Cadigan is one of the few women writing in that
subgenre. Textually, *Synners* displays the verbal inventiveness and stylistic
bricolage characteristic of the best of the new science fiction, but in Cadigan's case her verbal playfulness invokes Dr. Seuss, and the plot melds a
Nancy Drew mystery with a Kathy Acker-hacked Harlequin romance.
The mystery plot includes familiar cyberpunk devices such as illegal corporate maneuvers and heroic hacking; the romance plot offers a gentle
critique of women's propensity to fall for men who can't be there for them
(in this case, though, it's because the guy has abandoned his meat for the
expanse of cyberspace). More interesting is the manner in which her refrain, "Change for the machines?" morphs from a literal question at a
vending machine to a philosophical comment about the nature of the
technologized human.

One way to investigate the interpretive and ideological dimensions of
contemporary cyberculture is to situate cyberpunk mythologies in relation to the emergence of a new cultural formation built in and around
cyberspace.[8] Although we could map the discursive terrain of cyberpunk
science fiction through an analysis of the lists of (best) book titles, author
anecdotes, critical interpretations, readers' reviews, and the contradictions among them, this would only partially describe the practices of
dispersion and interpretation that serve as the infrastructure of a much
broader formation.[9] To fully investigate the *cultural* formation of what
Mondo 2000 calls "The New Edge" would require investigating related
discursive forms such as comic books, 'zines, and other forms of popular

Figure 26. Cover of *Mondo 2000*
User's Guide to the New Edge, edited
by Rudy Rucker (New York:
HarperCollins, 1992).

print culture, as well as new hybrid *social-textual* forms such as electronic newsgroups, bulletin boards, discussion lists, MUDs (multi-user domains), on-line journals, E-zines, and IRChats (Internet Relay Chat) (figure 26).[10] Given that these textually mediated social spaces are often constructed and populated by those who participate in related subcultural practices such as CONS (popular fan conventions), raves, body piercing, smart drugs, computer hacking, and video art, what is needed for a more developed and historically specific analysis of the New Edge as a cultural formation is a multidisciplinary analysis of other spaces of popular culture where material bodies stage cyberpunk identities.[11] Although constructing such a multiperspectival analysis is a challenging task, my intent is to demonstrate that such a project is already under way. In synthesizing this material, I want to suggest what is needed to produce a critical analysis of a specific sociohistorical conjunction that attends both to the expressive practices of cyberpunk science fiction and to the political aims of feminist cultural studies, and that can draw meaningful connections between them. My goal, then, is to read *Synners* as both cognitive map and cultural landmark.

Cyberpunk as a Feminist Imaginary

Teresa de Lauretis anticipated the critical response that cyberpunk science fiction enjoys from postmodern readers when she provisionally suggested (in 1980) that in "every historical period, certain art forms (or certain literary forms . . .), have become central to the episteme or historical vision of a given society. . . . If we compare it with traditional or postmodern fiction, we see that SF might, just might, be crucial from now on."[12] In one of the first reports on cyberpunk as a new science fiction subgenre, Darko Suvin, quoting Raymond Williams, argues for its cultural significance by claiming that cyberpunk novels (especially those by William Gibson) articulate a new structure of feeling: "a particular quality of social experience and relationship . . . which gives the sense of a generation or of a period."[13] Several critics have discussed the details of the relationship between cyberpunk and a postmodern sensibility.[14] For example, in her essay "Cybernetic Deconstructions: Cyberpunk and Postmodernism," Veronica Hollinger reads cyberpunk through a poststructuralist antihumanism to claim that cyberpunk is "an analysis of the postmodern identification of human and machine."[15] Her main point is that cyberpunk participates in the (postmodern) deconstruction of human subjectivity. According to her reading, cyberpunk narratives "radically decenter the human body, the sacred icon of essential self, in the same way that the virtual reality of cyberspace works to decenter conventional humanist notions of an unproblematic 'real.' "[16] By the end of her analysis, though, we discover that the antihumanist critique of cyberpunk doesn't hold. Cyberpunk collapses under the weight of its own genre determinations. It is still, Hollinger argues, about the "reinsertion of the human into the reality which its technology is in the process of shaping."[17] In support of Hollinger's conclusion, it is more useful to think of cyberpunk as offering a vision of posthuman existence where "technology" and the "human" are understood in contiguous rather than oppositional terms. This notion suggests a continuum between the terms "human" and "technology" that considers the relationship between them not a dichotomy but rather a relationship of degree; human identity, according to this schema, is understood as a value somewhere between the two (idealized) ends.

As an example of the cyberpunk meditation on the posthuman condition, *Synners* posits a world populated by "Homo datum," people whose natural habitat is "the net," synners for whom disconnection from the information economy is not an option (figure 27). This leads one character to speculate that there are three species of technological humans: "synthe*sizing* humans, synthe*sized* humans," and the "bastard offspring of both" — artificial intelligences.[18] The original syn, in this case, is neither an act nor a transgression, but rather the human condition of being "incur-

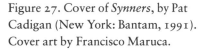

Figure 27. Cover of *Synners*, by Pat Cadigan (New York: Bantam, 1991). Cover art by Francisco Maruca.

ably informed." Death, according to this logic, is defined as a brain-scan flatline.

To the extent that we read cyberpunk through postmodern social theory, one of the most obvious thematic connections between the two is the way in which each discourse configures the space of the social as a landscape structured by the network of relations among multinational capitalist corporations. As Fredric Jameson suggests, the generic structure of cyberpunk science fiction represents an attempt to "think the impossible totality of the contemporary world system."[19] This space of "the decentered global network," metaphorically known as cyberspace, is a bewildering place for the individual/subject who is left to his/her own devices to construct a map of the relationship between a corporeal locale and the totality of "transnational corporate realities."

The focal tension in *Synners* concerns the multinational Diversifications' takeover of two small companies: Eye-Traxx, an independent music-video production company, and Hall Galen Enterprises, a company that employs the medical researcher who invented and patented the procedures for brain socket implants. As a result of the takeover, two of the four main characters, Gina and Visual Mark, become Diversifications' corporate property. Visual Mark was one of Eye-Traxx's original synners, a human synthesizer who is now nearing the age of 50: "It was as if he had a pipeline to some primal dream spot, where music and image created each other, the pictures suggesting the music, the music generating the pictures, in a synesthetic frenzy."[20] Diversifications intends to market its new brain sockets by offering virtual reality rock videos: Visual Mark is the best music-video synner in the business. Diversifications' brain sockets not only allow music videos to be fed into a receiving brain; they also provide a direct interface between a brain and a computer. This type of brain-to-computer connection proves to have dire consequences. While Diversifications tries to corner the market on a lucrative new form of electronic addiction — by providing the sockets and what is fed into the sockets — their socket clients encounter a fatal side effect: "inter-cranial meltdown" in the form of cerebral stroke.

In elaborating the distinctions between cyberpunk science fiction and its generic antecedents, namely New Wave and feminist science fiction from the late 1960s and 1970s, Fred Pfeil writes: "I am tempted to say [cyberpunk novels] have no 'political unconscious': [but are rather] a kind of writing in which, instead of delving and probing for neurotic symptoms, we are invited to witness and evaluate a relatively open acting out."[21] That a cyberpunk work's neurotic symptoms are easily identified does not disqualify it as an interesting cultural text; on the contrary, Pfeil argues that this is a productive, creative mutation:

> This new SF hardly requires the literary analyst's ingenuity in order for us to find or fathom its real social content; the collective anxieties and desires that fuel it are relatively openly evoked and worked through. And the shift from formal and aesthetic experimentation back to experiments in social thought itself suggests that in at least some senses and sectors we have indeed moved on from that earlier humanist debate on freedom, power and order to some new or at least mutated social and ideological ground, which is once again open and fresh enough to be explicitly tried on and explored.[22]

In the case of *Synners,* the "real social content," according to Pfeil's formulation, is not simply the plottings of a hostile corporate takeover, but also what we can read off its textual surface about the technological configuration of human life in multinational capitalism. Several topics nominate themselves as experiments in thinking through the social consequences of new technologies, any one of which could serve as the organizing perspective for elaborating an interpretive map of Cadigan's cosmology: the capitalist production of electronic addictions, the recording practices of video vigilantes, or the multiplication of television channels devoted to new forms of pornography: disasterporn, medporn, foodporn. In addition to speculating about the dynamics of new communication technologies, *Synners* also offers a critical account of the commodification of information.

> Truth is cheap, but information costs. . . . "Besides being rich," Fez said, "you have to be extra sharp these days to pick up any real information. You have to know what you're looking for, and you have to know how it's filed. Browsers need not apply. Broke ones, anyway. I miss the newspaper."[23]

This subtext also includes a political critique of the availability of information and of the difficulty of determining relevance in the midst of the "Instant Information Revolution."

> "Good guess, but the real title is *Need to Know*," said the same voice close to his ear. "It's an indictment of our present system of information dispersal. You're allowed to know only those things the information czars decide that you need to know. They call it 'market research' and 'efficient use of resources' and 'no-waste,' but it's the same old shit they've been doing to us for more than one-hundred years — keep 'em confused and in the dark. You gotta be a stone-ham super-Renaissance person to find out what's really going on."[24]

Pfeil is right when he says that isolating passages such as these hardly requires literary ingenuity to identify expressions of collective anxieties. Indeed, such skeptical statements about information overload and information manipulation resonate strongly with Baudrillard's reading of the postmodern scene: "We are in a universe where there is more and more information, and less and less meaning."[25] And yet, in contrast to the reading Baudrillard offers, Carolyn Marvin argues that "information cannot be said to exist at all unless it has meaning, and meaning is established only in social relationships with cultural reference and value."[26] In her critique of the dominant notion of information-as-commodity (a notion that is at the heart of the ideology of the information age), Marvin redefines information, not as a quantifiable entity but rather as a "state of knowing," which reasserts a knowing *body* as its necessary materialist foundation. This embodied notion of information is at the heart of *Synners*. Moving around a postmodernist reading of cyberpunk science fic-

GINA	VISUAL MARK
(the marked body)	*(the disappearing body)*
SAM	GABE
(the laboring body)	*(the repressed body)*

Figure 28. Matrix of four characters and their VR embodiments in Pat Cadigan's cyberpunk novel *Synners*.

tion that would focus on its figuration of multinational capitalism and the technological deconstruction of human identity, I would like to elaborate an alternative reading of *Synners* that focuses on the relation of the material body to cyberspace.

In the course of developing an ideological critique of a capitalist information economy, Cadigan focuses attention on an often repressed dimension of the information age: the constitution of the informed body. The problem is not just that information "costs," or even that it replicates exponentially, but rather that information is never merely discursive. What we encounter in the Cadigan novel is the narrativization of four different versions of cyberpunk embodiment: the marked body, the disappearing body, the laboring body, and the repressed body. In this sense, the four central characters symbolize the different *embodied* relations one can have, in theory and in fiction, to a nonmaterial space of information access and exchange. Figure 28 illustrates how Sam, Gabe, Gina, and Visual Mark represent four corners of an identity matrix constructed in and around cyberspace. Where Sam hacks the net through a terminal powered by her own body, Visual Mark actually inhabits the network as he mutates into a disembodied, sentient artificial intelligence (AI). Although both Gina and Gabe travel through cyberspace on their way to someplace else, Gabe is addicted to cyberspace simulations and Gina endures them. Each character plays a significant role in the novel's climactic confrontation in cyberspace: a role determined in part by their individual relationships to Diversifications and in part by their bodily identities.

Sam, Gabe's daughter and the only real hacker among the four, is a virtuoso at gaining access to the net. She is the character who best describes the labor of computer hacking and the virtual acrobatics of cyberspace travel: "If you couldn't walk on the floor, you walked on the ceiling. If you couldn't walk on the ceiling, you walked on the walls, and if you couldn't walk *on* the walls, you walked *in* them, encrypted. Pure hacking."[27] As competent as she is in negotiating the cyberspatial landscape of the net, Sam tries to live her embodied life outside of any institutional structure. Her only affiliations are to other punks and hackers, who form a community of sorts and who live out on "the Manhattan-Hermosa strip, what the kids called the Mimosa, part of the old postquake land of the lost."[28] Sam trades encrypted data and hacking talents for stray pieces of equipment and living necessities. In what proves to be a critically important "information commodity" acquisition, Sam hacks the specifications for an insulin-pump chip reader that runs off of body energy. When every terminal connected to "the System" is infected by a debilitating virus, Sam's insulin-pump chip reader is the only noninfected access point to the net. Connected by thin needles inserted into her abdomen, the chip reader draws its power from Sam's body. Seventeen-year-old Sam is a cyberspace hacker of considerable talent who shuns the heroic cowboy role. And for the most part, she is content to provide the power while others, namely Gina and Gabe, go in for the final showdown.

Recoiling from a real-time wife who despises him for his failure to live up to his artistic potential, Gabe spends most of his working time, when he should be designing advertising campaigns, playing the role (Hotwire) of a film noir leading man in a computer simulation built from pieces of an old movie thriller; his two female cyberspace sidekicks are "templates [that] had been assembled from two real, living people."[29] Where Visual Mark cleaves to cyberspace because the world isn't big enough for his expansive visual mind, Gabe becomes addicted to cyberspace because the world is just too big for him. He retreats to the simulation pit for the safety and familiarity it offers. "He'd been running around in simulation for so long, he'd forgotten how to run a realife, real-time routine; he'd forgotten that if he made mistakes, there was no safety-net program to jump in and correct for him."[30] Throughout the novel, Gabe moves in and out of a real-time life and his simulated fantasy world. In real time, his body is continually brought to life, through pain, intoxication, and desire caused by Gina, first when she punches him in the face with a misplaced stab intended for Mark, then later when he gets toxed after she feeds him two LotusLands (a "mildly hallucinogenic beverage"). After they make love for the first time, Gina wonders if Gabe has ever felt desire before: "She didn't think Gabe Ludovic had ever jumped the fast train in his life. Standing at the end of fifteen years of marriage, he'd wanted a lot more than sex. The wanting had been all but tangible, a heat that surprised both of them."[31] After a climactic cyberspace struggle, his repressed body reawakens; Gabe learns to feel his body again (or for the first time) with Gina's help.

Like Visual Mark, Gina is a synner who synthesizes images, sound, and special effects to produce virtual reality music videos. For all her disdain and outright hostility toward other people and institutions, "Bad-ass Gina Aiesi" has an intense emotional connection to Mark, her partner of 20 years, which she romanticizes in an odd way:

> They weren't smooch-faces, it didn't work that way, for her or for him. . . . One time, though . . . one time, three-four-five years into the madness, there'd been a place where they'd come together one night, and it had been different. . . . He'd been reaching, and she'd been reaching, and for a little while there, they'd gotten through. Maybe that had been the night when the little overlapping space called *their life* had come into existence.[32]

Gina's body, marked by its color, "wild forest hardwood," and her dread-locks, figures prominently in the narrative description of her sexual en-counters, first with Visual Mark and then with Gabe. After both she and Visual Mark have brain sockets implanted by Diversifications' surgeon-on-contract, they jack in together and experience a visual replay of shared memories: "The pov was excruciatingly slow as it moved across Mark's face to her own, lingering on the texture of her dreadlocks next to his pale, drawn flesh, finally moving on to the contrast of her deep brown skin."[33] The characteristics that mark Gina are her anger, her exasperated love for Mark, and the color of her skin.

Like others who bought sockets for jacking in, Visual Mark begins to spend less and less time off-line and more and more time plugged in to the global network known as "the System." This leads him to reflect on the metaphysical nature of his physical body: "he lost all awareness of the meat that had been his prison for close to fifty years, and the relief he felt at having laid his burden down was as great as himself."[34] After suffering a small stroke (one of the unpleasant side effects of brain sockets) while he was jacked in, Visual Mark prepares for "the big one"—a stroke that will release his consciousness into the system and allow him to leave his meat behind.

> He was already accustomed to the idea of having multiple aware-nesses and a single concentrated core that were both the essence of

self. The old meat organ would not have been able to cope with that kind of reality, but out here he appropriated more capacity the way he once might have exchanged a smaller shirt for a larger one.[35]

And sure enough, while his body is jacked in, Mark strokes out. He tries to get Gina to pull his plugs, but she is too late. As his meat dies, both his consciousness and his stroke enter "the System." In the process, his stroke is transformed into a deadly virus (or spike) that initiates a worldwide network crash.

Like the dramatic climax in recent cyberpunk films such as *Circuitry Man, Lawnmower Man,* and *Mindwarp,* the final showdown in *Synners* takes place in cyberspace.[36] Working together, a small community of domestic exiles, hackers, and punks assemble a workstation (powered by Sam's insulin-pump chip reader) that enables Gina and Gabe to go on-line to fight the virus/stroke — an intelligent entity of some dubious ontological status that now threatens the integrity of the entire networked world. Like a cyberspace Terminator, the virus/stroke is rationally determined to infect/destroy whoever comes looking for it. In the course of their cyberspace brawl, Gabe and Gina confront the virus's simulation of their individual worse fears. A "reluctant hero" till the very end, Gabe's cyberspace enemy is a simple construct: the fear of embodiment. "I can't remember what it feels like to have a body," he repeats obsessively during his final confrontation in cyberspace. What he learns through the encounter is that his whole body is a hotsuit; that is, he learns to feel the body that he has technologically repressed.

Gina's cyberspace struggle is with an embodiment of her own deepest fears about missed chances, lost love, and suffocating commitment. Her cyberspace showdown replays her obsessive 20-year-long search for Mark: "Old habits, they do die hard, don't they. That's yours, ain't it — looking for Mark."[37] "Why do you still want to love?" she is asked by the omniscient virus. In one sense her struggle is to confront the fact that she loves an addict and still wants to save him. The crucial decision Gina faces is whether to stay with Mark in cyberspace — where there is no pain, no separation — or to renounce him and return to the real world where such love is impossible. In the end, Gabe and Gina defeat the virus and the global network shortly reestablishes connections. But when Gina finally wakes to reunite with Gabe, we find out that although *they* have changed for the machines, the machines didn't change for them. "The door only swings one way. Once it's out of the box, it's always too big to get back in.

Can't bury that technology. . . . Every technology has its original sin. . . . And we still got to live with what we made."[38]

Darko Suvin asks two additional questions about the shape of a cyberpunk sensibility: whose structure of feeling? and to what ideological horizons or consequences does it apply? As if in response, Fred Pfeil suggests that most cyberpunk science fiction "remains stuck in a masculinist frame," in that cyberpunk dramas, like most video game narratives, remain "focused on the struggle of the male protagonist . . . to wend his lonely way through the worlds."[39] Andrew Ross concurs with Pfeil's assessment and adds: "One barely needs to scratch the surface of the cyberpunk genre, no matter how maturely sketched out, to expose a baroque edifice of adolescent male fantasies."[40]

In reading *Synners* as a *feminist* imaginary, I would argue that it offers an alternative narrative of cyberpunk identity that begins with the assumption that bodies are always gendered and always marked by race. In one sense, Cadigan's novel is implicitly informed by Donna Haraway's cyborg politics: the gendered distinctions among characters hold true to a cyborgian figuration of gender differences, whereby the female body is coded as a body-in-connection and the male body as a body-in-isolation. *Synners* illuminates the gendered differences in the way that the characters relate to the technological space of information. Sam and Gina, the two female hackers, actively manipulate the dimensions of cybernetic space in order to communicate with other people. Gabe and Visual Mark, on the other hand, are addicted to cyberspace for the release it offers from the loneliness of their material bodies.

The racial distinctions between characters are revealed through the novel's representation of sexual desire. Gina is the only character to be identified by skin color. She is also the focal object and subject of heterosexual desire, for a moment by Mark and more frequently by Gabe; and we know both men's racial identities by their marked differences from Gina's. In this way, the unmarked characters (Visual Mark and Gabe) are marked by the absence of identifying marks. Although we are never directly told their racial identities, both Visual Mark and Gabe are contextually identified as white in contrast to Gina, whose skin color and hair texture is explicitly described. In different ways and with different political connotations, *Synners* reasserts that gender and race are defining elements of posthuman identity. So even as *Synners* discursively represents different forms of technological embodiment, it also reasserts the critical importance of the materiality of bodies in any analysis of the information age.

THE MARKED BODY	THE VIRTUAL BODY
Gina (present/marked)	*Visual Mark (absent/marked)*
Multicultural Bodies	Cosmetic Surgery
Tattoos, Piercing	Bioengineering
THE LABORING BODY	THE REPRESSED BODY
Sam (present/unmarked)	*Gabe (absent/unmarked)*
Female Bodybuilders	Virtual Reality
Mothers as Wombs	Computer Communication

Figure 29. Postmodern forms of technological embodiment

Maybe Pfeil is right in his claim that cyberpunk novels have no political unconscious, in that their symbolic preoccupations are relatively easy to access. But in constructing this reading of *Synners,* not to emphasize its cyberpunk characteristics but rather to point to its feminist preoccupations, I am implicitly arguing that it expresses some form of allegorical narrative; as a work of the feminist imagination, it narrativizes certain tensions and obsessions that animate feminist thinking across cultural discourses. I've argued that Cadigan's narrative symbolically represents the female body as a material body and as a body that labors. The male body, in contrast, is repressed or disappearing. This reading suggests a slight revision of Arthur Kroker's theory of the postmodern body, where he argues that the signal form of postmodern embodiment is the "disappearing body." Consider figure 29 as it extends the *Synners* character matrix discussed earlier. In this matrix (a modified semiotic square), each of Cadigan's characters represents a different form of technological embodiment endemic to postmodernity.[41] These fictional characters suggest the other kinds of bodies (in contrast to Kroker's claim) that populate the (technological) postmodern scene. Some of these I've already discussed in earlier chapters of this book: the bodies of cosmetic surgery clients, maternal bodies, and female bodybuilders. In chapter 5 I discussed the repressed bodies of virtual reality users, and I continue the discussion of these bodies in the final section of this chapter. Other bodies require additional investigation by cultural critics. For example, what are the biopolitics surrounding the multicultural bodies used as mannequins for high-fashion messages? Who will determine who will receive the artificial body parts engineered to replace failing organic ones? To this end, this matrix suggests new body projects that are likely to occupy feminist scholars in the near future. In offering gendered descriptions of multiple forms of post-modern embodiment, *Synners* sets the stage for the elaboration of a feminist theory of the relationship of material bodies to cyberspace and of the construction of agency in technological encounters. But even in saying this, I must assert that the final horizon of this reading is not Cadigan's novel, but rather the insights it offers for a feminist analysis of the politics of new information technologies. To this end, *Synners* suggests a beginning point in the elaboration of a map of contemporary cyberculture, where technology serves as a site for the reinscription of cultural narratives of gender and race identities.

The Biopolitics of New Information Technology

This reading of *Synners* also implies that a political judgment of any technology is difficult to render in the abstract. Technologies always have multiple effects. Determining the meaning of those effects is not a simple process. For example, several news articles about the phenomenon of virtual reality boldly assert that VR applications, such as "Virtual Valerie" and 900-number phone sex services, are technologies of safe (fluidless) sex. One Atlanta-based sex expert goes so far as to say that VR will be a mainstream sex aid by the end of the decade, stimulating yet pathogenically prudent. And yet I notice how the very same phenomenon enables new forms of social and cultural autism. Brenda Laurel, a VR researcher and designer, reports: "I've had men tell me that one of the reasons they got into this business was to escape the social aspects of being a male in America — to escape women in particular."[42]

   Sandy Stone studies electronic communities and the bodies that labor in cyberspace — including VR systems engineers as well as phone sex workers. In her analysis of the virtual body, she concludes that cyberspace both disembodies and re-embodies in a gendered fashion: "the desire to cross the human/machine boundary, to penetrate and merge, which is part of the evocation of cyberspace . . . shares certain conceptual and affective characteristics with numerous fictional evocations of the inarticulate longing of the male for the female." But, as she goes on to argue, "to enter cyberspace is to physically put on cyberspace. To become the cyborg, to put on the seductive and dangerous cybernetic space like a garment, is to put on the female."[43] Even as she elaborates the gendered dimensions of cyberspace connection, Stone sees an inherent ambiguity in cyberspace technologies that is tied to the facticity of the material body. For as much as they offer the opportunity for new forms of virtual engagement, Stone rightly asserts that "no refigured virtual body, no matter how beautiful, will slow the death of a cyberpunk with AIDS. Even in the age of the technosubject, life is lived through bodies."[44]

If on the one hand new communication technologies such as VR create new contexts for knowing/talking/signing/fucking bodies, they also enable new forms of repression of the material body. Studies of the new modes of electronic communication, for example, indicate that the anonymity offered by the computer screen empowers antisocial behaviors such as "flaming" and borderline illegal behaviors such as trespassing, E-mail snooping, and MUD-rape.[45] And yet, for all the anonymity they offer, many computer communications reproduce stereotypically gendered patterns of conversation.[46]

In the Jargon File,[47] the entry "Gender and Ethnicity" claims that although "hackerdom is still predominantly male," hackers are gender- and color-blind in their interactions with other hackers due to the fact that they communicate (primarily) through text-based network channels. This assertion rests on the assumption that "text-based channels" represent a gender-neutral medium of exchange, that language itself is free from any form of gender, race, or ethnic determinations. Both of these assumptions are called into question not only by feminist research on electronic communication and interpretive theory, but also by female network users who participate in cyberpunk's virtual subculture.[48] This was dramatically, or rather textually, illustrated in an exchange that occurred on FutureCulture, an electronic discussion list devoted to cyberpunk subculture. The thread of discussion concerned a floating utopia called "Autopia."[49] The exchange about women in "Autopia" began innocently from the cyberdeck of a student:

> It may just be my imagination, but it seems that the bulk of the people participating in Autopia discussions are men.
>
> And hasn't anyone else noticed that most people on FutureCulture are men? Not to mention the over-all population of the net generally speaking. I'd like to get women into this discussion but I'm not even sure if there are any women on FC.
>
> Are there?

In response, a male participant pointed out:

> If you haven't noticed, the bulk of the people on these networks are
> men. It is about 80% male with higher percentages in some places.
>
> Yeah. Clearly the Internet is dominated by men. It just seems that
> some outreach to women might be in order. Hanging out on a
> ship with hundreds of male computer jocks isn't exactly my idea of
> utopia. :)

A female participant wrote back:

> Now, this is a loaded question. A lot of women will not open them-
> selves to possible net harassment by admitting they are listening.
> Of course, if they've come this far, they are likely to be the more
> bold/brave/stupid type.
>
> Which leaves me where?
>
> Cuz, yes, I am a woman & I hang out on the Internet, read cyber-
> punk, do interesting things with locks and computers. I don't pro-
> gram, I don't MU*/D/SH. I do technical work/repair. I write. I read.
> I'm a relatively bright individual.

This posting was followed by a self-acknowledged sexist statement from a
male participant who asked others if they too found that women on the
net were extremely unattractive. After being flamed from several other
men in the discussion, one reply rebuked the original poster:

> Concepts of physical beauty are hold overs from 'MEAT' space. On
> the net they don't apply. We are all just bits and bytes blowing in the
> phospor stream.

Concepts of physical beauty might be a "meat thing," but gender identity
persists in the "phospor stream" whether we like it or not. Eventually the
thread returned to the question of what a woman might say about "Autopia," the floating utopia idea. Several postings later, the same female participant responded:

> And, would you like to know why, overall, I am uninterested in the
> idea of Autopia? Because I'm a responsible person. (Over-responsi-
> ble, if you want to get into the nit-picky psychological semantics, but
> that's another point.) As a responsible person, I end up doing/am
> expected to do all the shit work. All the little details that others don't
> think of; like setting up laundry duty, dishes, cooking, building, re-

pairs, handling garbage. This is not to say that I fall into the typical "FEMALE" role, because both women and men have left these duties to fall in my lap. And, it's not a case that if I leave it, it will eventually get done either — you'd be amazed at how long people will ignore garbage or dishes; at how many people can't use a screw driver or hold a hammer correctly.

Plus, how about security? There is a kind of assumption that goes on, especially on the net, that folks on whatever computer network are a higher intelligence, above craven acts of violence. If you end up with 50 men for every woman, how are you going to insure her safety?

So, talk about security issues, waste disposal, cooking and cleaning duties, the actual wiring of whatever ship for onboard computers, how you're planning on securing hard drives for rough seas, how you're going to eat, in what shifts are you going to sleep, who's going to steer, how you are going to get navigators.

Where will you get the money for the endeavor? If you decide against a ship, and go for an island, how are you going to deal with the overrunning the natural habitat? What are you going to do if you cause some species that only lived on *that* island to become extinct? What are you going to do with refugees from the worlds of hurt on this planet, who are looking for someplace to escape to?

As one other (male) participant in the discussion pointed out, these are imminently practical concerns, but not ones that were raised until the female participant emerged from the silence she was lurking in. Her original point was passed over quickly, even as it was enacted in the course of the subsequent discussion: electronic discussion lists are governed by gendered codes of discursive interchange that often are not hospitable to female participants. This suggests that on-line communication is structured similarly to communication in other settings, and is overtly subjected to forms of gender, status, age, and race determinations.

Hoai-An Truong, a member of Bay Area Women in Telecommunications (BAWIT), writes:

Despite the fact that computer networking systems obscure physical characteristics, many women find that gender follows them into the on-line community, and sets a tone for their public and private interactions there — to such an extent that some women purposefully choose gender neutral identities, or refrain from expressing their opinions.[50]

Thus we see an interesting paradox in action. Cyberspace is a place where bodies aren't suppose to matter, but many women discover that they do matter. The false denial of the body (mainly by male users) requires the defensive denial of the body (mainly by female users) so that communication can occur. For some women, this denial of the body is simply not worth the effort. Most men apparently never notice.

Gendered Geographies of Cyberspace Landscapes

In *Landscape for a Good Woman,* a genre-bending theoretical critique of psychoanalysis and working-class social history, Carolyn Steedman asserts that autobiography is useful for the production of cultural criticism because "[p]ersonal interpretations of past time — the stories that people tell themselves in order to explain how they got to the place they currently inhabit — are often in deep and ambiguous conflict with the official interpretive devices of a culture."[51] Steedman describes the conflict she experiences when she takes cultural theory personally:

> the structures of class analysis and schools of cultural criticism . . . cannot deal with everything there is to say about my mother's life. . . . The usefulness of the biographical and autobiographical core of the book lies in the challenge it may offer to much of our conventional understanding of childhood, working-class childhood, and little-girlhood.[52]

In writing stories that aren't central to a dominant culture, specifically the story of her working-class childhood and a deauthorized father — Steedman simultaneously revises the insights of psychoanalytic theory and the discursive conventions of cultural criticism. More specifically, she links an autobiographical account of her working-class childhood with a biographical account of her mother's class determinations to serve as the context for a narrative critique of a classic psychoanalytical case study (Freud's story of Dora); Steedman's intent is to articulate the relationship between narratives of the self and narratives of history. Her broader point is to demonstrate that working-class histories, in whatever form they are found, as case studies or autobiographical narratives, often contradict the official "interpretive devices" of a dominant culture. Implicit in Steedman's work is the argument that provoking such a conflict creates the opportunity to interfere with the ongoing codification of official interpretations.

Although different accounts of this conflict could be written, I suggest that the "ambiguous conflict" between the autobiographical notes which opened this chapter and the dominant, if not exactly official, interpretive theory of our era — postmodernism — concerns the penchant to celebrate the perpetual present. Steve Best and Doug Kellner identify this tendency as "radical presentism" and argue that "the erasure of depth also flattens out history and experience, for lost in a postmodern present, one is cut off from those sedimented traditions, those continuities and historical memories which nurture historical consciousness and provide a rich, textured, multidimensional present."[53] Presentism augments two ideological projects of the information age: the construction of social theories narrated by disembodied virtual minds, and the construction of technological histories written without women, without workers, and without politics.[54]

I would like to conclude by discussing the gendered aspects of the development of those technologies that have been identified as central to the New Edge and the age of information: microelectronics, telecommunications networks, and other forms of computer technologies. To read accounts of the development of information technologies, for example, one might conclude that women have only just begun to show an interest in and aptitude for technological knowledge, innovation, and employment. This signals yet another pervasive myth of the information age: namely that everything that is important to know is transparently accessible with the right access codes. Feminist thinkers know differently.

The Gendering of Technological Histories

Gathering even basic biographical material about the women who participated in traditionally male-dominated technical and professional fields — including the physical and natural sciences, engineering, mathematics, military science, and astronomy — is not an easy project.[55] The historical material that is available illuminates the daunting structural barriers that many women had to overcome in order to pursue their interests and research in scientific and technological fields. The structural barriers range from formal prohibition against women's education to legal restrictions of women's property rights, which caused many women inventors to patent their inventions under brothers' or husbands' names. In reporting on the treatment of gender and women's subjects in the 24-year history of the journal *Technology and Culture* (the journal of the Society for the History of Technology), Joan Rothschild asserts that one of the reasons for the *lack* of discussion about gender in the historiography of technology is a consequence of a "literal identification of the male with technology."[56] This association has been seriously challenged by recent feminist studies that seek not only to recover women's contribution to the historical development of different technologies, but also to rethink the history of technology from a feminist perspective. Autumn Stanley, for one, argues that the history of technology omits women in part because of a categorical exclusion of the technologies that women were specifically instrumental in developing as not "proper" technologies: here she lists food preparation, nursing and infant care, and menstruation technologies.[57] Other feminists investigate social arrangements that reproduce the masculinist identification with technologies that intimately affect women's lives, such as domestic technologies, as well as studies of specific domains that are still dominated by male scientists, engineers, and medical researchers, such as the new reproductive technologies.[58]

As I implied in the opening remarks about my mother's computer employment history, women's relationship to the technology of the workplace has been a troubled one. The expansion of clerical occupations after World War I resulted in the feminization of such occupations; women were preferentially hired over men because they were less expensive to employ. This kept the costs of expansion contained. After World War II, many forms of female office work were subjected to the analysis of scientific management. Tasks were routinized and rationalized; bookkeepers and other office workers became "machine attendants who performed standardized repetitive calculating operations."[59] This repetitive work was the perfect material for automated calculators. Although some labor historians assert that the introduction of electronic calculators and computers occurred during a time of economic expansion, and thus had the effect of actually increasing the number of clerical jobs available for displaced workers, the new jobs were often sex-stratified such that better paying data-processing positions were staffed by men. I offer this brief note to point to the fact that women have been involved with implementing electronic information technologies in U.S. businesses and industries at least since World War I. These technologies had contradictory effects on women's employment, increasing the opportunity for new jobs, but at the same time downgrading the skill level of office workers who were employed to attend the new machines.[60] In forming a judgment about the impact of these technologies on women's lives, it is also important to remember that it is likely that the women who were displaced from their bookkeeping positions in the 1950s by the introduction of electronic technology did not necessarily experience this as an employment failure. No doubt some of them, like my mother, were eager to get on with the real business of their lives, which was getting married, having children, and raising families.

In the 10 years since the personal computer became widely available as a mass-produced consumer item, it has become an entirely naturalized fixture in the workplace, either at home or at the business office.[61] It is also becoming common to criticize the claims that computers increase office worker productivity — the primary marketing line for the sale of personal computers to businesses and industries. Some critics protest that the real impact of computers and word-processing systems has been to increase the quantity of time spent producing documents, while others argue that the computerized office decreases the quality of work life due to physical discomfort and information overload.[62] Sociological studies of the gendered aspects of computer employment focus on the de-skilling and displacement of female clerical workers in different industries. While these studies on women as laborers are vital for an understanding of the social and economic impact of computers, there is less research available about women's creative or educational use of information technologies or their role in the history of computing. But there is also a class bias reflected in these investigations: by focusing on women's computer *use* in the workplace, such studies restrict their critical investigation to those women who have access to what remains a costly technology that is beyond the reach and skill level of many women in the United States today. The question of women's employment and computer technology can be asked another way. For example, Les Levidow studies the women who make the tiny silicon chips that serve as the electronic guts for cheap computer gadgets. Both in affluent (until recently) Silicon Valley and in a relatively poor Malaysian state (Penang), the large majority of chip makers are poorly paid immigrant women.[63]

Yet another way to approach the question of women and technological histories, one more sensitive to class-related issues, is to ask "Who counts?" This leads to the investigation of both those who determine who counts as instances of what identities, and also those who are treated as numbers or cases in the construction of a database. The politics of data-bases will be a critical agenda item for the 1990s as an increasing number of businesses, services, and state agencies go "on-line." Determining who has access to data and how to gain access to data that is supposedly available to the "public" is a multidimensional project that involves the use of computers, skill at network access, and education in locating and negotiating access to government-supported databases. Even a chief data coordinator with the U.S. Geological Survey asserts that "data markets, data access, and data dissemination are complicated, fuzzy, emotional topics right now." She "predicts that they likely will be the major issues of the decade."[64]

Questions of public access and the status of information in the com-puter age are just now attracting public attention. As Kenneth B. Allen argues, the same technologies that enable us to "create, manipulate, and disseminate information" also, ironically, "threaten to diminish public access to government information."[65] The issue of citizens' rights to infor-mation needs to be monitored by computer-savvy citizen advocates. The question becomes, where will such advocates come from? Two immediate answers come to the fore: they will be either educated or elected. Feminist scholars and teachers can contribute to both by encouraging women stu-dents to address information policy issues in their research projects and by supporting women candidates who will serve on the federal and state boards that govern information access.[66]

These candidates and policy students will certainly face several dif-ficult issues involving bodies, information, and criminal charges. The Council for State Governments describes one item of state legislation pro-posed in 1993: the Prenatal Exposure to Controlled Substances Act. This act would require "substance abuse treatment personnel to report to the state department of children and family services any pregnant woman who is addicted to drugs or alcohol."[67] The positive consequence of such an act would require states to "bring treatment services to alcohol and/or substance abusing pregnant women." Negative consequences, such as the criminalization of pregnant women for delivering a controlled substance to a minor, are not mentioned. This act could, as Jennifer Terry suggests, serve as a "technology of surveillance," whereby the unborn fetus is guar-anteed certain rights denied to the pregnant woman: "[for] poor women, interventions into daily life through social welfare and the criminal justice system render recourse to the right to privacy somewhat moot."68

The Cultural Formation of the New Edge

In synthesizing this account of an emergent cultural formation, with its emphasis on signifying practices and forms of embodiment, it becomes clear that there is much work to be done to elaborate its connections to dominant cultural forms of production, consumption, communication, and control. I've tried to show how ongoing ideological projects such as the repression of history, of the body, of feminist foremothers are rearticulated through the use of new information technologies. Certainly an investigation of the broader cultural formation suggests new subjects for feminism now and in the future: global workers, homeworkers, knowledge engineers, corporate scientists, brain police, and permanent temporary workers. In telling the cyberpunk story of the coordination between technology and technical expertise and how it becomes subject to corporate control, *Synners* offers a countermythology of the information age — not that information wants to be free, but rather that access to information is going to cost, and cost a lot. Through its postfeminist portrayal of empowered female bodies who play off and against repressed or hysterical male bodies, *Synners* offers an alternative vision of technological embodiment that is consistent with a gendered history of technology: where technology isn't the means of escape from or transcendence of the body, but rather the means of communication and connection with other bodies. *Synners* also raises questions about the meaning of race in a technological age. How is technological disembodiment also a comment on the desire to transcend racial identities? How are material bodies race-marked through technological encounters? How are racial identities articulated to myths of technological progress?69 Despite our condition of being incurably informed, we don't have enough information about the embodied aspects of new information technologies. Simply put, we need a great deal more in order to construct analyses of the information age that can serve as a foundation for critical political interventions.

Synners also suggests the importance of a cyberpunk mythology for the construction of feminist cultural studies of scientific and technological formations. Gina and Sam make interesting subjects for feminist theory in that their technological competencies and synner talents emphasize

the need for feminist activists to encourage women to develop technological skills and for feminist teachers to promote educational efforts to increase technological literacy. The challenge is how to harness the power
of technological knowledge to a feminist agenda while struggling against
an increasing industrial imperialism that eagerly assimilates new techno-
workers to labor in the interests of private enterprise.[70] The question is
how to empower technological agents so that they work on behalf of the
right kind of social change.

EPILOGUE

The Role of the Body in Feminist Cultural Studies
of Science and Technology

In the introduction to the 1988 edition of the book *Women's Oppression Today,* Michele Barrett laid out a revised map of the terrain of contemporary feminist thought — a terrain that had changed significantly in the eight years since the first edition of the book. One of the new areas of feminist research she discussed was "corporeal feminism," first identified in the work of several Australian feminists, most notably Elizabeth Grosz. For Grosz, corporeal feminism names "an understanding of corporeality that is compatible with feminist struggles to undermine patriarchal structures and to form self-defined terms and representations" (3).[1] With this statement, Grosz describes the project that occupied many feminists during the late 1980s and early 1990s: how to recuperate a notion of the body that does not imply an unchanging, essentialist identity for sexed bodies. This project was greeted with mixed responses; while some feminists thought the reinvigorated attention to the body was a retrogressive topic that set the stage for the recontainment of women to the body, others claimed that the body was, and would continue to be, the premier battleground for women's rights in the late twentieth century.[2] In this final chapter, I briefly review Grosz's work on "corporeal feminism" and the insight it offers for this study of the techno-body.

Grosz asserts that her book *Volatile Bodies* "is a refiguring of the body so that it moves from the periphery to the center of analysis, so that it can now be understood as the very 'stuff' of subjectivity."[3] Her argument rests on a thorough examination of the key works of body philosophy — from Freud, Lacan, Merleau-Ponty, Nietzsche, Foucault, and Deleuze and Guattari. Her intent in focusing extensively, at first, on work by male theorists was to elaborate the historical foundation for the treatment of the body as a universal construct invested with certain qualities. The final part of her book, though, focuses on the work of women and feminists who seek to reconceptualize the body in its sexed specificity.[4] Grosz goes to the heart of the debate about "corporeal feminism" when she poses a series of questions about the ontological status of the material body:

> What, ontologically speaking, is the body? What is its "stuff," its matter? What of its form? Is that given or produced? Or is there some relation between givenness and the cultural order? Are sexually neutral, indeterminate, or hermaphroditic bodies inscribed to produce the sexually specific forms with which we are familiar? Or do bodies, all bodies (even nonhuman bodies, it must be presumed), have a specifically sexual dimension (whether it be male or female or hermaphroditic) which is psychically and culturally inscribed according to its morphology? In other words, is sexual difference primary and sexual inscription a cultural overlay or rewriting of an ontologically prior differentiation? Or is sexual differentiation a product of various forms of inscription of culturally specific bodies?[5]

In short the question becomes: which is ontologically primary — the sexual differences of the material body or the cultural assignment of sexual differentiation? When Grosz argues that producing answers to these questions would require multifaceted investigation into the intertwining practices that make the body meaningful not only to a self but within a social system more broadly, she sets forth a dense research agenda for other feminist scholars. Grosz's broader point is to elaborate a model of analysis that ties subjectivity to "the specificities of sexed bodies" and that sees the subject "no longer as an entity — whether psychical or corporeal — but fundamentally an effect of pure difference that constitutes all modes of materiality."[6]

I find this notion of sexual difference as that which is at once originary and constantly displaced, as an "alterity," very useful for elaborating the technological production of gendered bodies. Technologies of the body not only manipulate alterity, but also reproduce it. Sexual differences are both the input and the output of the technological production of gendered bodies. In offering this book as a contribution to the development of corporeal feminism, I have been less concerned about discussing the philosophical underpinnings of a new materiality of sexed subjectivity than about describing the ways in which gendered identities are technologically produced for material bodies. Here technology is understood in a Foucauldian sense — to mean not only machines and devices but also social, economic, and institutional forces.

The new body technologies discussed in this book are part of an emergent cultural formation of the techno-body. The discursive elements of this formation include dissimilar forms, from newspaper reports and magazine images to medical research and pages from the Sears catalogue. I think of this study as the investigation of the cultural apparatus that constructs gendered bodies. The particular configuration of institutional practices, social relations, forms of discourse, and systems of logic I examine is one manifestation of this cultural apparatus isolated through my interpretive act of "reading the body in contemporary U.S. culture." To call this manifestation an apparatus, following Foucault, suggests that it is a structured phenomenon that produces specific material effects at the level of the body. The term is a bit misleading in that the notion of an apparatus or machine suggests a bounded entity, managed by a sentient agent, deployed for rational and intentional ends. If the cultural apparatus of the gendered body has delimited boundaries, I have yet to discover them; every investigation of a discursive site suggested other sites for examination. Relatedly, I have yet to identify a singular responsible agent guiding the production of gendered bodies. This is a dynamic formation; agency, intention, and political consequences are wildly dispersed among people, institutions, and technologies. In the end it is important to remember that these chapters offer an account of a *historically* specific manifestation of the cultural formation of the techno-body.

In addition to contributing something to future historical studies, I have also attempted to describe the range of forms of technological embodiment available in postmodern culture. Technological practices such as bodybuilding, cosmetic surgery, and virtual reality depend on and indeed contribute to the repression, conceptual fragmentation, and commodification of the material body. Technologically fragmented body parts are articulated to a culturally determined "system of differences" that attributes differential value to different bodies according to traditional, dualistic "natures." In this way, the abstract concept of gender "difference" is reified as discrete gender identities. In tracking the development and deployment of new body technologies, I have described the different technological mechanisms whereby traditional narratives of gender identity are replicated and reinscribed on material bodies.

As discussed in chapter 1, it is clear that the material body is a critical symbolic resource for cultural expression, and although "the body" can be studied as a discursive construction, its symbolic form is *always* constructed in interaction with real material bodies. I start with the assumption that gender functions as an organized system of differentiation that grounds relations of power and knowledge, the chapters focus attention on the ways in which the meaningfulness of gender identity is *reproduced* in the application of new technologies.

For example, in examining the visualization technologies used in the practice of cosmetic surgery, we can witness the process whereby new technologies are articulated with traditional and ideological narratives about gender — an articulation that keeps the female body positioned as a privileged object of a normative gaze. Male bodies, in contrast, are treated as fully able, laboring bodies whose aesthetic proportions are important only as they serve as a business asset. And yet, upon closer reading of the medical literature on plastic surgery techniques, it becomes clear that a binary code of gender identity is only one of the semiotic systems that influence the practice of surgical procedures. Codes of racial identity also structure the meaning of technological operations. Whereas the quantified proportions of white faces are the taken-for-granted foundation for the construction of ideal surgical goals, black and Asian facial features are defined as abnormal, sometimes requiring special "corrective" surgery, as in the case of the "oriental eyelid."

In a slightly different sense, reproductive technologies also reinscribe dominant narratives of gender identity on the material body by providing the means for exercising power relations on the flesh of the female body. They do so in two ways: first by intervening in the physiological functioning of the female body, and secondly by providing the technological infrastructure for the institutionalization of surveillance practices. Moreover, the reality engendered by these new technologies requires the reformation of rights and responsibilities. With the deployment of the new reproductive technologies comes the cultural construction of a new set of possibilities and a new set of social agents — the fetus, the surrogate parent, the egg/sperm donor — each of whom can now stake a claim on the outcome of the reproductive encounter. Thus are born new ethical, social, and political dilemmas. Furthermore, these possibilities set the stage for the development of other social arrangements. Because these new conditions emerge in diverse settings and as a consequence of a variety of institutional events, it is difficult to see the ways in which reality is slowly being transformed. The purpose of feminist criticism — in fiction and in theory — is to provide a perceptual framework for understanding the transformations as they happen to our bodies and behind our backs.

New technologies of communication such as virtual reality and computer networks literally serve as cultural stages for the performance and enactment of gender identity. In the cybernetic realm of the techno-senses, the technological transformation of gender identity is more virtual than real. Promises of bodily transcendence, gender "neutrality," and race-blindness are the main planks of the ideology of the information age; the *re*presentation of gender is supposed to have given way to its technological effacement. And yet, gender distinctions persist in the new social spaces of virtual worlds. Computer simulations of the body replicate traditional gendered identities for sexed participants; Virtual Valerie and Penthouse Playmates are now available on CD-ROM. Whereas cyberpunk appeals to the pleasure of the interface seem to reassert a material body at the heart of new technological encounters, in actuality they are appeals that rest on repression of the material body. When one broadens the scope of analysis to include the network of relations whereby computer-mediated realities are produced—in hardware, software, and wetware—it becomes clear that the liberation of the few is bought at the expense of the many. Although computer-mediated communication networks are often promoted as the means to the realization of democratic ideals, the cultural politics enacted on these technological stages are in fact deeply conservative.

The project of feminist cultural studies more broadly is to write the stories and tell the tales that will connect seemingly isolated moments of discourse—histories and effects—into a narrative that helps us make sense of transformations as they emerge. Fictional narratives serve dual purposes in this effort. On the one hand, they can thematize cultural preoccupations—as was evident in my reading of cyberpunk science fiction novels that plot the masculinist, heterosexual construction of desire. However, they also serve as expressive resources that offer cognitive maps of emergent cultural arrangements. Both Atwood's novel *The Handmaid's Tale* and Cadigan's novel *Synners* exemplify this practice of map making. Reading textual maps is only part of the critical work of feminist cultural studies, especially as it turns its attention to the study of scientific and technological formations. This effort also requires an investigation into the structured relations of power and knowledge that serve as the foundation for both the practices of science and medicine and the development and deployment of new technologies. Although this necessarily involves

an analysis of the production and enactment of scientific and technological knowledge, in this book I have been more concerned with the way in
which such knowledge circulates in popular culture and everyday life and
how it structures the material conditions of women's lives. By focusing on
the intertextual connections between cultural narratives and scientific and
technological discourse, I hope to illuminate the cultural work of science
and technology. I consider both to be preeminent technologies of culture
as much as they are technologies that gender material bodies.

The purpose in reading the body in contemporary culture is not only
to tease out dominant cultural preoccupations, especially as they concern
the status of the gendered body in postmodernity, but also to suggest an
agenda for future feminist work. The aim of these readings of the techno-
body is to specify sites for immediate political intervention and social
change. I have argued throughout that gender is not simply an effect of
the circulation of representations and discourse, but also the effect of specific social, economic, and institutional relations of power. These arrangements are historical articulations that must be continually reproduced,
which explains the obsessive reinscription of dualistic gender identity in
the interactions between material bodies and technological devices. But
the fact that these arrangements must be continually reproduced also
suggests the possibility that these articulations can be disrupted. I have
implicitly argued that in order to engage in the struggle to rearticulate the
gendered identity of the technological body, feminists must understand
how its meaning is technologically and ideologically stitched into place.
On the horizon are critical issues for feminist cultural studies of science
and technology: the politics of information, the global division of technological labor, and the reproductive exploitation of women. These issues
are not, in a simple determinist sense, brought into being solely through
the development of new technologies; rather they emerge through the
articulation between technologies, cultural narratives, social, economic,
and institutional forces.

Throughout this book, I have offered polemical arguments about the
consequences of deploying these technologies; they do not always serve
women's best interests, however diverse these may be. Although I am
suspicious of the promises of corporeal transformation, I still remain thoroughly fascinated by these new body technologies. I have also discussed
other issues more central to the scholarly and political aims of feminist
cultural studies: issues concerning the construction of historical narratives, the writing of cultural criticism, the education of women, and the

political imperative to educate ourselves about new scientific and technological formations. In all these accounts, I have treated the body as a site of the mutually constitutive interaction between discourses *about* the body and the materiality *of* specific bodies. The body also serves as the locus for thinking differently about both feminist histories and feminist futures, and the political aims of feminist cultural criticism more broadly.

NOTES

※

Introduction

1   The man in the cover photograph wears liquid screen glasses that come with a handheld computer and earphones. For his viewing pleasure, the computer can transmit video images and other audiovisual material to the eyeglass screens. The cover photo is a striking visual emblem of the future high-tech body, which, from *LIFE*'s point of view, is gendered male. "The Future and You," A 30-Page Preview: "2000 and Beyond," *LIFE* Feb. 1989.

2   The 1987 Humana annual report implies that one of the reasons for Humana's success is the "solid foundation of credibility [established] through innovative activities such as the artificial heart program," which is considered a key strategy designed to give Humana hospitals a competitive edge in building patient volumes in a time of otherwise decreasing hospital admissions. Financial information is quoted from The Humana Inc. *1987 Annual Report,* "American Health Care: A World of Dramatic Change."

3   Michel Feher uses the Foucauldian term "thick perception" to describe one way to study the cultural relationship between the body and technology. Michel Feher, "Of Bodies and Technologies," *Discussions in Contemporary Culture,* ed. Hal Foster, DIA Art Foundation (Seattle, Wash.: Bay, 1987) 159–65. He further elaborates this concept in his introduction to *Zone 3, Fragments for a History of the Human Body,* part 1 (New York: Urzone, 1989) 11–17.

4   Michel de Certeau's chapter on "Reading as Poaching" is an eloquent discussion of the active practice of reading. I draw on John Frow's explication of de Certeau's theory of reading as not being solely an "experiential" practice without its systemic determinations. Apparently, I am less worried than Frow is though, about de Certeau's "politically fraught substitution of the voice of a middle-class intellectual for that of the users of popular culture" (Frow, 59–60). This is likely because I identify quite strongly with a working-class sensibility, even if, in institutional terms, I qualify as a "middle-class" academic. Michel de Certeau, *The Practice of Everyday Life,* trans. Steven Rendall (Berkeley: U of California P, 1984); John Frow, "Michel DeCerteau and the Practice of Representation," *Cultural Studies* 5.1 (1991): 52–60.

5   The process of body definition is one of the key cultural operations I investigate in this book. In one sense the proper discipline of the body in the American academy is the field

of kinesiology, which identifies itself as the study and science of the movement of the human body. In addition to the study of physical activity, recent work in kinesiology includes the study of bioenergetics, somatometry, body symbolism, and human social anatomy. A foundational analysis of the meaningfulness of body motion is Ray Birdwhistell, *Kinesics and Context: Essays on Body Motion Communication* (Philadelphia: U of Pennsylvania P, 1970).

The fields of medicine and biology also lay claim to the body. Of all the biomedical sciences of the body, immunology is probably the field with the most urgent social and political agenda: AIDS, cancer, germ warfare, environmentally induced allergies, legal issues related to paternity—each requires the practical application of immunological research. Immunology is concerned with the maintenance of the structural and functional integrity of complex organisms. As such it is concerned with issues of identity and difference, coding and self-recognition, and maintenance and surveillance. One work that discusses the epidemiological and forensic applications of immunology is F. M. Burnet, *The Integrity of the Body: A Discussion of Modern Immunological Ideas* (Cambridge: Harvard UP, 1963).

In the field of psychology, body image and body consciousness are mediating constructs in the study of how experiences are anchored in the body. From a slightly different perspective, symbolic interactionists join ethnomethodologists in claiming the body as a properly sociological object of study by exploring the social construction of the body and the physical self. See, e.g., Virginia Olesen, Leonard Schatzman, Nellie Droes, Diane Hatton, and Nan Chico, "The Mundane Complaint and the Physical Self: Analysis of the Social Psychology of Health and Illness," *Social Science of Medicine* 30.4 (1990): 449–55; Harold Garfinkel, "Passing and the Managed Achievement of Sex Status in an Intersexed Person," *Studies in Ethnomethodology* (Englewood Cliffs, N.J.: Prentice-Hall, 1967); Norman K. Denzin, "Harold and Agnes: A Narrative Undoing," paper presented to the symposium on Writing the Social Text: Anthropological, Sociological and Literary Perspectives, University of Maryland, College Park, 18–19 Nov. 1989.

Philosophy too has demonstrated its claim to the body as an object of theory both within traditions of existentialism and phenomenology and in Nietzsche's critique of metaphysics. Martin Heidegger, Maurice Merleau-Ponty, and Friedrich Nietzsche are key figures in the philosophical treatment of the human body. See also David Michael Levin, *The Body's Recollection of Being: Phenomenological Psychology and the Deconstruction of Nihilism* (London: Routledge & Kegan Paul, 1985).

What we find, given the wealth of scholarship on the human body, is that the body as an "object of study" changes as different fields take up the "fact" of the body in human life.

6 Robert Bud, "Biotechnology in the Twentieth Century," *Social Studies of Science* 21 (1991): 415–57.

7 The fear of death by contamination is certainly not a new phenomenon. In the 1950s, for example, Marshall McLuhan, in his book, *The Mechanical Bride* observed that:

> [the American] bathroom has been elevated to the very stratosphere of industrial folklore, it being the gleam, the larger hope, which we are appointed to follow. But in a world accustomed to the dominant imagery of mechanical production and consumption, what could be more natural than our coming to submit our bodies and fantasies to the same processes? The anal-erotic obsession of such a world is

inevitable. And it is our cloacal obsession which produces the hysterical hygiene ads, the paradox here being much like our death and mayhem obsession in the pulps on one hand, and on the other our refusal to face death at all in the mortician parlor. (62)

In many ways, the cult of personal hygiene reaches a sensible conclusion in the AIDS epidemic. Contact between the body and the nonbody (the foreign, the other, the enemy) creates anxieties connected to a loss of control and fear of contamination. Pleasurable aspects of body-to-body (self-to-other) contact are now replaced by fears of infection: of herpes, genital warts, syphilis, HIV. No doubt that the AIDS epidemic is one of the most significant body issues in recent history. In some way it manifests subterranean cultural fears about the final technological "death" of the body. With the continuing increase in technological developments, we are lulled, and willfully lead ourselves into thinking that disease can be cured with only a few more dollars of research, more drug testing, more expensive imaging equipment. Technological immortality is presented as a real possibility. McLuhan, *The Mechanical Bride: Folklore of Industrial Man* (Boston: Beacon, 1951).

8   A Texas antidrug program (D-FY-IT) provides rewards in the form of discounts at restaurants, clothing stores, and game rooms, to teenagers who volunteer to participate in random urine drug tests. Membership in the program is contingent upon successful tests and works through the process of reverse peer pressure. Continued membership requires participation in a drug test within 48 hours' notice. Teenagers who don't participate feel the suspicion that they must be on drugs; others fear that such a Big Brother-like program will encourage snitching and peer surveillance. A board of student directors sets policies and dispenses punishment and allows students to anonymously report other students. "Texas Antidrug Program Talks Teens' Language," *Chicago Tribune* 15 June 1989, sec. 1: 1, 9. In Lafayette, Indiana, high school athletes began random urine drug testing in August 1989. But some believe that administering random drug tests to teenage students is an infringement of their basic rights. According to Marcida Dodson:

School officials should be aware that drug testing is considered a search and seizure under the Fourth Amendment to the Constitution, and that the U.S. Supreme Court, in a 1985 case, ruled that searches by school officials must be based on "reasonable suspicion." (36)

Simply being a member of a demographic age group is not reasonable grounds for suspicion, though. Marcida Dodson, "New Kind of School Test — for Drugs," *Los Angeles Times* 2 June 1989, part 1: 1, 36–37.

Random drug testing promises to provoke many legal debates and casts a cloud over the issues of teenage friendship. Mike Royko reports that many teenagers (900 out of a nonrandom sample of 1,500) say that they would blow the whistle on friends who use drugs: "they'd rather lose the friendship of a living person than go to the funeral of a friend" (Mike Royko column, 11 June 1989). All this attention to teenage drug use and abuse is fueling the field of youth psychiatry, the fastest growing part of American health care. It is estimated that up to a quarter of a million teenagers will be admitted for psychiatric treatment during the next year; many will be admitted for drug- and alcohol-related "dependencies." John Kass, "Youth Psychiatry: What's the Bottom Line?" *Chicago Tribune* 28 May 1989, sec. 1: 1, 18.

9   Of course, this gendered system of differences develops through diverse contexts. One

important source is modern, social-scientific, origin-of-life stories. In a chapter titled "How Your Life Began," from a pamphlet on sexual education (*A Story about You*), the mystery of the beginning of life is explained through the use of biological concepts and pseudoscientific diagrams:

> In a human being there are many different kinds of cells. These are muscle cells, skin cells, bone cells, nerve cells and blood cells. And there are two very special kinds of cells that are needed to start the life of a new human being. These are egg cells from the mother, and sperm cells from the father. . . . The egg cell from which you grew was made inside your mother in a special place called an ovary (o va re). . . . Girls and women have ovaries, a uterus, and a vagina. Boys and men do not have these parts of the body. . . . Sometimes an egg cell stays in the uterus and starts growing into a baby. This happens when a sperm cell from the father joins the egg cell made by the mother. . . . When a baby boy is born, he already has testicles and a penis. Girls and women do not have these parts of the body. . . . These organs make the chief differences between the sexes. . . . Sometimes people call the sex organs "reproductive organs" because they are the parts of the body that "reproduce," by passing life on to make new human beings.* (*If parts of this chapter are hard for you to read, you might ask your mother or father to read it with you.) (12–13)

Marion O. Lerrigo, Helen Southard, Milton J. E. Senn, MD, *A Story About You*, prepared for the Joint Committee on Health Problems in Education of the National Education Association and the American Medical Association, Chicago, 1964.

10   Silicone breast forms are the only artificial body part available in the *Sears Health Care Specialog* (Sears, Roebuck and Co., 1988). They take up one page of a two-page layout on "Post Mastectomy Needs," opposite the catalog page of mastectomy bras. "Classique" prostheses (the registered trademark name of the Sears silicon breast forms) are said to "recreate the natural appearance, comfortable softness and gentle movement of a woman's breast. . . . [They] fit simple, modified and radical mastectomies." There are four different models, including an asymmetrical form, a "youthful, symmetrical" form, and an oval-shaped form with nipple. In the March 1988 catalog the prices for these forms ranged from $60 to $160.

11   In her book *The Cancer Journals*, Audre Lorde denounces the "travesty of prosthesis" and suggests that women who choose a breast prosthesis in a fantasy effort to be "the same as before" participate in the cultural coverup of institutionally induced causes of breast cancer. Although Lorde acknowledges the pressures of conformity and the loneliness of difference that compel some women to wear a breast form, she is unflinching in her critique of the ideological function of such a prosthesis.

> When other one-breasted women hide behind the mask of prosthesis or the dangerous fantasy of reconstruction, I find little support in the broader female environment for my rejection of what feels like a cosmetic sham. But I believe that socially sanctioned prosthesis is merely another way of keeping women with breast cancer silent and separate from each other. For instance, what would happen if an army of one-breasted women descended upon Congress and demanded that the use of carcinogenic, fat-stored hormones in beef-feed be outlawed? (16)

Lorde goes on to describe postmastectomy interactions with women and nurses who tried to counsel her and shame her into wearing a breast form:

the insistence upon breast prostheses as decent rather than functional is an additional example of the wipe-out of self in which women are constantly encouraged
to take part. I am personally affronted by the message that I am only acceptable if I
look right or normal, where those norms have nothing to do with my own perceptions of who I am . . . When I mourn my right breast, it is not the appearance of it I
mourn, but the feeling and the fact. But where the superficial is supreme, the idea
that a woman can be beautiful and one-breasted is considered depraved, or at
best, bizarre, a threat to morale. (65)

Audre Lorde, *The Cancer Journals* (San Francisco: Spinsters Ink, 1980).

12 Throughout my discussion of these body technologies I am interested in determining
how codes of gender cross-cut the discussions, the framing of the issues, and application
of these body practices. I rely on a binary model of female and male sets of codes, more
as a template for reading the signs of gender associated with each practice. Traditional
codes of gender suggest that female bodies are signed by (1) a concern for appearance,
(2) expressions of sexuality, and (3) a reproductive capacity. In contrast, although not
simply oppositional, the male body is marked by (1) a concern to establish identity,
(2) the privilege of the gaze, and (3) a productive capability.

13 I am implicitly drawing on Teresa de Lauretis's transformation of Foucault's notion of
the "technology of sex" into the "technologies of gender." In her book *Technologies of
Gender,* she uses the term "technologies of gender" to name the process by which
gender is "both a representation and self-representation produced by various social
technologies, such as cinema, as well as institutional discourses, epistemologies, and
critical practices" (ix). Her crucial contribution is her understanding that "gender is not
a property of bodies or something originally existent in human beings, but the set of
effects produced in bodies, behaviors, and social relations" (3). This uncovers a central
paradox in feminist theory: how Woman is at once both a representation and an object,
and the very condition for that representation and objectification. An important question for feminism remains to consider how these representations are constructed and
then accepted, embodied, and reproduced. Teresa de Lauretis, *Technologies of Gender:
Essays on Theory, Film, and Fiction* (Bloomington: Indiana UP, 1987).

14 For an elaboration of theories of articulation within cultural studies, see Lawrence
Grossberg, *We Gotta Get Out of This Place: Popular Conservatism and Postmodern
Culture* (New York: Routledge, 1992).

15 Judy Wajcman, *Feminism Confronts Technology* (University Park: Pennsylvania State
UP, 1991) 149.

16 Judith Butler, *Gender Trouble: Feminism and the Subversion of Identity.* (London:
Routledge, 1990) 33.

17 Gregory Bateson, *Steps to an Ecology of Mind* (New York: Ballantine, 1972) 319.
Bateson describes a cybernetic system as an information-transmitting network of connections between receivers' nodes. Although he considers human culture to be one such
cybernetic system — the intent of his analysis is to enhance the development of an
orderly approach to scientific cultural investigation — he does not go so far as to "name"
the human members/participants of such a system.

18 Grosz first uses the term in her introduction and article ("Notes Towards a Corporeal
Feminism") in a special issue of *Australian Feminist Studies* on feminism and the body
(Vol. 5, Summer 1987: 1–16). Michele Barrett, in her revised introduction to the 1988

edition of *Women's Oppression Today,* situates Grosz's work on "corporeal feminism" on her equally revised map of the terrain of contemporary feminist theory. See Michele Barrett, *Women's Oppression Today: The Marxist/Feminist Encounter* (London: Verso, 1980; rev. ed. 1988); and Elizabeth Grosz, *Volatile Bodies: Toward a Corporeal Feminism* (Bloomington: Indiana UP, 1994).

19 *Newsweek* calls the new ideals of muscle as beauty "The New Flex Appeal." Charles Leerhsen and Pamela Abramson, "The New Flex Appeal," *Newsweek* 6 May 1985: 82–83. And a Gallup survey proves it: today's women want to be strong, not skinny; Elle Macpherson, curvy but also athletic, is announced as the new beauty ideal. Reported in A. G. Britton, "Thin Is Out, Fit Is In," *American Health* July/Aug. 1988: 66–71.

20 Ernesto Laclau and Chantal Mouffe make a distinction between elements of social relations and *moments,* which are articulated parts of discourse. Elements are not discursively articulated but are available to be. Moments, in contrast, have an articulated identity within any discursive totality. That is, moments are elements that have been taken up in the process of meaning construction — articulated within discourse. But "because no discursive formation is a sutured totality . . . the transformation of the elements into moments is never complete." Ernesto Laclau and Chantal Mouffe, *Hegemony and Socialist Strategy: Toward a Radical Democratic Politics* (London: Verso, 1985) 107.

1. Reading Cyborgs, Writing Feminism

1 From the song "Monkey's Paw," *Strange Angles* album, 1989. Also quoted in Laurie Anderson, *Stories from the Nerve Bible: 1972 Retrospective 1992* (New York: HarperCollins, 1994). The "nerve bible" is Anderson's term for the body.

2 See Michel Foucault, *The History of Sexuality: Vol. 1, An Introduction* (New York: Vintage, 1978); *The Use of Pleasure: Vol. 2 of The History of Sexuality* (New York: Vintage, 1985); *The Care of the Self: Vol. 3 of the History of Sexuality* (New York: Vintage, 1986). See also Bryan S. Turner, *The Body and Society: Explorations in Social Theory* (Oxford, Eng.: Basil Blackwell, 1984); Susan Rubin Suleiman, ed., *The Female Body in Western Culture: Contemporary Perspectives* (Cambridge: Harvard UP, 1985); Catherine Gallagher and Thomas Laqueur, eds., *The Making of the Modern Body: Sexuality and Society in the Nineteenth Century* (Berkeley: U of California P, 1987); Emily Martin, *The Woman in the Body: A Cultural Analysis of Reproduction* (Boston: Beacon, 1987).

Other works that take a sociocultural approach to the history of the human body include: Barry Glassner, *Bodies* (New York: Putnam, 1989); Stephen Kern, *Anatomy and Destiny: A Cultural History of the Human Body* (Indianapolis, IN: Bobbs-Merrill, 1975); John O'Neill, *Five Bodies: The Human Shape of Modern Society* (Ithaca: Cornell UP, 1985); Robert Brain, *The Decorated Body* (New York: Harper and Row, 1979); Nancy M. Henley, *Body Politics: Power, Sex, and Nonverbal Communication* (Englewood Cliffs, N.J.: Prentice-Hall, 1977); Ted Polhemus, ed., *The Body Reader: Social Aspects of the Human Body* (New York: Pantheon, 1978).

3 Hubert L. Dreyfus and Paul Rabinow quote Foucault's elaboration of these concrete relations in their book *Michel Foucault: Beyond Structuralism and Hermeneutics* (Chicago: U of Chicago P, 1982) 223.

4 Jana Sawicki provides a useful overview of the points of contention and agreement between some feminist theory and Foucault's work. Although she rebukes "radical feminism" for its dismissal of Foucault, she does acknowledge that Foucault failed to specifically consider the treatment of women's bodies in his *History of Sexuality*. She defends this by noting that he intended to write a volume entitled "Women, Mother and Hysteric." Although I am entirely sympathetic to her aim asserting the importance of many of Foucault's insights for the feminist study of the gendered body, she does less "disciplining" of Foucault than she does of other feminists. Jana Sawicki, *Disciplining Foucault: Feminism, Power and the Body* (New York: Routledge, 1991).

5 Irene Diamond and Lee Quinby, eds., *Feminism & Foucault: Reflections on Resistance* (Boston: Northeastern UP, 1988); see also Biddy Martin, "Feminism, Criticism and Foucault" (3–19) and Francis Bartkowski, "Epistemic Drift in Foucault" (43–60).

6 Bartkowski, "Epistemic Drift in Foucault," Diamond and Quinby 47.

7 Susan Rubin Suleiman, ed., *The Female Body in Western Culture: Contemporary Perspectives* (Cambridge: Harvard UP, 1985).

8 Mary Douglas, *Natural Symbols: Explorations in Cosmology* (1970; New York: Pantheon Books, rev. ed. 1982). See also Mary Douglas, *Purity and Danger: An Analysis of the Concepts of Pollution and Taboo* (1966; London: Ark Paperbacks, 1984).

9 Douglas, *Natural Symbols* 90. Douglas relies heavily on Marcel Mauss as an authority for this point; she describes how Mauss "boldly asserted that there can be no such thing as natural behavior. Every kind of action carries the imprint of learning, from feeding to washing, from repose to movement and above all, sex" (*Natural Symbols* 65). See Marcel Mauss, "Techniques of the Body," *Sociologie et Anthropologie,* intro. by Claude Levi-Strauss, 4th ed. (Paris: Presses Universitaires de France, 1968) 364–86. This essay was most recently reprinted in English in Jonathan Crary and Sanford Kwinter, eds., *ZONE 6: Incorporations* (New York: Urzone, 1992) 454–77.

10 Beverley Brown and Parveen Adams, "The Feminine Body and Feminist Politics" *m/f* 3 (1979): 35–50.

11 Thomas Laqueur, "Organism, Generation, and the Politics of Reproductive Biology," Gallagher and Laqueur 1–41. Quotation is from pages 2–3.

12 Mary Poovey, " 'Scenes of an Indelicate Character': The Medical Treatment of Victorian Women," Gallagher and Laqueur 137–68. Quotation is from page 139.

13 Arthur Kroker and Marilouise Kroker, eds., *Body Invaders: Panic Sex in America* (New York: St. Martin's, 1987). I first heard Arthur Kroker present the disappearing body thesis on a panel we were on at the International Communication Association Meetings in May 1987.

14 In *Technology and the Canadian Mind,* Arthur Kroker describes McLuhan's discourse as taking "its working premise that the most insidious effect of technology lay in its deep colonization of biology, of the body itself" (71–72). Kroker elaborates McLuhan's understanding of technology:

> for the first time, the central nervous system itself has been exteriorized. It is our plight to be processed through the technological simulacrum; to participate intensively and integrally in a "technostructure" which is nothing but a vast simulation and "amplification" of the body senses. (57)

According to Kroker, McLuhan is a technological humanist (and radical empiricist) whose "intention was to create anti-environments by which the silent message of the electronic media could be revealed" (54). McLuhan's humanism seeks to evoke the creative possibilities that come from understanding how the new media work. It is not only the content of McLuhan's work that enacts a critique of the mind-numbing influence of media technology, but also his writing and presentation style. Kroker explicitly addresses the process of reading McLuhan:

> McLuhan makes the reader a "metonymy" to his "metaphor": he transforms the act of "reading McLuhan" into dangerous participation in a radical experiment which has, as its end, the exploration of the numbing of consciousness in the technological massage. (58)

McLuhan remains rooted in an existentialist philosophy that posits the notion of "epiphany" as something to be released from the media experience with cultural objects. Arthur Kroker, *Technology and the Canadian Mind: Innis/McLuhan/Grant* (New York: St. Martin's, 1984).

15 This question is also raised by Greg Ostrander in his essay, "Foucault's Disappearing Body," Kroker and Kroker 169–82.

16 In "Unwrapping the Postmodern," I argue that, from a feminist perspective, the *crises* that preoccupy postmodernism do not appear as crises, largely because the break between modernism and postmodernism is indistinct and arbitrary; patriarchal relations of domination continued undeterred. Women's voices are still actively suppressed within postmodern discourse. Indeed, feminists might interpret postmodern*ism* as an instance of patriarchy valorizing its own epistemological crises as a new cultural and historical age. Given that postmodernism has gained such widespread theoretical and cultural currency, it threatens to eclipse the feminist scholarship that examines the dawning of a new epistemology as a specifically feminist epistemology. Anne Balsamo, "Unwrapping the Postmodern: A Feminist Glance" *Journal of Communication Inquiry* 11.1 (1987): 64–72.

17 Arthur Kroker and David Cook specify the new French feminism of Cixous, Irigaray, and Gauthier as the best situated to theorize the body issues that they (Kroker and Cook) identify as arising within postmodernism: "to theorize the equivalence between the repression of sexual difference and the sexual division of labor; to relativize misrecognition as being based on gender displacement ..." (19). These issues, of course, are not unique to postmodernism, but have long been items on the feminist agenda. Arthur Kroker and David Cook, *The Postmodern Scene: Excremental Culture and Hyper-Aesthetics* (New York: St. Martin's, 1986).

18 Alice Jardine, *Gynesis: Configurations of Woman and Modernity* (Ithaca: Cornell UP, 1985) 37.

19 Norbert Wiener was among the first scholars to explicitly describe the relationship between the human body and information processing technologies, through his elaboration of the science of cybernetics. Wiener's work was from the beginning an interdisciplinary endeavor; disparaging the increasing specialization of science, he sought to work in what he saw as the most fruitful areas of the sciences — the spaces between the fields of mathematics, physics, and biology. Wiener was the first to specify the requirements of a computing machine in terms of processing time and economics of action. One such requirement stipulated the use of the binary system as the basic computing scale. Norbert Wiener, *Cybernetics of Control and Communication in the Animal and the Machine* (New York: John Wiley & Sons [The Technology Press], 1948).

From the very beginning, Wiener hoped that cybernetics would accomplish something *practical* for mankind. Artificial limbs were another practical application Wiener proposed; these were not simply parts that would replace limbs in their support function, but artificial parts that would be "wired" into the body's central nervous system and would reproduce the cybernetic information network of the human body's sense organs:

> There is a manifest possibility of doing something in the case of artificial limbs. The loss of a segment of limb implies not only the loss of the purely passive support of the missing segment or its value as mechanical extension of the stump, and the loss of the contractile power of its muscles, but implies as well the loss of all cutaneous and kinesthetic sensations originating in it. The first two lessons are what the artificial-limbmaker now tries to replace. The third has so far been beyond our scope. (35–36)

Here he describes the scientific basis of cyborg design: replaceable body parts that are not just artificial limbs, but actually connected to the body, controlled by the body's nervous system, and capable of transmitting physical sensations. One such application of cybernetics was the development of what he called the "ultra-rapid computing machine." Wiener argued that an "ultra-rapid computing machine" should function like an ideal central nervous system, that is, as an apparatus for automatic control, in which machine output would direct motors, photoelectric cells, thermometers, and other sense apparatuses, and in which this output would then in turn regulate the machine (i.e., an apparatus with a feedback loop). His broader point was to prescribe "feedback" as the governing technique of a new age of technology, which could be observed in any of a number of scientific phenomenon, including the body, society, and culture. Describing three major ages of technique, Wiener identifies the seventeenth and early eighteenth centuries as the age of clocks, the late eighteenth and early nineteenth centuries as the age of steam engines, and the present time (which for him was 1948) as the age of communication and control. Each age is marked by a definable technique — the present by the technique of feedback, the process whereby a mechanical-electronic device not only performs an action but also receives a report of the consequences of that performance, which in turn can be used to effect the next action. According to Wiener, the technique of feedback is fundamentally a communication process. Thus Wiener and his colleagues designed the term "cybernetics" in 1947 to name the field of control and communication theory. It is clear that Wiener grounded his notion of cybernetics in a conceptualization of the human body as an organized information-processing system of communicational parts. In doing so, he articulated two founding assumptions of cybernetics — (1) that the human body is the best model for the development of automatic machines and (2) the belief that, in subtle contrast to Foucault's analysis of the body as machine, the body was now not simply mechanical or anatomical but processual and communicative. Wiener's cybernetic science of communication and control operates at several levels: not only is the human body itself a cybernetic system (with feedback mechanisms and information process), but so too is the broader social system within which it is embedded.

20 Like Wiener, Marshall McLuhan defines technologies (especially communication technologies) as extensions of the senses of the human body. It is not simply that technologies create the *concept* of the body, but rather that communication technologies

reproduce the body itself. To this end, McLuhan critically examines a variety of images and texts from popular culture to demonstrate how communication technologies function as the new body sensorium. We know our bodies through technological sense organs (self-surveillance devices), and the bodies we know have been irrevocably transformed by technological practices. If Wiener shows how cybernetics was founded on a simulation of the human body, McLuhan suggests the converse — that people have begun to simulate machines. We can read in McLuhan's work the elaboration of a relationship between sex and technology in which human bodies become the sex organs of machines, facilitating their reproduction, evolution, and immortality through the exhaustion of our corporeal mortality. In similar ways, both Wiener and McLuhan offer readings of the cybernetic body that inform the production of postmodern theories of the body. Marshall McLuhan, *The Mechanical Bride: Folklore of Industrial Man* (Boston: Beacon, 1951).

21   Andreas Huyssen, "Mapping the Postmodern." *New German Critique* 33 (1984): 5–52.

22   Donna Haraway, "A Manifesto for Cyborgs: Science, Technology, and Socialist Feminism in the 1980s," *Socialist Review* 80.2 (1985): 65–108. Quotation is from page 96.

23   Sandra Harding, *The Science Question in Feminism* (Ithaca: Cornell UP, 1986); Ruth Bleier, *Science and Gender: A Critique of Biology and Its Theories on Women* (New York: Pergamon, 1984); Paula A. Treichler, "AIDS, Gender, and Biomedical Discourse: Current Contests for Meaning," *AIDS: The Burdens of History,* ed. Elizabeth Fee and Daniel M. Fox (Berkeley: U of California P, 1990) 190–266. The voluminous feminist work on science, technology, epistemology, and methodology includes the following collections: Rita Arditti, Pat Brennan, and Steve Cavrak, eds., *Science and Liberation* (Boston: South End, 1980); Carolyn Merchant, *The Death of Nature: Women, Ecology, and the Scientific Revolution* (New York: Harper and Row, 1980); Sandra Blaffer Hrdy, *The Woman That Never Evolved* (Cambridge: Harvard UP, 1981); Ruth Hubbard, Mary Sue Henifin, and Barbara Fried, eds., *Biological Woman: The Convenient Myth* (Cambridge, Mass.: Schenkman, 1982); Margaret Rossiter, *Women Scientists in America: Struggles and Strategies to 1940* (Baltimore: Johns Hopkins UP, 1982); Sandra Harding and Merrill Hintikka, eds., *Discovering Reality: Feminist Perspectives on Epistemology, Metaphysics, Methodology and Philosophy of Science* (Dordrecht: Reidel, 1983); Joan Rothschild, ed., *Machina ex Dea: Feminist Perspectives on Technology,* (New York: Pergamon, 1983); Jan Zimmerman, ed., *The Technological Woman: Interfacing with Tomorrow* (New York: Praeger, 1983); Evelyn Fox Keller, *Reflections on Gender and Science* (New Haven: Yale UP, 1985); Anne Fausto-Sterling, *Myths of Gender: Biological Theories about Women and Men* (New York: Basic, 1985); Sandra Harding ed., *Feminism and Methodology: Social Science Issues* (Bloomington: Indiana UP, 1987); Sandra Harding and Jean F. O'Barr, eds., *Sex and Scientific Inquiry* (Chicago: U of Chicago P, 1987); Cheris Kramarae, ed. *Technology and Women's Voices: Keeping in Touch* (New York: Routledge, 1988); Sally Hacker, *Pleasure, Power, and Technology: Some Tales of Gender, Engineering, and the Cooperative Workplace* (Boston: Unwin Hyman, 1989); Donna J. Haraway, *Primate Visions: Gender, Race, and Nature in the World of Modern Science* (New York: Routledge, 1989); Alison M. Jagger and Susan R. Bordo, eds., *Gender/Body/Knowledge: Feminist Reconstructions of Being and Knowing* (New Brunswick, N.J.: Rutgers UP, 1989); Ludmilla Jordanova,

Sexual Visions: Images of Gender in Science and Medicine Between the Eighteenth and Twentieth Centuries (Madison: U of Wisconsin P, 1989); Marcel C. LaFollette, *Making Science Our Own: Public Images of Science 1910–1955* (Chicago: U of Chicago P, 1990); Mary Jacobus, Evelyn Fox Keller, and Sally Shuttleworth, eds., *Body/Politics: Women and the Discourses of Science* (New York: Routledge, 1990); Helen E. Longino, *Science as Social Knowledge: Values and objectivity in scientific inquiry* (Princeton: Princeton UP, 1990); Donna J. Haraway, *Simians, Cyborgs, and Women: The Reinvention of Nature* (New York: Routledge, 1991); Sandra Harding, *Whose Science? Whose Knowledge?: Thinking from Women's Lives* (Ithaca: Cornell UP, 1991); Londa Schiebinger, *The Mind Has No Sex? Women in the Origins of Modern Science* (Cambridge: Harvard UP, 1991); Gill Kirkup and Laurie Smith Keller, eds. *Inventing Women: Science, Technology and Gender* (Cambridge: Polity, in conjunction with the Open University, 1992).

24 Haraway, "A Manifesto" 82.

25 Paula A. Treichler, "AIDS, Homophobia, and Biomedical Discourse: An Epidemic of Signification" *Cultural Studies* 1.3 (Oct. 1987): 263–305.

26 Treichler, "AIDS, Gender, and Biomedical Discourse: Current Contests for Meaning," *AIDS: The Burdens of History*, ed. Elizabeth Fee and Daniel M. Fox, 190–266.

2. Feminist Bodybuilding

1 Lynda I. A. Birke and Gail Vines, "A Sporting Chance: The Anatomy of Destiny?" *Women's Studies International Forum* 10.4 (1987): 337–47.

2 Helen Lenskyj, *Out of Bounds: Women, Sport and Sexuality* (Toronto: The Women's Press, 1986) 18.

3 Patricia Vertinsky, "Exercise, Physical Capability, and the Eternally Wounded Woman in Late Nineteenth Century North America," *Journal of Sport History* (Special issue: "Sport, Exercise, and American Medicine") 14.1 (1987): 7–27.

4 "Prizewinning Bodybuilder Quits Taking Steroids Because . . . Drugs Were Turning Me Into a Man," *National Enquirer* 22 Sept. 1987: 4.

5 Phil Hersch, "Griffith-Joyner Sets U.S. Record in Style," *Chicago Tribune* 23 July 1988, sec. 4: 1.

6 The quotation from Duffy is from an article by Phil Hersch, sportswriter for the *Chicago Tribune*. This article appeared in the "Tempo" section of the newspaper rather than in the sports section. ("Tempo" is a light news section focusing on current social issues and the arts, the section that carries the Dear Abby and Bob Greene columns.) The explicit focus of the article was Griffith-Joyner's track outfits and her running history. The article included a comment by rival runner Gwen Torrence, who said that she wouldn't be interested in the one-legged outfit that Griffith-Joyner wears: "We're out there to run like Superwoman, not look like Superwoman." Phil Hersch, "Running Style," *Chicago Tribune* 22 July 1988, sec. 2: 1, 2.

7 Jennifer A. Hargreaves analyzes the ideology of masculinity that is prominent in sport in her article "Where's the Virtue? Where's the Grace? A Discussion of the Social Production of Gender Relations in and through Sport," *Theory, Culture and Society* 3.1 (1986): 109–21. Another excellent study of the ideological system of the body is Sander L. Gilman, "Black Bodies, White Bodies: Toward an Iconography of Female

Sexuality in Late Nineteenth-Century Art, Medicine, and Literature," *Critical Inquiry* 12 (Autumn 1985): 96–117.

8 Robert Kennedy and Vivian Mason, *The Hardcore Bodybuilder's Source Book* (New York: Sterling, 1984).

9 Laurie Jane Schulze analyzes a made-for-TV movie, *Getting Physical,* in terms of the economic conditions of television production and the narrative form of television movies. In her reading, the movie presents several iconographic strategies to disrupt a hegemonic recuperation of a potentially problematic figure: a female bodybuilder. Laurie Jane Schulze, "*Getting Physical:* Text/Context/Reading and the Made-For-Television Movie," *Cinema Journal* 25.2 (Winter 1986): 16–30.

10 *Pumping Iron II: The Women,* dir. George Butler with Carla Dunlap, Bev Francis, and Rachel McLish, 1985.

11 Kennedy and Mason, *Hardcore Bodybuilder's Source Book* 181.

12 Physiologically, this is a matter of fat content and water retention. Stripping off fat allows the muscle to bulge, producing the "ripped" look that many men popularize. Being "ripped" means that every sinew, tendon, and vein stands out under the skin, demonstrating very little fat content of the skin. The softer, rounder, smoother muscle definition of women occurs because there is more fat between the skin's outer layer and the muscle. Since women also battle a physiological sensitivity to fluid retention, to achieve better muscularity they are advised to minimize sodium intake during "peaking cycles" (the final four days before a competition). Given women's physiological predisposition for higher body fat composition, the decision to remove fat is more than a question of appearance. It is a matter of altering the biological composition of the female body. Fat removal is accomplished primarily through diet and a strenuous workout regimen with machines and weights, which work to burn off all unnecessary body fat.

13 The film was created by Charles Gaines and George Butler based on their book *Pumping Iron II: The Unprecedented Woman* (New York: Simon and Schuster, 1984).

14 The film includes a sequence that shows Carla performing a synchronized swimming routine. Her biography in the book *Women of Iron: The World of Female Bodybuilders* describes her as a compulsive athlete who is expert in floor gymnastics, yoga, speed swimming, and dance. As one of the few black women in bodybuilding (for most of the early 1980s), she was often asked if this caused any problems. Her reply: "No. She had never been taught that color was a limitation . . . Her father was a chemist in Newark, and his children were provided with everything they needed. Carla had four sisters and a brother. They lived in a huge house. There were horses and boats, and lots of space to breathe in. A typical American middle-class background, she called it" (59). Early in her bodybuilding career, Carla reports being plagued by a physical structure that was deemed to be "too muscular" by various judges. Nik Cohn and Jean-Pierre Laffont, *Women of Iron: The World of Female Bodybuilders* (New York: Wideview Books, 1981).

15 Annette Kuhn, "The Body and Cinema: Some Problems for Feminism," *Grafts: Feminist Cultural Criticism,* ed. Susan Sheridan (London: Verso, 1988) 11–23. Quotation is from page 18.

16 bell hooks, *Feminist Theory: From Margin to Center* (Boston: South End, 1984) 13.

3. On the Cutting Edge

1 The technical literature on biomedical imaging discusses everything from the architecture of computer systems for the creation and analysis of biological images, to the medical models that underlie such imaging systems. With respect to this last point, a 1989 editorial in the journal *Computerized Medical Imaging and Graphics* pointed out that one factor that is often overlooked in the discussions of computer imaging is "the quality of the physiological model underlying the creation of the image itself. If the physiological model is seriously in error, then the best computerized image analysis conceivable will simply perpetuate misconceptions" (2). Donald L. McEachron, "Editorial," *Computerized Medical Imaging and Graphics* 13.1 (Jan.–Feb. 1989): 1–2.

   Medical imaging programs are also being used in nonmedical cases. For example, a new computer program developed by two medical illustrators at the University of Illinois at Chicago produces age-progressed illustrations of missing children. A 1985 broadcast of the computer-aged pictures of two young girls abducted by their father eight years previously resulted in their return to their mother. Richard Brunelli, "Picturing Age: A Computer Breakthrough Can Help Find Long-Lost Kids," *Chicago Tribune* 17 Nov. 1989, sec. 3: 1, 9.

2 In the early 1980s, doctors performed computer-assisted surgery that combined a computer graphics program with a series of CT scans to create a 3-D model of an infant's congenitally deformed skull, which helped surgeons determine before surgery how to reconstruct the skull. Glenn Garelik, "Putting a New Face on Surgery," *Discover* May 1983: 86–90. A. Lee Dellon describes how CT permits a better understanding of massive facial trauma. A. Lee Dellon, MD, "Plastic Surgery," *Journal of the American Medical Association* 265.23 (19 June 1991): 3160–61.

3 Stefan Hirschauer offers a fascinating ethnographic account of the handling of human bodies during surgery in his article "The Manufacture of Bodies in Surgery," *Social Studies of Science* 21 (1991): 279–319.

4 Carole Spitzack, "The Confession Mirror: Plastic Images for Surgery," *Canadian Journal of Political and Social Theory* 12.1–2 (1988): 38–50.

5 The relationship between disabled women and manufactured feminine beauty is addressed by several contributors in the anthology edited by Susan E. Browne, Debra Connors, and Nanci Stern, *With the Power of Each Breath* (Pittsburgh: Cleis Press, 1985).

6 Spitzack 39.

7 Mary Ann Doane, "The Clinical Eye: Medical Discourses in the 'Woman's Film' of the 1940s," *The Female Body in Western Culture: Contemporary Perspectives,* ed. Susan Suleiman (Cambridge: Harvard UP, 1986) 152–74.

8 In this article, the underlying aesthetic theory of plastic surgery is elaborated through the annotated meaning of A (awareness), R (relativity), and T (technique), where awareness means awareness of "universal qualities of form, content, lighting, color and symmetry coupled with a medical understanding of underlying anatomy and physiology"; relativity means understanding features in relation to a "norm"; and technique refers to measuring, rendering, and sculpting techniques. Stewart D. Fordham, "Art for Head and Neck Surgeons," *Plastic and Reconstructive Surgery of the Head and Neck*

(Proceedings of the Fourth International Symposium of the American Academy of Facial Plastic and Reconstructive Surgery), *Vol. 1: Aesthetic Surgery,* ed. Paul H. Ward and Walter E. Berman (St. Louis, Mo.: C. V. Mosby, 1984) 5.

9   Anthropometry "can be further divided into [subfields]: somatometry — measurement of the body of the living and of cadavers; cephalometry — measurement of the head and face; osteometry — measurement of the skeleton and its parts; and craniometry — measurement of the skull." William M. Bass, *Human Osteology* (Columbia: Missouri Archaeological Society, 1971) 54. One of the well cited texts on anthropometry is M. F. Ashley Montagu, *A Handbook of Anthropometry* (Springfield, IL: Charles C. Thomas, 1960).

10   Richard G. Snyder (and Highway Safety Research Institute, University of Michigan), "Anthropometry of Infants, Children, and Youths to Age 18 for Product Safety Design," *Final Report, Prepared for Consumer Product Safety Commission* (Warrendale, Pa.: Society for Automotive Engineers, 1977).

11   Stephen Pheasant, *Bodyspace: Anthropometry, Ergonomics, and Design* (Philadelphia: Taylor & Francis, 1986).

12   Melville Herskovits, *The Anthropometry of the American Negro* (New York: AMS Press, 1969); L. G. Farkas and J. C. Kolar, "Anthropometrics and Art in the Aesthetics of Women's Faces," *Clinics in Plastic Surgery* 14.4 (1987): 599–616.

13   Nelson Powell, DDS, MD, and Brian Humphreys, MD, *Proportions of the Aesthetic Face* (New York: Thieme-Stratton, 1984).

14   Powell and Humphreys ix. Powell and Humphreys go on to claim that "Beauty itself is then a relative measure of balance and harmony, but most find it difficult to quantitate; however, lines, angles, and contours may be measured and gauged. Standards then can be established to evaluate the elusive goal of beauty" (ix). Thus the rest of their volume reports the geometrical constitution of the "Ideal Face." According to Powell and Humphreys, the ideal face is divided into five "major aesthetic masses," each of which is described in mathematical and geometrical detail in terms of anatomical distances, contour lines, and facial angles. The authors outline a method of analysis in which an "aesthetic triangle relates the major aesthetic masses of the face, forehead, nose, lips, chin and neck to each other" and propose that this method be used as a diagnostic tool, whereby dentofacial deformities are defined as deviation from the ideal proportions. Powell and Humphreys 51.

15   Powell and Humphreys 4.

16   Napoleon N. Vaughn, "Psychological Assessment for Patient Selection," *Cosmetic Plastic Surgery in Nonwhite Patients,* ed. Harold E. Pierce, MD (New York: Grune & Stratton, 1982) 245–251.

17   In fact, one of the most central issues discussed in Pierce's *Cosmetic Plastic Surgery in Nonwhite Patients* is that black patients, Oriental patients, and patients with dark ruddy complexions have a greater propensity to form keloids or hypertrophic scars than do Caucasian patients. Macy G. Hall Jr., MD, "Keloid-Scar Revision," Pierce 203–08.

18   Howard E. Pierce, "Ethnic Considerations," Pierce 37–49.

19   Arthur Sumrall, "An Overview of Dermatologic Rehabilitation: The Use of Corrective Cosmetics," Pierce 141–54.

20   Jackie White, "Classic Schnozz Is 80s nose," *Chicago Tribune* 8 July 1988, sec. 2: 1, 3.

21   The U.S. edition of *Elle* magazine offers several examples of a refashioned primitivism

as high-fashion statement, where both fashion and fashion figures display lines and angles that depart significantly from the ideal (white) facial geometry discussed earlier. Two "alternative" fashion spreads feature the deconstructivist designs of Martin Margiela and provide a glimpse of the new antifashion movement: "From Our Chicest Radicals: Alternative Fashion Routes," *Elle* (Sept. 1991): 324–29; and Stephen O'Shea, "Recycling: An All-New Fabrication of Style," *Elle* (Oct. 1991): 234–39. For a discussion of the appeal of "the exotic woman" and the rise of new multicultural supermodels, see Glenn O'Brien, "Perfect Strangers: Our Love of the Exotic," *Elle* (Sept. 1991): 274–76. Two striking covers that feature both a black model and a white model — symbolizing the multicultural refashioning of ideals of feminine beauty — appear on the May 1988 and Nov. 1991 issues of *Elle*.

22 Bardach also reports that many Iranian women reportedly seek to replace their "strong arched noses" with small pert upturned ones. "The Dark Side of Cosmetic Surgery: Long Term Risks Are Becoming Increasingly Apparent," *New York Times Magazine* 17 Apr. 1988: 24–25, 51, 54–58.

23 Bradley Hall, Richard C. Webster, and John M. Dobrowski, "Blepharoplasty in the Oriental," Ward and Berman 210–25. Quotation is from page 210.

24 Hall et al. 210.

25 Richard T. Farrior and Robert C. Jarchow, "Surgical Principles in Face-lift," Ward and Berman 297–311.

26 J. S. Zubiri, "Correction of the Oriental Eyelid," *Clinical Plastic Surgery* 8 (1981): 725. For a discussion of the discursive strategies whereby Western scholars (anthropologists, scientists) construct "Oriental" as an ideological system of reference, see Edward Said, *Orientalism* (New York: Vintage, 1979).

27 Hall et al. 210.

28 Marwali Harahap, MD, "Oriental Cosmetic Blepharoplasty," Pierce 77–97. Quotation is from page 78.

29 The six-year-old girl was born with cryptopthalmos ("hidden eyes") — without normal eyelids or eye openings. She was treated by a University of Illinois surgeon who developed a technique for reconstructing normal openings. An ultrasound examination revealed that the girl had one eye, so the surgeon created a cavity around the eye and refashioned a "normal-appearing" set of upper and lower eyelids; hopefully, this will allow her to see. "Surgery Will Give Girl a Chance for Sight," *Chicago Tribune* 17 Jan. 1988, sec. 2: 1.

30 A 1989 article in *Longevity* magazine described in grisly detail the stitch-by-stitch procedure of a "tummy tuck" — which they identified as one technique of "youth surgery." John Camp, "Youth Surgery: A Stitch-by-Stitch Guide to Losing Your Tummy," *Longevity* June 1989: 33–35.

31 Shirley Motter Linde, ed., *Cosmetic Surgery: What It Can Do for You* (New York: Award, 1971) 7.

32 Martha Smilgis, "Snip, Suction, Stretch and Truss: America's Me Generation Signs Up for Cosmetic Surgery," *Time* 14 Sept. 1987: 70. One of the most ridiculous descriptions of cosmetic surgery applications appeared in the advertisement for a B.P.I. (Body Profile Improvement) consultation by an Atlanta plastic surgeon, who claimed to offer services for "cellulite correction" and "vertical gravity liposuction." Advertising slide show at Hoyt's Midtown Theater, opening night of *Death Becomes Her,* 31 July 1992.

33   Ruth Hamel, "Raging Against Aging," *American Demographics* 12 (Mar. 1990): 42–
44. In a related article, another journalist speculated that the rising popularity of plastic
surgery was evidence of the baby boomers' obsession with death and their search for
some measure of control over their mortality. Debra Goldman, "In My Time of Dying:
Babyboomers Experience Interest in Death," *ADWEEK* 33 (2 Mar. 1992), Eastern ed.:
18.

34   An article by Peter Jaret in *SELF* magazine describes the new tooth technology in a
cavity-free era. Tooth cosmetics are a growing business and include such techniques as
bonded porcelain veneers, dental implants to replace missing or decayed teeth, and
ceramic braces that replace the metal ones of old. Peter Jaret, "Future Smiles," *SELF*
Apr. 1989: 186–89.
     Although this fear of aging might appear to be a new phenomenon, brought on by
the aging baby boomers' confrontation with body deterioration, it is actually the case
that from the early 1900s on, crow's-feet, the tiny wrinkles formed at the corner of the
eyes, have been defined as an aging "condition" treatable through surgical methods.
Sylvia Rosenthal, *Cosmetic Surgery: A Consumer's Guide* (Philadelphia: J. B. Lippin-
cott, 1977).
     Retin-A, a cream used for almost 20 years as an acne treatment, recently has been
launched as a new "youth cream." Retin-A not only treats acne but also is effective in
removing wrinkles and liver spots. John Voorhees, the scientist who first confirmed the
ability of Retin-A to reverse skin damage is quoted as saying: "I don't want to say that
this is the fountain of youth, but it's the closest thing we have today." An editorial in the
Journal of the American Medical Association, referring to the significance of Voorhees's
study, announced, "A new age has dawned." The day after the editorial appeared the
stock value of Johnson & Johnson (the parent firm of Ortho Pharmaceutical) rose three
points. Tim Friend, "Youth Cream: 'A New Age Has Dawned,' " *USA Today* 22 Jan.
1988, sec. 1: 1.
     Other rejuvenation drugs tested in Europe but not available in the United States
include: Gerovital, a mixture of procaine and stabilizers that seems to improve memory,
muscular strength, and skin texture; Centrophenoxine, a compound that slows the skin
aging process; DHEA (dehydroepiandrosterone), a naturally occurring hormone found
in young adults that has been found to increase survival and improve immune function
in animals; Piracetam, a nootropic which shows some signs of improving memory
function; and cerebral vasodilators, a category of drug that improves blood circulation
to the brain, which in turn is supposed to improve mental ability. Lynn Payer, "Rejuvenation Drugs," *Longevity* June 1989: 25.

35   The news item read: "Dr. Charles D. Smithdeal's ad in *Los Angeles* magazine is a
definite eye-catcher. In full color, on a full page, model Rebecca Ferratti leans her nearly
bare body on a red Ferrari. Her flawless proportions are credited to Smithdeal, a Los
Angeles cosmetic surgeon." Donna Kato, "A Shot of Glitz for Medical Marketing."
Chicago Tribune 30 Jan. 1989, sec. 2: 1, 3.

36   Farrior and Jarchow 298.

37   Several papers in the Ward and Berman collection emphasize the point that prospective
patients should be made to understand the serious nature of surgical procedures; however, they also acknowledge that a "patient's desire to remain attractive and to improve

their self-image is understandable and a paramount consideration that has bearing on their business, social and emotional areas." Farrior and Jarchow 297.

38   G. Richard Holt and Jean Edwards Holt, "Indications for and Complications of Blepharoplasty," Ward and Berman 251.

39   Mike Mitka, "Recession Hits Some Specialists Doing Elective Procedures," *American Medical News* 34 8 Apr. 1991: 9; and "Cosmetic Surgeons See Slowdown in Procedures: Recession, Breast Implant Controversy Cited," *American Medical News* 34 (23 Sept. 1991): 18.

40   Luiz F. DeMoura and Patricia DeMoura, "Rhytidoplasty in the Otolaryngologic Practice," Ward and Berman 324–329. Quotation is from page 324.

41   Mary Wright, "The Elective Surgeon's Reaction to Change and Conflict," Ward and Berman 525–29. Quotation is from page 525.

42   In discussing the nonwhite patient's motivation for rhinoplasty, Harold Pierce rejects the argument that "the non-white patient who seeks rhinoplasty is attempting, symbolically to deny his heritage"; rather, Pierce asserts that these patients want "a nose that is smaller, more symmetrical and pleasing in three dimensional contour — a desire shared by patients requiring rhinoplasty in all racial groups" ("Ethnic" 48). He notes the irony that in an era marked by increased displays of ethnic pride, the number of black and Asian cosmetic surgery patients is increasing. He explains this paradox by suggesting that economic forces demand an "attractive appearance" as a professional attribute.

43   Kathryn Pauly Morgan, "Women and the Knife: Cosmetic Surgery and the Colonization of Women's Bodies," *Hypatia* 6.3 (Fall 1991): 25–53. Quotation is from page 28.

44   Suzanne Dolezal, "More Men Are Seeing Their Future in Plastic — the Surgical Kind," *Chicago Tribune* 4 Dec. 1988, sec. 5, p. 13. Quote from page 13.

45   Michael M. Gurdin, MD, "Cosmetic Problems of the Male," Linde 105–14. Quotation is from page 107.

46   Dolezal, "More Men Are Seeing Their Future in Plastic," 13. A 1989 Ann Landers column reported that Texas prisons often provide free cosmetic surgery as therapy for convicts: "A convicted rapist serving time in Louisiana received an implanted testicle at Charity Hospital in New Orleans that cost the state an estimated $5,000. The implanted testicle replaced one that was diseased and had been surgically removed in 1987. The rationale offered by the Texas prison system suggests that cosmetic surgical procedures performed on inmates provide practice for plastic surgeons and that cosmetic surgery makes a person feel better about himself. Studies were cited to prove that inmates were less likely to return to prison if they had a higher level of self-esteem." Ann Landers column, 13 July 1989.

47   Numerous articles on "the cost of beauty" suggest that as women earn more money they will demand better cosmetic services and conveniences. *Vogue* reports that many companies are responding by offering convenient maintenance programs, which for "the new breed of executive woman" can become a substantial investment and part of her business style; for some executives, in fact, an important perk is a contract that covers the cost of image upkeep and exercise. This would suggest that the differences between men's and women's rationalizations for cosmetic surgery are eroding: women, too, are beginning to justify cosmetic alterations within a logic of the workplace. Dorothy Schefer, "The Real Cost of Looking Good," *Vogue* Nov. 1988: 157–68.

48   The horror stories of women who justify cosmetic surgery for business-related reasons are often reported with an exceedingly critical edge. A female real estate agent in Beverly Hills felt pretty enough in her own way, but totally inadequate when compared to the glamorous female clients she worked with. After three years of silicone treatments to produce artificial "high cheekbones," her face began changing grotesquely; relentless calls to her plastic surgeon went unanswered, and two years later he committed suicide. She is still plagued by shifting silicone lumps under her face skin, and though she has undergone surgery several times to repair the damage, she will never regain her previous unconstructed features. She is described as a woman who just wanted to get "an edge" on the competition, but ended up getting more than she bargained. Bardach, "The Dark Side of Cosmetic Surgery" 24–25, 51, 54–58.

49   Dull and West offer an interesting analysis of the social process whereby gender is constructed. They label this process "the accomplishment of gender," which they describe as "an ethnomethodological view of gender as an accomplishment, that is, an achieved property of situated social action" (64). Building on their work, my essay is concerned with the elaboration of how gender is also a fully *cultural* accomplishment. Diana Dull and Candace West, "Accounting for Cosmetic Surgery: The Accomplishment of Gender," *Social Problems* 38.1 (Feb. 1991): 54–70. Quotation is from page 67.

50   Blair O. Rogers, MD, "Management after Surgery in Facial and Eyelid Patients," Linde, 53–61. Quotation is from page 57.

51   Wendy Chapkis, *Beauty Secrets: Women and the Politics of Appearance* (Boston: South End, 1986) 14.

52   Several advertisements for liposuction procedures published in the *Chicago Tribune* circa 1988 used illustrations of the female body — waist to midcalf — to demonstrate the difference that liposuction can accomplish. An advertisement for The Liposuction Institute (Chicago-Water Tower Place, Arlington Heights, Oakbrook) shows a "before" illustration of a female rear end that bulges with "saddle-bag thighs"; the "after" illustration shows smooth slender thighs. The ad claims that "liposuction, or fat suction-extraction, is a remarkable in-office surgical procedure that reshapes and streamlines your body through the permanent removal of fat that does not respond to dieting or exercise, especially: Pot-bellies, Love handles, Saddle bags, Hips, Double chins, Calves, Thighs, buttocks and large male breasts." The identification of breasts as male here suggests that the assumed reader/client of liposuction would be a female in search of a technological fix for undesirable body fat. A different advertisement for the Vein Specialists (also located in Water Tower Place, Arlington Heights, and Oakbrook) announces that "gentlemen prefer LEGS . . . not veins." Again, women are the intended readers/clients for their varicose vein removal service. *Chicago Tribune Sunday Magazine* 26 June 1988: 24.

53   Eye surgeon Giora Angres of Las Vegas implants a permanent eyeliner just under the skin, so it is always there. The most popular colors are earth-tone shades of gray and brown. Implanted pigments look very natural and last about 10 years. It takes 20 minutes to complete the tattooing effect, and costs from $800 to $1,000. "It's probably one of the most effective tattooing methods yet developed," says a spokesman for the American Academy of Ophthalmology. *American Health* Dec. 1984: 33. Removing tattooed eyeliner is becoming a common "spin-off" surgery. As reported in the *Chicago Tribune*, two Chicago surgeons describe the difficulties of surgery performed on a

woman unhappy with the appearance of her tattooed eyeliner. "Medical Notes," *Chicago Tribune* 21 Aug. 1988, sec. 2: 5.

54 In a 1990 survey, DuraSoft found that 43 percent of black women were interested in hazel lenses, 26 percent in blue, and 14 percent in green. Leslie Savon, "Green looks very natural on Black women; but in blue, they look possessed," *Village Voice* 2 May 1988: 52.

55 Carol Lynn Mithers, "The High Cost of Being a Woman," *Village Voice* 24 Mar. 1987: 31.

56 In the medical literature, patients who show an insatiable desire or addiction to surgery are said to display a "Polysurgical Syndrome." In her article, "How to Recognize and Control the Problem Patient," Mary Ruth Wright argues that "surgical addiction reflects deep psychological conflicts" (532). Wright goes on to report that her research on the psychological profile of the cosmetic surgery patient supports the argument that "all cosmetic surgery patients are psychiatric patients" and that all are "potential problem patients" (530). According to Wright, paranoid schizophrenics are the most dangerous. She notes that "homicides involving elective surgeons are increasing as elective surgery increases" (532). She refers to the case of Dr. Vasquez Anon who was assassinated after he refused to see a patient who wanted more surgery. Mary Ruth Wright, "How to Recognize and Control the Problem Patient," Ward and Bermen 530–35. For more information on Dr. Anon, see U. T. Hinderer, "Dr. Vasquez Anon's Last Lesson," *Aesthetic Plastic Surgery* 2 (1978): 375.

57 Annette C. Hamburger, "Beauty Quest," *Psychology Today* May 1988: 28–32.

58 "Scalpel Slaves Just Can't Quit," *Newsweek* 11 Jan. 1988: 58–59.

59 David M. Sarver, DMD, Mark W. Johnston, DMD, and Victor J. Matukas, DDS, MD, "Video Imaging for Planning and Counseling in Orthognatic Surgery," *Journal Oral and Maxillofacial Surgery* 46 (1988): 939–45. Quotation is from page 939. The authors point out that mismatched goals are a common occurrence: "what surgeons or orthodontists consider ideal may not be the same as the patient's desires" (939).

60 Wayne F. Larrabee Jr., John Sidles, and Dwight Sutton describe the traditional two-dimensional methods of facial analysis and the new three-dimensional digitizers that offer a new approach to facial analysis. Wayne F. Larrabee Jr., MD, John Sidles and Dwight Sutton, "Facial Analysis," *Laryngoscope* 98 (Nov. 1988): 1273–75.

61 Kathryn Pauly Morgan does an excellent job of uncovering the "idea of pain" associated with the surgical instruments used by cosmetic surgeons: "Now look at the needles and at the knives. Look at them carefully. Look at them for a long time. Imagine them cutting into your skin. Imagine that you have been given this surgery as a gift from your loved one." Morgan, "Women and the Knife" 26.

62 Larrabee et al. 1274.

63 J. Regan Thomas, MD, M. Sean Freeman, MD, Daniel J. Remmler, MD, and Tamara K. Ehlert, MD, "Analysis of Patient Response to Preoperative Computerized Video Imaging," *Archives of Otolaryngol Head and Neck Surgery* 115 (July 1989): 793–96.

64 Thomas et al., "Facial Analysis" 793.

65 One Atlanta cosmetic surgeon uses a proprietary image-processing system designed by Truevision, Inc. (Indianapolis), which includes an IBM computer (with peripherals), mouse and tablet, analog RGB monitor and video camera, and Truevision's TARGA+ board and Imager-1 software (by Cosmetic Imaging Systems, Inc., Santa Monica, Calif.).

66   Sarver et al., "Video Imaging" 940.

67   The use of new medical imaging devices is well documented through the 1980s. A. Favre, Hj. Keller, and A. Comazzi, "Construction of VAP, A Video Array Processor Guided by Some Applications of Biomedical Image Analysis," *Proceedings of the First International Symposium on Medical Imaging and Image Interpretation,* Vol. 375 (Berlin, FRG, 26–28 Oct. 1982).

Computer imaging is also being tested in instructional uses where, in one report, resident plastic surgeons are taught how to conduct a patient planning session — normally a skill that is considered very difficult to teach. Ira D. Papel, MD, and Robert I. Park, MD, "Computer Imaging for Instruction in Facial Plastic Surgery in a Residency Program," *Archives of Otolaryngol Head and Neck Surgery* 114 (Dec. 1988): 1454–60.

In another article, the use of video imaging as a "means of predicting results of orthognatic surgery" is said to increase a surgeon's treatment-planning skills. Sarver et al., "Video Imaging" 939.

68   Dido Franceschi, MD, Robert L. Gerding, MD, and Richard B. Fratianne, MD, "Microcomputer Image Processing for Burn Patients," *Journal of Burn Care and Rehabilitation* 10.6 (Nov.–Dec. 1989): 546–49.

69   The release form includes five statements that must be signed by the patient, the physician, and a witness. A copy of the disclaimer appears in William B. Webber, MD, "A More Cost-Effective Method of Preoperative Computerized Imaging," *Plastic and Reconstructive Surgery* 84.1 (July 1989): 149.

70   In a recent newspaper article, one New York ad man claimed that he showed "a client how to use such in-motion retouching techniques in political advertising [by showing] how we could take Michael Dukakis and make him as tall as Bill Bradley. . . . We also made Bush look drunk. That's possible." "Image 'Morphing' Changes What We See — and Believe," *Atlanta Journal-Constitution* 29 June 1992: sec. 4, p. 6.

71   According to Frigga Haug and The Frauenformen Collective, the process of subjectification requires an active participant. In their investigation of the process of female sexualization, the Frauenformen Collective were explicitly looking for the ways in which girls and women "construct themselves into existing structures and are thereby themselves formed" (42). The question for the Collective was not how are women passively manipulated by socialization clichés or media images, but rather how are gendered bodies actively reproduced by women themselves? According to Haug and the Frauenformen Collective, this transformation is the motor of the process of subjectification: "the process by which individuals work themselves into social structures they themselves do not consciously determine" (59). Frigga Haug, *Female Sexualization: A Collective Work of Memory* (London: Verso, 1987).

4. Public Pregnancies and Cultural Narratives of Surveillance

1   Janice Kaplan, "Public Pregnancy," *SELF* April 1989: 155.

2   Patricia Spallone discusses the significance of naming the fetal entity and the politics of deciding when an embryo becomes an embryo in her review of the Warnock Report on human embryo research. Patricia Spallone, "Introducing the Pre-embryo or What's in a

Name," *Beyond Conception: The New Politics of Reproduction* (Granby, Mass.: Bergin & Garvey, 1989): 50–55.

3 Although I am walking dangerous ground here, my iconoclastic rhetoric about the "romance of motherhood" is offered as an attempt to assert that for some women, motherhood holds no magical promise or wonderment. Survivors of childhood violence, for example, know the haunting shame of growing up in a family where children were not treated as "blessings" of any sort. For a discussion of different models of the mother-fetus relationship, see Barbara Katz Rothman, *In Labor: Women and Power in the Birthplace* (London: Norton, 1991).

4 Margaret Atwood, *The Handmaid's Tale* (Boston: Houghton Mifflin, 1986). All page numbers of quoted passages refer to this edition.

5 E. Peter Volpe, *Test-Tube Conception: A Blend of Love and Science* (Macon, Ga.: Mercer UP, 1987) 63–64. In a footnote, Volpe reports the going rate: "Typically, the commissioning couple will need at least $22,000: $10,000 for the surrogate mother's fee, $5,000 for medical expenses, $5,000 for legal fees to draw up the contract and arrange the eventual adoption of the baby, and about $2,000 for miscellaneous expenses" (65).

6 For a related study of the role of ultrasound as a technology of the gendered body, see Lisa Cartwright, *Screening the Body: Tracing Medicine's Visual Culture* (Minneapolis: U of Minnesota P, 1995). See also Carole Stabile, "Shooting the Mother: Fetal Photography and the Politics of Disappearance," *Camera Obscura* 28 (1992): 179–205; and Jennifer L. Stone, "Contextualizing Biogenetic and Reproductive Technologies," *Critical Studies in Mass Communication* 8 (1991): 309–32.

7 For a discussion of the way in which legal decisions and policy statements fail to differentiate between the female body and the mother's body, see Zillah R. Eisenstein, *The Female Body and the Law* (Berkeley: U of California P, 1988).

8 Reviewers disagree about the quality of Atwood's dystopia. See, for example, Christopher Lehmann-Haupt, rev. of *The Handmaid's Tale,* by Margaret Atwood, *New York Times* 27 Jan. 1986: C24; Joyce Johnson, "Margaret Atwood's Brave New World," *Washington Post* 2 Feb. 1986, "Book World": 5; Mary McCarthy, "Breeders, Wives and Unwomen," *New York Times Book Review* 9 Feb. 1986: 1, 35; Peter S. Prescott, "No Balm in this Gilead," *Newsweek* 17 Feb. 1986: 70; Jane Gardam, "Nuns and Soldiers," *Books and Bookmen* Mar. 1986: 29–30; Barbara Ehrenreich, "Feminism's Phantoms," *New Republic* 17 Mar. 1986: 33–35; Bruce Allen, rev. of *The Handmaid's Tale,* by Margaret Atwood, *Saturday Review* 12.2 (May–June 1986): 74; Gayle Greene, "Choice of Evils," *Women's Review of Books* 3.10 (July 1986): 14.

9 As many reviewers point out, a close reading of her "Tale" reveals that the handmaid's name is probably June, one of the names listed in the opening chapter and the only one not attached to another handmaid in the novel.

10 See Paula Treichler, "Feminism, Medicine and the Meaning of Childbirth," *Body/Politics: Women and the Discourses of Science,* ed. Mary Jacobus, Evelyn Fox Keller, and Sally Shuttleworth (New York: Routledge, 1990): 113–38.

11 William Ray Arney, *Power and the Profession of Obstetrics* (Chicago: U of Chicago P, 1982) 123. Although their review is not as detailed, Samuel Osherson and Lorna AmaraSignham explore the cultural role of the machine model in the history of child-

birth practices in America in their essay "The Machine Metaphor in Medicine," *Social Contexts of Health, Illness and Patient Care,* ed. Elliot G. Mishler, Lorna R. Amara-Singham, Stuart Hauser, Samuel D. Osherson, Nancy E. Waxler, and Ramsay Liem (London: Cambridge UP, 1981): 218–49.

12   This is the argument at the heart of Emily Martin's essay "Ideologies of Reproduction" — namely, that reproduction is an area of social life saturated with ideological forms of thought about the "naturalness" of certain predispositions. She especially challenges feminists to scrutinize our thinking about reproduction for class-biased ideological beliefs. Emily Martin, "The Ideology of Reproduction: The Reproduction of Ideology," *Uncertain Terms: The Negotiation of Gender in American Culture,* ed. Faye Ginsburg and Anna Lowenhaupt Tsing (Boston: Beacon, 1990): 300–14.

13   Paula Treichler illuminates how the earlier definition of obstetrics that I refer to here — that is, as "a specialized practice that involves the exercise of professional judgment" — is itself a consequence of a power struggle between midwives and early physicians, which established the institutionalized authority of those newly professionalized obstetricians over the pregnant female body. For a fuller discussion of this cultural struggle, see Treichler, "Feminism, Medicine and the Meaning of Childbirth."

14   In his 1978 book, Stanley Joel Reiser traced the historical development of "technological advances in the art and practice of medicine during the past four centuries" (ix). Although his study was concluded before the wide-scale use of new reproductive technologies, he claimed even in the 1970s that "modern medicine has now evolved to a point where diagnostic judgments based on 'subjective' evidence — the patient's sensations and the physician's own observations of the patient — are being supplanted by judgments based on 'objective' evidence provided by laboratory procedures and by mechanical and electronic devices" (ix). Stanley Joel Reiser, *Medicine and the Reign of Technology* (Cambridge: Cambridge UP, 1978).

15   For a discussion of the politics of fetal imaging, see Rosalind Pollack Petchesky, "Fetal Images: The Power of Visual Culture in the Politics of Reproduction," *Feminist Studies* 13.2 (Summer 1987): 263–92. For a discussion of the dimensions of a "fetal teleology," see Sarah Franklin, "Fetal Fascinations: New Dimensions to the Medical-Scientific Construction of Fetal Personhood," *Off-Centre: Feminism and Cultural Studies,* ed. Sarah Franklin, Celia Lury, and Jackie Stacey (London: HarperCollins Academic, 1991). Faye Ginsburg discusses the role of the public fetus in the abortion debate: "The 'Word-Made' Flesh: The Disembodiment of Gender in the Abortion Debate," *Uncertain Terms: Negotiating Gender in American Culture,* ed. Faye Ginsburg and Anna Lowenhaupt Tsing (Boston: Beacon, 1990): 59–75. See also the special issue of *Science as Culture* 3.4, no. 17 (1993) on "Procreation Stories," with related essays by Sarah Franklin, "Postmodern Procreation: Representing Reproductive Practice" 522–61; Barbara Duden, "Visualizing 'Life' " 562–600; and Janelle Sue Taylor, "The Public Foetus and the Family Car: From Abortion Politics to a Volvo Advertisement" 601–18.

16   Jana Sawicki offers an insightful appraisal of the consequence of new monitoring devices when she writes that new reproductive technologies "facilitate the creation of new objects and subjects of medical as well as legal and state intervention.... infertile, surrogate and genetically impaired mothers, mothers whose bodies are not fit for pregnancy . . . mothers whose wombs are hostile environments for fetuses" (84). Jana Sawicki, *Disciplining Foucault: Feminism, Power and the Body* (New York: Routledge, 1991).

17 Barbara Duden, *Disembodying Women: Perspectives on Pregnancy and the Unborn* (Cambridge: Harvard UP, 1993) 52. See Duden for an elaboration of the historical antecedents of the construction of the public body and the public fetus.

18 Timothy J. McNulty, "Growing Pains Afflict Birth Technology," *Chicago Tribune* 28 July 1987, sec. 1: 1, 9. Quotation is from page 9.

19 Although not the subject of this study, the rise of biotechnology as a lucrative new industry represents the broader context for the economic and policy impact of the development of new reproductive services. See Edward Yoxen, *The Gene Business: Who Should Control Biotechnology?* (New York: Oxford UP, 1983); David J. Webber, ed. *Biotechnology: Assessing Social Impacts and Policy Implications* (New York: Greenwood, 1990); Robert Teitelman, *Gene Dreams: Wall Street, Academia, and the Rise of Biotechnology* (New York: Basic, 1989).

20 Price information from an article by Timothy J. McNulty, "Science Turns Birth into New Industry," *Chicago Tribune* 9 Aug. 1987, sec 1: 1, 10.

21 Volpe, *Test-Tube Conception* 4. In other cases, ultrasound scans are used to visualize mature eggs in the ovary; the process of retrieval is similar to that using a laparoscopy, but only one abdominal incision is required. In place of an optical device for viewing the ovaries, the ultrasound scanner provides a visual guide for inserting the hypodermic needle that is used to aspirate the egg.

22 Volpe, *Test-Tube Conception* 33.

23 Marney Rich, "A Question of Rights," *Chicago Tribune* 18 Sept. 1988, sec. 6: 1, 7.

24 Gena Corea, *The Mother Machine: Reproductive Technologies from Artificial Insemination to Artificial Wombs* (New York: Harper & Row, 1985) 303. The Mead quotation is reported on page 35.

25 Elkie Newman also describes how reproductive technology is implicated in a struggle for control over woman's childbearing facility. Elkie Newman, "Who Controls Birth Control?" *Smothered by Invention: Technology in Women's Lives*, ed. Wendy Faulkner and Erik Arnold (London: Pluto, 1985): 35–54. Robyn Rowland argues that in the process of trying to appropriate procreation and birth from women in the development of new technologies of human reproduction, men organize the procreative alienation of women, turning them into "the experimental raw material in the masculine desire to control the creation of life; patriarchy's living laboratories" (14). Robyn Rowland, *Living Laboratories: Women and Reproductive Technologies* (Bloomington: Indiana UP, 1992).

26 Rebecca Albury, "Who Owns the Embryo?" *Test-Tube Women: What Future for Motherhood?* ed. Rita Arditti, Renate Duelli Klein, and Shelley Minden (London: Pandora, 1984) 58–72. Quotation is from page 14.

27 See Treichler, "Feminism, Medicine, and the Meaning of Childbirth."

28 In Wajcman, *Feminism Confronts Technology*, see especially the chapter titled "Reproductive Technologies: Delivered into Men's Hands," 54–80. In Sawicki, *Disciplining Foucault*, see especially the chapter "Disciplining Mothers: Feminism and the New Reproductive Technologies," 67–94.

29 Spallone, *Beyond Conception* 190. Spallone elaborates a critique of new reproductive technologies grounded in a "women-centered ethics."

30 Michelle Stanworth, ed., *Reproductive Technologies: Gender, Motherhood, and Medicine* (Minneapolis: U of Minnesota P, 1987).

31   Feminist treatments of these issues, again by some of the feminists named above, such as
      Corea, are offered in Rita Arditti, Renate Duelli Klein, and Shelley Minden, eds. *Test-
      Tube Women: What Future for Motherhood?* (London: Pandora, 1984); Ann Oakley,
      The Captured Womb: A History of the Medical Care of Pregnant Women (Oxford,
      Eng.: Basil Blackwell, 1984); and H. Patricia Hynes, *Reconstructing Babylon: Essays
      on Women and Technology* (Bloomington: Indiana UP, 1991). A representative sample
      of nonfeminist work includes Amitai Etzioni, *Genetic Fix: The Next Technological
      Revolution* (New York: Harper Colophon, 1973); Philip Reilly, *Genetics, Law and
      Social Policy* (Cambridge: Harvard UP, 1977); Yvonne M. Cripps, *Controlling Technol-
      ogy: Genetic Engineering and the Law* (New York: Praeger, 1980); R. C. Lewontin,
      Steven Rose, and Leon J. Kamin, eds., *Not in Our Genes: Biology, Ideology, and
      Human Nature* (New York: Pantheon, 1984); Daniel J. Kevles, *In the Name of Eu-
      genics: Genetics and the Uses of Human Heredity* (New York: Alfred A. Knopf, 1985);
      Ruth F. Chadwick, ed. *Ethics, Reproduction and Genetic Control* (London: Routledge,
      1987); Anthony Dyson and John Harris, eds. *Experiments on Embryos* (London: Rout-
      ledge, 1990); Joel Davis, *Mapping the Code: The Human Genome Project and the
      Choices of Modern Science* (New York: John Wiley, 1990); Derek Chadwick, Greg
      Bock, and Julie Whelan, eds., *Human Genetic Information: Science, Law and Ethics —*
      Proceedings from the Ciba Foundation Symposium (Chichester, Eng.: John Wiley &
      Sons, 1990); Daniel J. Kevles and Leroy Hood, eds., *The Code of Codes: Scientific and
      Social Issues in the Human Genome Project* (Cambridge: Harvard UP, 1992).

32   A 1989 ruling by an Australian state government decided the fate of embryos that had
      been frozen since 1981. The donor parents of the frozen embryos died in a plane crash
      in April 1983. The couple, who were unable to conceive "naturally," used in vitro
      fertilization and were storing the embryos for future implantation. The legal status of
      the embryos was debated because someone raised the possibility that they (it) may have
      a legal claim to the dead parents' estate. In this case, the judge ruled that the embryos
      have no legal claim and that any children born from the implanted embryos in other
      mothers likewise have no legal claim to the estate. "Ruling Takes Frozen Embryos Out
      of a 4-Year Legal Limbo," *Chicago Tribune* 2 Dec. 1987, sec. 1: 14.

33   Ellen Goodman takes issue with the judge's ruling, especially his definition of the "fro-
      zen seven" as embryos, variously identified by him as "children," "little children," and
      once as "little people." The embryos are factually, pre-embryos: a group of undifferenti-
      ated cells, that "deserve respect because it can become a child, not because it is one."
      Goodman rightly argues that this judgment leads to murky waters: what about the six
      that are left if the first one "takes"? What about birth control devices that inhibit
      implantation but not fertilization? Of course, pro-life advocates fully supported this
      decision. Ellen Goodman, "The Frozen Seven: Judge Misses Larger Picture in Micro-
      scopic Ruling," *Chicago Tribune* 1 Oct. 1989, sec. 5: 8.

34   Associated Press, "Woman Gets Custody of Frozen Embryos," *Chicago Tribune* 1 Oct.
      1989, sec. 1: 3. This response is consistent with the antiabortion rhetoric that argues
      that "abortion on demand laws give to one person (a mother) the legal right to kill
      another (an embryo) in order to solve the first person's social problem." Quotation
      taken from an antiabortion pamphlet, "Did You Know?" distributed by the Hayes
      Publishing Co., Inc., 6304 Hamilton Ave., Cincinnati, Ohio, 45224.

35   One Chicago obstetrician/gynecologist described the impossible situation that results

when a woman refuses to allow surgery on her fetus: "If you perform a surgical procedure despite the explicit refusal of a competent adult, you could be liable for battery or assault on the woman. If, on the other hand, you respect the women's refusal and do not intervene and some harm happens to the baby, you might be sued by the woman's husband or family for neglect of the fetus. The only way to get out from under that double liability is to give it to somebody else to decide. So the incentive to go to court is very big in these cases." Rich, "A question of rights" 7. The moral status of the embryo is discussed in Volpe, *Test-Tube Conception.*

36　Green was the first woman charged with manslaughter due to delivery of a controlled substance to an infant in the womb. *People of the State of Illinois v. Green,* 88-CM-8256, Cir. Ct., filed 8 May 1989 (cited in Cynthia Daniels, *At Women's Expense: State Power and the Politics of Fetal Rights* (Cambridge: Harvard UP, 1993).

37　Patrick Reardon reported on the case in a series of articles in the *Chicago Tribune:* " 'I Loved Her,' Mother Says: 'Shocked' Over Arrest in Baby's Drug Death," 11 May 1989, sec 1: 1, 8; "When Rights Begin: Baby's Cocaine Death Adds to Debate on Protection of the Unborn," 14 May 1989, sec. 5: 8–9; "Drug and Pregnancy Debate Far from Resolved," 28 May 1989, sec. 1: 1, 5.

38　Anna Lowenhaupt Tsing, "Monster Stories: Women Charged with Perinatal Endangerment," *Uncertain Terms: Negotiating Gender in American Culture,* ed. Faye Ginsburg and Anna Lowenhaupt Tsing (Boston: Beacon, 1990): 282–99.

39　Valerie Hartouni, "Breached Birth: Reflections on Race, Gender, and Reproductive Discourses in the 1980s," *Configurations* 1 (1994): 73–88. Quotation is from page 85.

40　Patricia Hill Collins, "Mammies, Matriarchs and Other Controlling Images," *Black Feminist Thought: Knowledge, Consciousness, and the Politics of Empowerment* (New York: Routledge, 1990): 67–90.

41　Cynthia R. Daniels, *At Women's Expense* 7.

42　Paddy Shannon Cook, Robert C. Petersen, and Dorothy Tuell Moore (ed. Tineke Bodde Haase), *Alcohol, Tobacco, and Other Drugs May Harm the Unborn,* U.S. Department of Health and Human Services (DHHS), Office of Substance Abuse Prevention, DHHS Publication #(ADM) 90-1711 (Rockville, Md.: U.S. DHHS, 1990) 45.

43　In the foreword to the booklet, Elaine M. Johnson, director of the Office for Substance Abuse Prevention, states, "ultimately, this booklet is intended for women of childbearing age and their partners. I include the father because, through his own abstinence, a man can make a major contribution to a woman's drug-free lifestyle and safe pregnancy and to their child's health" (iii). Other than this remark, the booklet makes no mention of paternal contribution to the welfare of the fetus.

44　See Ruth E. Little and Charles F. Sing, "Father's Drinking and Infant Birth Weight: Report of an Association, *Teratology* 36 (1987): 59–65; David A. Savitz and Jianhua Chen, "Parental Occupation and Childhood Cancer: Review of Epidemiological Studies," *Environmental Health Perspectives* 88 (1990): 325–37; Devra Lee Davis, "Fathers and Fetuses," *The Lancet* 337 (12 Jan. 1991): 122–23; Christine F. Colie, "Male-Mediated Teratogenesis," *Reproductive Toxicology* 7 (1993): 3–9; Andrew F. Olshan and Elaine M. Faustman, "Male-Mediated Developmental Toxicity," *Reproductive Toxicology* 7 (1993): 191–202.

45　When people discuss the distressing factor of low-birth-weight babies, it is not so much in the context of concerns about the baby's or the mother's quality of life, but related to the fact that these are very expensive babies to keep alive. As the authors of one report state: "Not only has concern been generated because the United States has a much higher rate of low birth-weight babies than other developed countries . . . but because these are 'expensive babies,' in monetary, familial, and societal terms. The initial cost of hospitalization for a low birth-weight baby is estimated to be over $13,000" (288). J. Brooks-Gunn, Marie C. McCormick, and Margaret C. Heagarty, "Preventing Infant Mortality and Morbidity: Developmental Perspectives," *American Journal of Orthopsychiatry* 58.2 (April 1988): 288–96.

46   Statistical information taken from the Report from the Assistant Secretary for Health, James O. Mason, MD, *Journal of the American Medical Association* 262.16 (27 Oct. 1989): 2202. Other sources for information on infant mortality rates of different races include: Edward G. Stockwell, David A. Swanson, and Jerry W. Wicks, "Economic Status Differences in Infant Mortality by Cause of Death," *Public Health Reports* 103.2 (Mar.–Apr. 1988): 135–42; Frank Dexter Brown, "Expanding Health Care for Mothers and Their Children," *Black Enterprise* (May 1990): 25–26, Teri Randall, "Infant Mortality Receiving Increasing Attention," *Journal of the American Medical Association* 263.19 (16 May 1990): 2604–06; Priscilla Painton, "$25,000,000: Mere Millions for Kids," *Time* (8 Apr. 1991): 29–30.

47   "From the beginning, MCH (Maternal and Child Health) activities have focused on medically underserved women and children — people barred from receiving health services by poverty, ignorance of how to enter the health care system, inability to communicate, lack of transportation, and lack of facilities and providers. And people from minority populations have been disproportionately affected by these barriers" (621). Vince Hutchins and Charlotte Walch, "Meeting Minority Health Needs through Special MCH Projects," *Public Health Reports* 104.6 (Nov.–Dec. 1989): 621–26.

48   For example, in Honolulu, HI, a project is underway to screen Asian American families for hereditary anemia, as distinguished from simple iron deficiencies, so that future health needs of this group can be assessed. Vince Hutchins and Charlotte Walch, "Meeting Minority Health Needs."

49   Jennifer Terry, "The Body Invaded: Medical Surveillance of Women as Reproducers," *Socialist Review* 19.3 (July/Sept. 1989): 13–43. Quotation is from page 14.

50   Seth Koven and Sonya Michel, eds., "Introduction: 'Mother Worlds,'" *Mothers of a New World: Maternalist Politics and the Origins of Welfare States* (New York: Routledge, 1993) 2.

51   Lisa Maher, "Punishment and Welfare: Crack Cocaine and the Regulation of Mothering," *The Criminalization of a Woman's Body,* ed. Clarice Feinman (New York: Harrington Park, 1993) 174.

52   Teri Randall, "Coping with Violence Epidemic," *Journal of the American Medical Association* 263.19 (16 May 1990): 2612–14. Quotation is from page 2612.

53   Reported in the *Morbidity and Mortality Weekly Report* (*MMWR*) under "Current Trends." M. VandeCastle, J. Danna, and T. Thomas, "Physical Violence During the 12 Months Preceding Childbirth — Alaska, Maine, Oklahoma, and West Virginia, 1990–1991," *MMWR* 43.8 (4 Mar. 1994): 132–37.

54   Michael D. Dogan, Milton Kotelchuck, Greg R. Alexander, and Wayne E. Johnson, "Racial Disparities in Reported Prenatal Care Advice from Health Care Providers," *American Journal of Public Health* 84.1 (Jan. 1994): 82–88.

55 Dogan et al., "Racial Disparities" 86.

56 This was counterindicated only in the case of white single women, who reported receiving more advice about illegal drug use than did black single women; income level was not discussed. Untangling the "facts" of risk is confusing, especially in light of more recent reports that smoking cigarettes may do more harm than ingesting cocaine. See the report by Paul Cotton, "Smoking Cigarettes May Do Developing Fetus More Harm Than Ingesting Cocaine, Some Experts Say," *Journal of American Medical Association* 271.8 (23 Feb. 1994): 576–77.

57 Norma Finkelstein, "Treatment Issues for Alcohol- and Drug-Dependent Pregnant and Parenting Women," *Health and Social Work* 19.1 (Feb. 1994): 7–15. Finkelstein is the director of the Coalition on Addiction, Pregnancy and Parenting in Cambridge, MA.

58 Donald E. Hutchings, "The Puzzle of Cocaine's Effects Following Maternal Use during Pregnancy: Are There Reconcilable Differences?" *Neurotoxicology and Teratology* 15.5 (1993): 281–86. Quotation is from page 286.

59 Ira Chasnoff, whose work has reported the most adverse effects of cocaine use among pregnant women patients at a drug treatment center, is the author of one of the studies that Hutchings discusses in great detail. Chasnoff's commentary immediately follows the Hutchings article in the same issue of *Neurotoxicology and Teratology*. Both agree that cocaine dangers to fetal health are a media-amplified phenomenon and that there are many missing pieces of the puzzle, due in part to the vicissitudes of "drug culture," which "guides [different] city's [and hence populations'] availability of drugs, use patterns, polydrug use patterns, and the role women are allowed to play within the culture." "As researchers," Chasnoff claims, "we have no idea what impact these issues can have on pregnancy and neonatal outcome" (287). Ira J. Chasnoff, "Commentary: Missing Pieces of the Puzzle," *Neurotoxicology and Teratology* 15.5 (1993): 287–88.

60 Adam Gelb, "State's Newborns to Get Cocaine Tests," *Atlanta Journal Constitution* 12 Mar. 1991: A1. To date there have been no follow-up reports. Funding for the study came largely from the March of Dimes.

61 This corresponds with Robyn Rowland's assertion that language, specifically "reprospeak," powerfully shapes the attitudes of a society. See her chapter " 'Reprospeak': The Language of the New Reproductive Technologies," *Living Laboratories: Women and Reproductive Technologies* (Bloomington: Indiana UP, 1992) 230–45.

62 Nancy L. Daly and Gale A. Richardson, "Cocaine Use and Crack Babies: Science, the Media, and Miscommunication," *Neurotoxicology and Teratology* 15.5 (1993): 293–94.

63 P. A. Stephenson and M. G. Wagner, "Reproductive Rights and the Medical Care System: A Plea for Rational Health Policy," *Journal of Public Health Policy* (Summer 1993): 174–82. Quotation is from page 176. Stephenson and Wagner cite the following article in their summary of the position of fetal rights advocates: M. A. Field, "Controlling the Woman to Protect the Fetus," *Law Medical Health Care* 17 (1989): 114–29.

64 Dorothy E. Roberts, "Drug-Addicted Women Who Have Babies," *Trial* April 1990: 56–61. Quotation is from page 58.

65 The case reference is *People v. Stewart,* no. M508097 California, San Diego Mun. Ct. 23 Feb. 1987, slip op. Cited in Dorothy E. Roberts, "Drug-Addicted Women Who Have Babies."

66 The quotation is from William Fraser, associate professor of obstetrics and gynaecol-

ogy, Laval University and Hospital St-Francois d'Assise, Quebec, in his article "Methodological Issues in Assessing the Active Management of Labor," *Birth* 20.3 (Sept. 1993): 155–56. Fraser's article was part of a roundtable discussion of the benefits and risks of the active management of labor. Other articles, all published in the same issue of *Birth*, included the following: Karyn J. Kaufman, "Effective Control or Effective Care?", 156–58; Barbara Katz Rothman, "The Active Management of Physicians," 158–59; and Marc J. N. C. Keirse, "A Final Comment . . . Managing the Uterus, the Woman, or Whom?" 159–61.

67   The recommendation is from the 1989 Report of the Public Health Service Expert Panel on the Content of Prenatal Care, "Caring for Our Future: The Content of Prenatal Care," discussed in Shannon Cook et al.

68   This work is in addition to other passive national surveillance systems set up to monitor cases of menstrual illnesses and the reproductive health effects on women due to occupational and workplace exposures. *Priorities for Women's Health: A Report from the Centers for Disease Control and Prevention* (Published by the CDC and the U.S. Department of Health and Human Services, Public Health Service, Spring 1993). For a history of the CDC and its role in the development of a practical science of epidemiology, see Elizabeth M. Etheridge, *Sentinel for Health: A History of the Centers for Disease Control* (Berkeley: U of California P, 1992).

69   "The Yellow Wallpaper," in *The Charlotte Perkins Gilman Reader: "The Yellow Wallpaper" and Other Fiction,* ed. Ann J. Lane (New York: Pantheon Books, 1980) 3–20.

70   Elaine Kendall, rev. of *The Handmaid's Tale, Los Angeles Times Book Review* 9 Feb. 1986: 15.

71   See Anne Balsamo, "Rethinking Ethnography: A Work of the Feminist Imagination," *Studies in Symbolic Interactionism* 11 (1990): 75–86.

72   Amin Malak situates the novel within a broader dystopian tradition in his article "Margaret Atwood's *The Handmaid's Tale* and the Dystopia Tradition," *Canadian Literature* 112 (Spring 1987): 9–16. David Ketterer calls it a "contextual dystopia" in his article "Margaret Atwood's *The Handmaid's Tale*: A Contextual Dystopia," *Science-Fiction Studies* 16 (1989): 209–17. Harriet F. Bergmann also classifies it as a dystopian novel in her article " 'Teaching them to Read': A Fishing Expedition in *The Handmaid's Tale,*" *College English,* 51.8 (1989): 847–54. Patrick D. Murphy explores its dystopic genre characteristics in his article "Reducing the Dystopian Distance: Pseudo-documentary Framing in Near-Future Fiction," *Science-Fiction Studies* 17 (1990): 25–39.

5. The Virtual Body in Cyberspace

1   Mike Godwin, staff counsel for the Electronic Frontier Foundation (EFF), describes the EFF in his article "The Electronic Frontier Foundation and Virtual Communities," *Whole Earth Review* (Summer 1991): 40–42. In many ways participants in the EFF are working to ensure the democratic application of electronic networking, so although they participate in the same postmodern schizo-subculture I describe in this chapter, their objectives resonate with the liberatory rhetoric of a 1960s counterculture.

2   John Perry Barlow, "Crime and Puzzlement: In Advance of the Law on the Electronic Frontier," *Whole Earth Review* (Fall 1990): 44–57. Quotation is from page 45.

3   Here I'm describing elements of Internet, "a vast network of networks that interconnect thousands of computing sites in government, industry, and academia. The Internet has evolved from primarily providing electronic mail services to become the infrastructure for significantly broader services of information exchange and collaborative work. Like CompuServe, the heart of the Internet is a vast collection of newsgroups in which participants from around the world post and comment on messages" (46). Pamela Samuelson and Robert J. Glushko, "Intellectual Property Rights for Digital Library and Hypertext Publishing Systems: An Analysis of Xanadu," *Hypertext '91 Proceedings* Dec. 1991: 39–50.

4   The term "virtual reality" has come under fire from some computer scientists who think that the term, like "artificial intelligence," names an impossible project; they offer the term "virtual worlds" as an alternative name for the space of virtuality. Brenda Laurel suggests the term "telepresence," to connote a medium rather than a place. Brenda Laurel, *Computers as Theatre* (Reading, Mass.: Addison Wesley, 1991).

5   The subculture of virtual reality was small enough in 1989–90 that the editors of a book titled *Virtual Reality: Theory, Practice, and Promise* (a reprint of the Summer 1990 issue of *Multimedia Review*) could include a directory of companies and individuals interested in VR. The list contained 63 entries. Sandra K. Helsel and Judith Paris Roth, eds. *Virtual Reality: Theory, Practice, and Promise* (Westport, Conn.: Meckler, 1991).

6   William Gibson, *Neuromancer* (New York: Ace Science Fiction, 1984). Although William Gibson is widely credited with introducing cyberspace to a mass audience and spawning a new subgenre of science fiction called cyberpunk, he is only one of the cyberthinkers at work on the new frontier of reality science. Some scholars claim that Vernor Vinge was the first to introduce the notion of an alternative, electronically mediated plane in his novella *True Names* (New York: Dell, 1981). (See Michael B. Spring, "Informating with Virtual Reality," Helsel and Roth, *Virtual Reality* 3–17.) However, I also am reminded of the empathy box in Philip K. Dick's novel *Do Androids Dream Of Electric Sheep?* (New York: Doubleday, 1968) as an earlier forerunner.

7   Gibson utilizes a wide range of technological metaphors and computer slang to describe data banks, net running, and the various practices associated with computer hacking. His description of the history of cyberspace has been quoted often:

> "The matrix has its roots in primitive arcade games," said the voice-over, "in early graphics programs and military experimentation with cranial jacks." ... "Cyberspace. A consensual hallucination experienced daily by billions of legitimate operators, in every nation, by children being taught mathematical concepts ... A graphic representation of data abstracted from the banks of every computer in the human system. Unthinkable complexity. Lines of light ranged in the nonspace of the mind, clusters and constellations of data. Like city lights, receding. ..."

Gibson, *Neuromancer* 51.

8   Lanier is the source of many of the prophetic statements about the potential of virtual reality. See, for example, Kevin Kelly, "An Interview with Jaron Lanier: Virtual Reality," *Whole Earth Review* Fall 1989: 119; Steven Levy, "Brave New World," *Rolling Stone* 14 June 1990: 92–100; John Perry Barlow, "Life in the DataCloud: Scratching your Eyes Back In" (interview with Jaron Lanier), *Mondo 2000* 2 (Summer 1990): 44–51.

9   There are several cultural critics — notably Arthur Kroker and Jean Baudrillard — who, either explicitly or implicitly, have continued to produce McLuhanesque criticism.

However, none of them has spawned an entire subculture, although Kroker's "panic postmodernism" comes close. See especially the chapter titled "The Mechanical Bride" in Marshall McLuhan, *The Mechanical Bride. Folklore of Industrial Man* (Boston: Beacon, 1951).

10 This list of topics refers to the following articles from *Mondo 2000* 4: "Winnelife: An Interview with Steve Roberts" by Gareth Branwyn, 32–35; "Durk and Sandy: Read This or Die" (on antioxidants), 42–44; "Avital Ronell on Hallucinogenres," interview by Gary Wolf, 63–69; "Antic Women" (an announcement about a new *ReSearch* issue by Avital Ronell, Kathy Acker, and Andrea Juno), 71; "Freaks of the Industry: An Interview with the Digital Underground," by Rickey Vincent, 88–92; "The Carpal Tunnel of Love, Virtual Sex with Mike Saenz," interview by Jeff Milstead and Jude Milhon, 142–45. This issue also features a conversation between William S. Burroughs and Timothy Leary and an article on Jim Morrison on the occasion of Oliver Stone's film *The Doors* ("Orpheus in the Maelstrom," by Queen Mu, 129–34).

11 The article is actually a review for a Dance Theater Workshop video screening project, "Cyberspatial Intersections," curated by Shalom Gorewitz, 21–23 Mar. 1991. As the press release describes, the series included video presentations about VPL products, special effects by Hollywood F/X companies, as well as computerized graphic art. Erik Davis, "Virtual Video," *Village Voice* 26 Mar. 1991: 41–42.

12 Although as recently as 1980 cultural critics were explaining why art and technology were constructed as mutually exclusive domains, the engagement with art and visual artists has been part of the virtual reality industry from the very beginning. The ties to art and entertainment are the signal issues at meetings of ACM–SIGGRAPH (Association for Computing Machinery–Special Interest Group on Computer Graphics) and important early work on the interdisciplinary potential of VR as an artistic medium shows up in SIGGRAPH conference proceedings of 1989. The connections between VR and artistic expression are a persistent subtheme even in less spectacular conferences that focus on more serious issues related to the technological development of the machine-human interface. For example, a research conference called "Virtual Worlds: Real Challenges," included sessions on applications for art and entertainment in addition to sessions on systems architecture, teleoperations, and biomedical applications. This conference, held 17–18 June 1991, was cosponsored by SRI International, the David Sarnoff Research Center, and VPL Research, Inc. (the company founded by Jaron Lanier in 1985). SRI and the David Sarnoff Research Center are electronic research organizations. Other events — such as "Art and Virtual Environments," a public symposium held as part of the Banff Center for the Arts' new project on virtual technologies as artistic media; the First and Second Artificial Life conferences, a Penn State symposium on computer learning; and special sessions of the Human Factors Society — have also taken up the issues of virtual reality and rely on VR "stars" such as Timothy Leary, Eric Gullichsen (president of Sense8), and researchers from the MIT Media Lab to draw crowds. Jack Burnham reviews the history of the art/technology schism as it has been constituted in the twentieth century in "Art and Technology: The Panacea that Failed," *The Myths of Information: Technology and Postindustrial Culture* ed. Kathleen Woodward (Madison, Wis.: Coda, 1980) 200–15.

13 Richard Kadrey is one of the regular reporters on the cyberspace beat, along with Howard Rheingold, Kevin Kelly for WER, Steve Diltea of *Omni,* and Randall Walser of

Autodesk. Kadrey is quoted in "Cyberthon No. 1: Virtual Reality Fair in San Francisco," *Whole Earth Review* Winter 1990: 145.

14   The irony has not been lost on the popular press; the page 1 headline in the *New York Times* announced " 'Virtual Reality' Takes its Place in the Real World." In addition to regular reports in the *Whole Earth Review, Omni* magazine, and *Mondo 2000,* other popular press articles include: Erik Davis, "Virtual Video," *The Village Voice* 26 Mar. 1991: 41; Philip Elmer-Dewitt, "Through the 3-D Looking Glass, *Time* 1 May 1989: 65–66; "(Mis)Adventures in Cyberspace," *Time* 3 Sept. 1990: 74–76; Trish Hall, " 'Virtual Reality' Takes Its Place in the Real," *New York Times* 8 July 1990, sec. 1: 1, 14; Jim Harwood, "Agog in Goggles: Shape of Things to Come Reshaping Hollywood's Future," *Variety* (56th anniversary issue) 1989: 66; Steven Levy, "Brave New World," *Rolling Stone* June 1990: 92–98; A. J. S. Rayl, "The New, Improved Reality," *Los Angeles Times Magazine* 21 July 1991: 17–20+; Sallie Tisdale, "It's Been Real," *Esquire* April 1991: 36; G. Pascal Zachary, "Artificial Reality: Computer Simulations One Day May Provide Surreal Experiences," *Wall Street Journal* 23 Jan. 1990, sec. 1: 1; Gene Bylinsky, "The Marvels of 'Virtual Reality,' " *Fortune* 3 June 1991: 138–43; D'arcy Jenish, "Re-creating Reality," *Macleans* 4 June 1990: 56–58; Peter Lewis, "Put on Your Data Glove and Goggles and Step Inside," *New York Times* 20 May 1990: 8; Douglas Martin, "Virtual Reality! Hallucination! Age of Aquarius! Leary's Back! *New York Times* 2 Mar. 1991: 11; Edward Rothstein, "Just Some Games? Yes, But These Are Too Real," *New York Times* 4 Apr. 1991: B4; Richard Scheinin, "The Artificial Realist," *San Jose Mercury News* 29 Jan. 1990: 1–2; Julian Dibbell, "Virtual Kool-Aid Acid Test," *Spin* 4 Mar. 1991.

15   David L. Wheeler, "Computer-Created World of 'Virtual Reality' Opening New Vistas to Scientists," *Chronicle of Higher Education* 37.26 (13 Mar. 1991): A6.

16   One of the earliest references cited in a 24-page bibliography on VR is the *Proceedings of a Symposium on Large-Scale Calculating Machinery* (Jan. 1947), reprinted in The Charles Babbage Institute Reprint Series for the History of Computing, Vol. 7 (Cambridge: MIT P, 1985). Norbert Wiener is known in some circles as "the father of cybernetics." Norbert Wiener, *Cybernetics or Control and Communication in the Animal and Machine,* New York: Technological Press, 1948; and *The Human Use of Human Beings: Cybernetics and Society* (New York: Doubleday, 1950).

17   Myron W. Krueger, "Artificial Reality: Past and Future," Helsel and Roth, *Virtual Reality* 19–25; quotation is from page 22. Krueger suggests that work by Ivan Sutherland in the early 1960s influenced his own work on artificial reality, which began in the late 1960s and developed throughout the 1970s; Krueger's book *Artificial Reality* wasn't published until the mid-1980s, though (Menlo Park, Calif.: Addison-Wesley, 1983). From other sources we learn that Sutherland's PhD thesis, titled *Sketchpad: A Man-Machine Graphical Communication System,* is dated 1963; other articles published by Sutherland in the mid-1960s were on the topic of a head-mounted, 3-D display. In 1974, working with Robert Burton, he published work on a 3-D computer input device. Ivan Sutherland, "The Ultimate Display," *Proceedings IFIP Congress* (1965): 506–08; Ivan Sutherland, "A Head-Mounted Three-Dimensional Display," *Fall Joint Computer Conference* 33 (1968): 757–64; Robert P. Burton and Ivan E. Sutherland, "Twinkle Box: A Three-Dimensional Computer Input Device, *Proceedings of the National Computer Conference* (1974): 513–20.

18   Although VPL had already developed the dataglove technology, it encountered difficulty finding a production source, so it licensed a version of the dataglove to Mattel Inc.,
which produced the "PowerGlove" for use with Nintendo video games. The other
examples listed are culled from industry product literature (VPL, Cyberware, Sense8,
Autodesk) and *Virtual World News,* the VPL newsletter.

19   Randal Walser, "Elements of a Cyberspace Playhouse," Helsel and Roth, *Virtual Reality* 51–64. Quotation is from page 59. The contributor notes to the Helsel and Roth
book state that Walser, manager of the Autodesk Cyberspace Project, has been interested in cyberspace for over 18 years as he has worked in many areas of artificial
intelligence.

20   From an article by A. J. S. Rayl, "Making Fun," *Omni* Nov. 1990: 42–48. Since 1990
several VR arcades featuring games such as "Dactyl Nightmare" and "Dactyl Nightmare II" have opened in malls across the United States. In Chicago there is a VR arcade
entirely devoted to the BattleTech game that includes eighteen game "pods." Atlanta
has "Dave and Busters" — an adult arcade and restaurant with VR games rigs, virtual
golf, skee ball, and assorted pinball and blackjack tables. In Albuquerque, Blockbuster
just opened its version of an adult arcade, called "Block Party," that includes not only
VR games ("Dactyl Nightmare II" and "Virtu Alley") but also interactive videos such
as "Go Motion Pictures" (moving seat films) and a new entertainment installation
called "The PowerGrid" (described in *Wired* magazine as a techno habitrail for adults).
"Romper Room for Grown-Ups," *Wired* June 1995: 43.

21   Jack Zipes, "The Instrumentalization of Fantasy: Fairy Tales and the Mass Media," *The
Myths of Information: Technology and Postindustrial Culture* ed. Kathleen Woodward
(Madison, WI: Coda, 1980) 88–110. Quotation is from page 101.

22   Sandra K. Helsel and Judith Paris Roth raise similar questions in their introduction to
their book *Virtual Reality: Theory, Practice, and Promise.* They pose no answers and, in
fact, comment on the lack of attention in their collection of articles to the issue of
perspective or viewpoint: "Many feminist historians assert that written history is history according to white males. How will any individual or group carefully and sen-
sitively, with a deep appreciation for cultural, racial, religious and gender bias, create
virtual reality systems?" They go on to ask, "Will virtual reality systems be used as a
means of breaking down cultural, racial, and gender barriers between individuals and
thus foster 'human values'? Will virtual reality systems be multicultural in nature or will
they only offer Western ways of assimilating knowledge? Will virtual realities systems
serve as supplements to our lives, enriching us, or will individuals so miserable in their
daily existences find an obsessive refuge in a preferred cyberspace?" (ix–x). Good
questions every one.

23   Andrew Ross, "Hacking Away at the Counterculture," *Technoculture,* ed. Constance
Penley and Andrew Ross (Minneapolis: U of Minnesota P, 1991) 107–34. Quotation is
from page 126. Ross examines the ways that the hacker subculture has been interpreted
by cultural critics. His intention is to complicate those interpretations in such a way as
to resist the totalizing picture of new information technologies that would disallow its
more liberatory use. He reminds readers that the meaning of any technology is constructed through a struggle among competing systems of understanding — those determined by broader social and institutional forces as well as those produced through
individual subjective encounters. In the end, he argues that while we need to maintain a

healthy "technoskepticism," we must also understand that "technology must be seen as a lived, interpretive practice for people in their everyday lives" (131–32). Cultural critics are encouraged to develop a hacker-like knowledge about contemporary culture: "to make our knowledge about technoculture into something like a hacker's knowledge . . . capable of . . . rewriting the cultural programs and reprogramming the social values that make room for new technologies . . . capable also of generating new popular romances around the alternative use of human ingenuity" (132).

24 This quotation is from Randal Walser, reported in an article by Therese R. Welter, "The Artificial Tourist: Virtual Reality Promises New Worlds for Industry," *Industry Week* 1 Oct. 1990: 66. Using VR as an architectural tool to design and then interact with spaces before they are built is one of its more immediately practical applications. Another cyberspace environment, called "Traumabase," uses three-dimensional computer graphics to access information collected during the Vietnam War, ostensibly to "show the realities of war in text, pictures, films, and sounds" (70). In this case, the information database is organized by "creating a computer graphic construct . . . representing contained information along important dimensions: location and severity of wounds, wound pattern clustering, wound pattern frequencies, survival patterns" (71). Joseph Henderson, "Designing Realities: Interactive Media, Virtual Realities, and Cyberspace," Helsel and Roth, *Virtual Reality* 65–73.

25 Eric Gullichsen, the president of a small software company called *Sense8*, allowed me to try out his bio-apparatus and VR program. The head-mounted apparatus was rather primitive, held together by fishing clips and duct tape; and the software, called World-Tools, was a bit underwhelming. But that was as much due to the fact that WorldTools is a program for other programmers that enables them to create their own virtual realities as it was due in part to the fact that VR technology is still in its infancy. Prospective clients for such programs include art gallery directors, interior decorators, architects, and engineers.

26 According to Jean Baudrillard, a cultural shift has already taken place when the relationship between the "real" and the image is transformed from a relation of reflection to a relation of simulation; the current phase of the image "bears no relation to any reality whatever: it is its own simulacrum" (11). Baudrillard's cultural criticism is evocative and his elaboration of the logic of the simulacrum helps make sense of U.S. media culture, but he remains within a logic of the image and the disembodied, which is not, in my opinion, a viable starting point for a feminist analysis of the cultural impact of VR technology. Jean Baudrillard, *Simulations* (New York: Semiotext(e), 1983).

27 Richard Bolton elaborates modernism as an epistemological position that includes "a faith in rationalism, the rise of science and technology and the growth of capitalism" (35). He goes on to discuss the problems associated with the "ocular metaphors that inform modernist science, epistemology, and art," which leads him to argue that "our understanding of the world is limited by the 'spectator theory of knowledge' . . . inherited from rationalism" (35). His point is to describe how postmodernism offers an alternative epistemological framework. Richard Bolton, "The Modern Spectator and the Postmodern Participant," *Photo Communique* Summer 1986: 34–45.

28 David Sudnow has provided the beginning description of such a phenomenology, although his trip through the microworld was confined to the two-dimensional space of a Pong game. David Sudnow, *Pilgrim in the Microworld* (New York: Warner, 1983).

29 Spring poses several questions about the mechanics of thinking, what he calls "the process of informating," and how it is related to visual metaphors and models; one of his questions is "How can the interconnectedness of ideas be visualized?" (14). See also Randal Walser, "Elements of a Cybernetic Playhouse."

30 For example, Michael Spring has defined language as "an abstraction of reality with words and symbols representing various information loadings to the receiver" (11–12). Spring, "Informating with Virtual Reality." In his essay "Artificial Reality: Past and Future," Krueger argues that the future of artificial reality must include communication because "it is possible to capture everything that passes between two people in ways never before possible" (24).

31 Randal Walser, "Elements of a Cyberspace Playhouse," 51.

32 The 24 Feb. 1990 Doonesbury strip by Gary Trudeau offered a frame-by-frame depiction of the bomb's-eye view of a bomb traveling into a chemical weapons facility "past startled Iraqi production managers and into the office of the facility administrator." The next frame indicates an explosion, while the narrator (a general in the next frame) states: "Unfortunately, it continues through an open window and explodes in a nearby parking lot." Earnest Larsen considers the implications of what we didn't see during the television coverage of the Gulf War. Ernest Larsen, "Gulf War TV," *Jump Cut* 36 (1991): 3–10.

33 Tisdale, "It's Been Real" 3.

34 Scott S. Fisher, "Virtual Environments: Personal Simulations and Telepresence," Helsel and Roth 101–10; quotation is from page 109.

35 Fred Pfeil, *Another Tale to Tell: Politics and Narrative in Postmodern Culture* (London: Verso, 1990) 88.

36 Outside of cyberspace, in an alternative universe, or some future postapocalyptic earth, heterosexual connections dominate the sexual scene. Consider two short stories in *Mirrorshades: The Cyberpunk Anthology*, edited by Bruce Sterling. In Marc Laidlaw's short story "400 Boys," the gangs in Fun City, which include a gang of girls called the "Galrogs," unite together to fight off a new gang, the "400 Boys," for control of the city. Rice, the main character in Bruce Sterling and Lewis Shiner's short story "Mozart in Mirrorshades," becomes fascinated with Marie Antoinette: She "sprawled across the bed's expanse of pink satin, wearing a scrap of black-lace underwear and leafing through an issue of *Vogue*. . . . 'I want the leather bikini,' she said. . . . Rice leaned back across her solid thighs and patted her bottom reassuringly" (231). Bruce Sterling, ed. *Mirrorshades: The Cyberpunk Anthology* (New York: Ace, 1986).

37 In their introduction, titled "Strange Attractor(s)," Rucker and Wilson describe contributions from three categories of writers: (1) "luminaries of the old New Wave: J. G. Ballard, Sol Yurick, and William Burroughs" (2) the loosely defined school of young writers sometimes called "cyberpunks" and (3) writers from the "underground world of xerox microzines and American samzidat: writers so radically marginalized they could never be co-opted, recuperated, reified, or bought out by the establishment" (13). Rudy Rucker and Peter Lamborn Wilson, eds., *Semiotext(e) SF* 5.2 (1989).

38 Andrew Ross, "Cyberpunk in Boystown," *Strange Weather: Culture, Science and Technology in the Age of Limits* (London: Verso, 1991).

39 Sherry Turkle and Seymour Papert argue that computer technologies may promote the development of epistemological pluralism. The most optimistic prophesy about virtual

reality technologies would be consistent with their argument. But they go on to remind readers that the computer culture may inhibit the realization of such possibilities. Sherry Turkle and Seymour Papert, "Epistemological Pluralism: Styles and Voices within the Computer Culture," *SIGNS* 16.1 (Autumn 1990): 128–57.

40   Using new imaging devices such as magnetic resonance imaging (MRI), scientists and physicians are able to look inside the brain to extract information about brain activity. Jon Van, "Understanding the Body through Imaging," *Chicago Tribune* 2 Aug. 1987: sec. 2, 1.

Positron emission tomography (PET) is another new imaging procedure that uses radioactive tracers to measure metabolic function as the brain "processes" information. Several scientists claim that the new imaging technologies will refine psychiatric diagnosis, so that trying to figure out what is "wrong" with someone won't be such a matter of guesswork anymore. As Dr. Floyd E. Bloom, chief of the Division of Preclinical Neuroscience and Endocrinology at the Research Institute of Scripps Clinic in LaJolla, explains, "We'll be able to be very precise, mechanical and quantitative about the differences between our brains at different times and between other brains under similar conditions. That kind of information will be totally useful in predicting what's wrong in mental illness." Ronald Kotulak, "Mind Readers: The Wondrous Machines That Let Scientists Watch Us Think," *Chicago Tribune* 9 May 1988: sec. 2, 2.

Magnetoencephalography (MEG) is a computer-based technology for looking inside the brain to determine whether thoughts are being generated. One recent article ("A Look Inside the Mysterious Brain") suggests that MEG and other new imaging techniques "are wonderful because they essentially turn the brain to glass so we can look inside and see what's going on. . . . This unprecedented view is expected to lead to methods for diagnosing mental disorders, predicting behavior and personality, evaluating mental capacities and basically determining when a brain is working well and when it is not." This would be an obvious benefit in treating coma patients, for example, but it has ominous overtones with respect to body privacy. Ronald Kotulak, "A Look Inside the Mysterious Brain," *Chicago Tribune* 8 May 1988: sec. 1, 1, 12. See also two other articles by Ronald Kotulak, all in the *Chicago Tribune*: "Down Memory Lane: The Ability to Learn Is Mankind's Greatest Possession," 8 May 1988: sec. 2, 1, 3; "Mind Readers," 9 May 1988: sec. 2, 1–2.

To peer inside the brain to see what areas light up when a person thinks about a hamburger may be an oblique way to "diagnose" obesity, but it also is a way to monitor subjective thoughts. Researchers working on brain-scanning devices unabashedly claim to want to find a way to "reveal people's inner thoughts as well as their innate mental talents" — a capability the military is interested in for selecting tank drivers and fighter pilots (Kotulak, "A Look Inside the Mysterious Brain," 1). In a study of Alzheimer's disease, electroencephalogram scans from Alzheimer's patients are compared to "healthy" people's brain scans and are found to have fewer alpha-range waves and more delta waves; however, the process whereby someone is diagnosed as "healthy" is rarely discussed in any of the popular media reports on brain imaging. Kathleen Doheny, "Alzheimer's Disease: Science Struggles to Ease the Nightmare," *Los Angeles Times* 5 June 1989: sec. 2, 7; and Jon Van, "New Image Scan's Value Is Unproven, AMA Says," *Chicago Tribune* 10 June 1988: sec. 2, 3.

These new technologies raise serious ethical questions tied not so much to the possibilities of treating "disease" or "mental disorders" but to the possibilities of using the very same technology to pigeonhole people according to brain activity profiles.

6. Feminism for the Incurably Informed

1 In her historical study of the gendering of the automobile, Virginia Scharff reports that the first woman in the United States to get a driver's license was Mrs. John Howell Phillips of Chicago in 1899, which suggests that women have been involved with the automobile (a "high-technology" at one point) from the beginning of its history. See Virginia Scharff, *Taking the Wheel: Women and the Coming of the Motor Age* (New York: Free, 1991) 25.

2 Jumping 30 years in this abbreviated history leaves several threads hanging. From World War I to the end of World War II, Chicago was the scene of several significant industrial and cultural transformations. Like thousands of other new immigrants, one set of my grandparents immigrated from southern Italy, the other set from Lithuania. Each family settled in an ethnically identified Chicago neighborhood and began working for one of several large corporate employers already dominating Chicago politics and economics: Grandfather Balsamo at International Harvester; Grandmother Martins at Hart, Schaffner and Marx; and Uncle Barnes at the Swift stockyards. As labor historian Lisabeth Cohen surmises: "The typical industrial worker in Chicago around 1920 needed little prior training before securing a job in one of Chicago's mass production industries. Ability to endure long hours in tough conditions was the only requirement for most of the jobs the city had to offer" (3). Cohen's book *Making a New Deal* investigates the social, cultural, and economic history of Chicago's working class between the wars; her objective is to "take a close look at the multiple ways that the lives of working-class people changed between 1919 and 1939." She criticizes what she sees in other historical studies of the twentieth century as a tendency to "erect . . . artificial barriers between people's experiences at work, in the community, and with politics; between different ethnic and racial groups; and between decades such as the twenties and thirties" (6). Her intent is to study the way that people's lives cross boundaries. In her own words, her "study address[es] itself to how people recombined their multiple identities in ways that led them to undertake new kinds of collective action, how, for example, workers' self-images as ethnic and working class became more compatible as a result of the upheavals of the Great Depression" (6–7). Cohen's project enacts a cyborgian logic to investigate a historical pattern of recombinant social identity, where we can read how mass culture played a significant role in the unification of previously disparate groups. See Lisabeth Cohen, *Making a New Deal: Industrial Workers in Chicago, 1919–1939* (Cambridge: Cambridge UP, 1990).

3 According to Sharon Hartman Strom, "the comptometer, developed by Felt and Tarrant in Chicago was often more popular than the calculator because it was key-driven, lightweight, and inexpensive. . . . Its chief drawback was that it was non-listing; that is, there was no printed tape which showed each item entered, only a window in which a running total appeared" (70). Sharon Hartman Strom, " 'Machines Instead of Clerks': Technology and the Feminization of Bookkeeping, 1910–1950," *Computer Chips and Paper Clips: Technology and Women's Employment,* Vol. 2: *Case Studies and Policy Perspectives,* ed. Heidi I. Hartmann (Washington, DC: National Academy P, 1987) 63–97.

4   Rose Balsamo was one of the 800 troops assigned to the (HHC) Fourth Aviation
    Brigade; she was assistant to the NCO in charge of medical support for the other U.S.
    troops and for Kurdistani refugees. She and her staff treated them for dysentery, chol-
    era, dehydration, and malnutrition. She has no idea how many Kurdistanis they treated
    because there was a constant "revolving door" of patients during the six months she
    was stationed there. The Fourth Brigade left by October 1991, although another force
    (members of the Eighth Brigade) remained behind for police and humanitarian support.
    For her service she received the following decorations: a Distinguished Unit Citation,
    Humanitarian Service Ribbon, the 3rd Infantry Division Combat Patch, and the South-
    west Asia campaign ribbon. But there were no "yellow ribbon" parades welcoming her
    and fellow soldiers back to West Germany or to the U.S., where she eventually returned.
    Even while they were there, nothing was ever mentioned in the media about the fact that
    this humanitarian effort was being conducted in the midst of a declared combat zone;
    there were a number of fly-by bombings and two perimeter alerts when troops were
    ordered to don full combat gear to defend camp. She was one of many troops (mostly
    medical personnel) dispatched to "clean up" the aftereffects of the Gulf War. What she
    encountered were the human casualties of war—a consequence hidden from sight
    during most of the media coverage of the spectacular technological display of smart
    bombs and SCUD missiles.

5   The "New Edge" is one of the most recent labels for a particular arrangement within
    contemporary culture. James Beniger constructs an exhaustive list of the ways that
    "modern social transformations [have been] identified since 1950," that is, as the "end
    of ideology" (Bell) or as the "technological society" (Ellul). James R. Beniger, *The
    Control Revolution: Technological and Economic Origins of the Information Society*
    (Cambridge: Harvard UP, 1986) 485. Beniger references are to Daniel Bell, *The Coming
    of Postindustrial Society* (New York: Basic, 1973) and to Jacques Ellul, *The Technologi-
    cal Society*, trans. John Wilkinson (New York: Knopf, 1964).
        My interest is in the cultural analyses of the historical conjuncture among forms of
    cultural expression, modes of social organization, and the materiality of the technologi-
    cal infrastructure of the U.S. In addition to the sources above, see: Norbert Wiener, *The
    Human Use of Human Beings: Cybernetics and Society* (New York: Anchor, 1954);
    Marshall McLuhan, *Understanding Media* (New York: Basic, 1964); Amitai Etzioni,
    The Active Society (New York: Free, 1968); Raymond Williams, *Television: Technol-
    ogy and Cultural Form* (New York: Schocken, 1974); J. David Bolter, *Turing's Man:
    Western Culture in the Computer Age* (Chapel Hill: U of North Carolina P, 1980);
    Yoneji Masuda, *The Information Society as Post-Industrial Society* (Washington, D.C.:
    World Future Society, 1981); Ithiel de Sola Pool, *Technologies of Freedom: On Free
    Speech in an Electronic Age* (Cambridge: Harvard UP, 1983); Gilles Deleuze and Felix
    Guattari, *Anti-Oedipus: Capitalism and Schizophrenia* (Minneapolis: U of Minnesota
    P, 1983); Paul Virilio and Sylvere Lotringer, *Pure War* (New York: Semiotext(e), 1983);
    Jean Baudrillard, *Simulations* (New York: Semiotext(e), 1983); Jean-François Lyotard,
    The Postmodern Condition: A Report on Knowledge, trans. Geoff Bennington and
    Brian Massumi (Minneapolis: U of Minnesota P, 1984); Sol Yurick, *Behold Metatron,
    The Recording Angel* (New York: Semiotext(e), 1985); Hakim Bey, *The Temporary
    Autonomous Zone, Ontological Anarchy, Poetic Terrorism* (New York: Autonomedia,
    1985); Arthur Kroker and David Cook, *The Postmodern Scene* (New York: St. Mar-

tin's, 1986); Andreas Huyssen, *After the Great Divide: Modernism, Mass Culture, Postmodernism* (Bloomington: Indiana UP, 1986); Jennifer Daryl Slack and Fred Fejes, eds., *The Ideology of the Information Age* (Norwood, N.J.: Ablex, 1987); Tom Forrester, *High-Tech Society: The Story of the Information Technology Revolution* (Boston: MIT P, 1987); Shoshana Zuboff, *In the Age of the Smart Machine: The Future of Work and Power* (New York: Basic, 1988); Jerry L. Salvaggio and Jennings Bryant, eds., *Media Use in the Information Age: Emerging Patterns of Adoption and Consumer Use* (Hillside, NJ: Lawrence Erlbaum, 1989); Marshall McLuhan and Bruce R. Powers, *The Global Village: Transformations in World Life and Media in the 21st Century* (New York: Oxford UP, 1989); Raymond Kurzweil, *In the Age of Intelligent Machines*, (Cambridge: MIT P, 1990); Mark Poster, *The Mode of Information: Poststructuralism and Social Context* (Chicago: U of Chicago P, 1990); Mike Featherstone, *Consumer Culture and Postmodernism* (London: Sage, 1991); Paul Virilio, *Lost Dimension* (New York: Semiotext(e), 1991); Fredric Jameson, *Postmodernism, or, The Cultural Logic of Late Capitalism* (Durham, NC: Duke UP, 1991); Andrew Ross, *Strange Weather: Culture, Science, and Technology in the Age of Limits* (London: Verso, 1991); Celeste Olalquiaga, *Megalopolis: Contemporary Cultural Sensibilities* (Minneapolis: U of Minnesota P, 1992).

6   Pat Cadigan, *Synners* (New York: Bantam, 1991) 3. Cadigan's first novel, *Mindplayers* (New York: Bantam, 1989), and most recent one, *Fools* (New York: Bantam, 1992) also belong to the genre of cyberpunk science fiction. *Fools* is much more experimental in its narrative construction, in a way similar to Joanna Russ's *The Female Man,* where the identity of the narrative "I" is fluid and fragmented.

7   Teresa de Lauretis writes: "Hence SF as a mode of writing and reading, as a textual and contextual production of signs and meanings, inscribes our cognitive and creative processes in what may be called the technological imagination. In tracing cognitive paths through the physical and material reality of the contemporary technological landscape and designing new maps of social reality, SF is perhaps the most innovative fictional mode of our historical creativity." Teresa de Lauretis, "Signs of Wa/onder," *The Technological Imagination: Theories and Fictions,* ed. Teresa de Lauretis, Andreas Huyssen, and Kathleen Woodward (Madison, Wis.: Coda P, 1980) 169.

8   In describing the structural definition of a cultural formation, Lawrence Grossberg states that a "formation is a historical articulation, an accumulation or organization of practices. The question is how particular cultural practices, which may have no intrinsic or even apparent connection, are articulated together to construct an apparently new identity. . . . It is not a question of interpreting a body of texts or tracing out their intertextuality. Rather the formation has to be read as the articulation of a number of discrete series of events, only some of which are discursive." Lawrence Grossberg, *We Gotta Get Out of This Place* (New York: Routledge, 1992) 70.

9   If we broaden the dimensions of a discursive formation such that it includes the way in which readers read the work and discuss it, reproduce it, and detourn it, then the possibility of producing Archimedian criticism of any form of popular fiction is all the more improbable. In this way, cyberpunk illustrates one of the key issues at the heart of our information-obsessed culture. As Darko Suvin argues, "an encompassingly extensive survey of cyberpunk sf looks . . . not only materially impossible but also method-

ologically dubious" (41). Darko Suvin, "On Gibson and Cyberpunk SF," *Foundation* 46 (1989): 40–51.

It has become increasingly difficult to claim any sort of mastery vis-à-vis a discursive dispersion or a properly historical genealogy because of the rate of publication and the shelf life of science fiction publications. Not only is it very difficult to keep track of all the writers of a particular style, it is equally difficult to keep track of a single author's output. Few libraries archive pulp science-fiction novels; even fewer catalog the early science-fiction magazines or any of the numerous fanzines that have appeared in the past decade. As with the situation for small press literature and poetry, the economics and politics of publishing and library archiving have more to do with the evaluation of the work in question than with any metaliterary notions of "value," "unity," or "genre." The field exists as an unpatterned dispersion — like the Internet, it is impossible to map exhaustively. Users who read the Internet newsgroup alt.cyberpunk report that several lists of cyberpunk fiction have circulated in the past three years. I have one compiled by Jonathan Drummey, dated 23 Feb. 1992, which lists 91 authors, including some who write only nonfiction. The *Beyond Cyberpunk* hypercard stack lists over 100 books, stories, and anthologies, whereas the FutureCulture list maintained by Andy Hawkins includes over 200. I list these fan bibliographies to illustrate how a community of readers constitutes a discursive field; it would be interesting to study how and why they determine who's in and who's not.

10   *Mondo 2000* has an interesting publishing history, having begun as a hacker's magazine, only to be transformed more recently into a slick, visually dense, techno-pop fanzine with high production values. Selections from the first eight issues have been collected into *The Mondo 2000 User's Guide to the New Edge*. Chapter topics include all the defining preoccupations of New Edge cyberpunks: smart drugs, computer graphics, chaos theory, electronic music/freedom, hip-hop, robots, street tech, vr, v-sex, wetware, multimedia, and the net (among other things). The book includes a bibliography titled "The Shopping Mall," which is a list of products, programs, music, journals, and books where you can "read/hear all about it." *The Mondo 2000 User's Guide to the New Edge,* ed. Rudy Rucker, R. U. Sirius, and Queen MU (New York: HarperPerennial, 1992).

11   Although clearly beyond the scope of this paper, such an analysis would also need to trace the enabling conditions for the emergence/convergence of the New Edge as cultural formation, notably the phenomenon of Star Trek fandom, the structure of feeling of punk rock & roll, phone phreaking, and the computerization of fantasy rpgs (role-playing games). Mixing in with these popular forms are a range of new technologies that are themselves being studied as important cultural phenomena; here I'm thinking of Brenda Laurel's work on computers as theater and Benjamin Woolley's study of virtual reality. Brenda Laurel, *Computers as Theater* (Reading, MA: Addison-Wesley, 1991); Benjamin Woolley, *Virtual Worlds: A Journey in Hype and Hyperreality* (Oxford, Eng.: Blackwell, 1992).

Other guides to the new technologies, new arts, and new cultural forms include: Stuart Brand, *The Media Lab: Inventing the Future at MIT* (New York: Viking Penguin, 1987); Constance Penley and Andrew Ross, eds., *Technoculture* (Minneapolis: U of Minnesota P, 1991); Michael Benedikt, ed., *Cyberspace: First Steps* (Cambridge: MIT P,

1991); Linda Jacobson, ed., *Cyberarts: Exploring Art and Technology* (San Francisco: Miller Freeman, 1992); journals such as *CyberEdge, Leonardo,* and *Presence;* magazines such as *Verbum, Wired, Mondo 2000, bOING bOING* and *Intertek;* E-zines and digests such as *Computer Underground Digest, Digital Free Press, Leri-L, Phrack, Surfpunk,* and *FutureCulture;* and catalogues from art exhibits such as *Bioapparatus* (Banff Arts Center, 1991) and Jeffrey Deitch, *Post Human* (New York: DAP, 1992).

12   De Lauretis, "Signs of Wa/onder" 160, 167, 170. Having identified the key periods in science fiction's literary history, de Lauretis puts the issue of periodization aside in favor of discussing the sign work of SF as a "mode of writing [and] a manner of reading." She points out two modes of signification unique to science fiction as an art form: (1) "SF uses language and narrative signs in a literal way" and (2) "technology is its diffuse landscape."

13   Suvin, "On Gibson and Cyberpunk SF" 49. Suvin uses William Gibson's novels to identify the genre conventions of "the best works" of cyberpunk science fiction, while Bruce Sterling's work serves as an "unworthy" example. However, Suvin's polarization of the two is somewhat reversed when he considers the two writers' more recent novels. Suvin claims that Gibson's third novel, *Mona Lisa Overdrive,* "confirms and solidifies his trajectory from critical to escapist use of cyberspace" (48).

14   Much of this work has focused on the postmodern qualities of Gibson's novels in particular. See, for example, David Porush, "Cybernauts in Cyberspace: William Gibson's Neuromancer," *Aliens: The Anthropology of Science Fiction,* ed. George Slusser (Carbondale: Southern Illinois P, 1987) 168–78; Miriyam Glazer, "'What Is Within Now Seen Without': Romanticism, Neuromanticism, and the Death of the Imagination in William Gibson's Fictive World," *Journal of Popular Culture* 23.3 (Winter 1989): 155–64; Glenn Grant, "Transcendence Through Detournement in William Gibson's *Neuromancer,*" *Science-Fiction Studies* 17 (1990): 41–49; Peter Fitting, "The Lessons of Cyberpunk," *Technoculture,* ed. Constance Penley and Andrew Ross (Minneapolis: U of Minnesota P, 1991) 295–315. Other writers elaborate the connection between cyberpunk and popular media: Brooks Landon, "Bet on IT: Cyber/Video/Punk/Performance," *Mississippi Review* 47/48 16.2/3 (1988): 245–51; George Slusser, "Literary MTV," *Mississippi Review* 47/48 16.2/3 (1988): 279–88. One of the first statements to thematize cyberpunk's generic characteristics was editor Bruce Sterling's preface to *Mirrorshades: The Cyberpunk Anthology* (New York: Ace, 1986).

15   Veronica Hollinger, "Cybernetic Deconstructions: Cyberpunk and Postmodernism," *Mosaic* 23.2 (Spring 1990): 29–44. Quotation is from page 31. If Hollinger misses anything in her careful reading, it is the multiplication of capitalist space, where the mise-en-scène of cyberpunk landscapes (cybernetic as well as the urban sprawl) don't signify just an excess of surface, but rather an excess of corporate territorialization. In this sense, Gibson's compulsive use of brand names is a testimony to the cybernetic expansion of multinationalist capitalism. On this point, see Hollinger; and Pam Rosenthal, "Jacked In: Fordism, Cyberpunk, Marxism," *Socialist Review* 21.1 (1991): 79–103.

16   Hollinger, "Cybernetic Deconstructions" 33.

17   Hollinger, "Cybernetic Deconstructions" 42.

18   Cadigan, *Synners* 386–87.

19   Jameson, *Postmodernism* 38.

20 Cadigan, *Synners* 109.

21 Fred Pfeil, *Another Tale to Tell: Politics and Narrative in Postmodern Culture* (London: Verso, 1990), 86.

22 Ibid.

23 Cadigan, *Synners*, 52–53.

24 Cadigan, *Synners*, 194.

25 Jean Baudrillard, *In the Shadow of the Silent Majorities . . . or the End of the Social,* trans. Paul Foss, Paul Patton, and John Johnston (New York: Semiotext(e), 1983) 95.

26 Carolyn Marvin, "Information and History," *The Ideology of the Information Age,* ed. Jennifer Daryl Slack and Fred Fejes (Norwood, N.J.: Ablex, 1987) 49–62. Quotation is from page 51.

27 Cadigan, *Synners*, 351.

28 Ibid., 7.

29 Ibid., 41.

30 Ibid., 239.

31 Ibid., 243.

32 Ibid., 213.

33 Ibid., 216.

34 Ibid., 232.

35 Ibid., 325.

36 Hollywood representations of technological hallucinations show an amazing visual similarity over time, using out-of-focus shots, swirling images that involve a pov sequence that moves through a worm hole, rapid edits, and illogically juxtaposed shots to suggest a technologically induced subjective state. See especially *The Trip* (1967), *Brainstorm* (1983), *Circuitry Man* (1989), *Freejack* (1992), *Until the End of the World* (1991).

37 Cadigan, *Synners* 400.

38 Ibid., 435.

39 Pfeil, *Another Tale* 89. In his study of Nintendo video games, Eugene Provenzo reports that when women are included as characters in video games they "are often cast as individuals who are acted upon rather than as initiators of action" (100). They are depicted as the princess or girlfriend in distress, who must be rescued by the male hero acting alone or as the leader of a team of fighters/magicians. Female characters may serve obliquely as the animating motive for the video search, journey, and fight narratives, but they do so only as victims who are unable to rescue themselves. Video games designed for other gaming systems show a similar stereotyping of female characters. In the Sega Genesis game *Phantasy Star III,* for example, the video player can choose female cyborgs as members of his team of adventurers; in the course of this game the hero's team encounters many powerful monsters depicted as seductive women. Even when the games include women characters on the fighting/journeying team, they still serve at the behest of the male warrior figure, who is the real agent in the gaming narrative. Girls who *play* video games have no other choice but to play the male main character who rescues the pretty princess or, in the case of Nintendo's *Maniac Mansion,* Sandy the Cheerleader. "Thus the games not only socialize women to be dependent, but also condition men to assume dominant gender roles" (100). Eugene F. Provenzo, Jr., *Video Kids: Making Sense of Nintendo* (Cambridge: Harvard UP, 1991).

40   Andrew Ross, *Strange Weather: Culture, Science, and Technology in the Age of Limits* (London: Verso, 1991) 145.

41   My thanks to Ron Schleiffer for helping me work out the nuances of the cells' relationship to one another. See Ronald Schleiffer, *A. J. Greimas and the Nature of Meaning: Linguistics, Semiotics, and Discourse Theory* (Lincoln: U of Nebraska P, 1987).

42   For an especially insightful discussion between Susie Bright and Brenda Laurel on the erotic possibilities of virtual sex, see "The Virtual Orgasm," *Susie Bright's Sexual Reality: A Virtual Sex World Reader* (Pittsburgh: Cleis, 1992) 60–70.

43   Allucquére Rosanne Stone, "Will the Real Body Please Stand Up?: Boundary Stories about Virtual Cultures," *Cyberspace: First Steps,* ed. Michael Benedikt (Cambridge: MIT P, 1992) 109. See also Sally Pryor, "Thinking of Oneself as a Computer," *Leonardo* 24.5 (1991): 585–90.

44   Stone, "Real Body" 113. I would argue that the repression of the material body is discursively accomplished in part because of the very intelligence of the techno-body: just as driving a car becomes physiologically intuitive, so too does using a VR rig. As a newly emergent popular cultural form, embodied encounters with VR are more virtual than real at this point (see chapter 5).

45   For discussions of the ethical/policy dimensions of computer communication, see: Jeffrey Bairstow, "Who Reads Your Electronic Mail?" *Electronic Business* 16.11 (11 June 1990): 92; Bob Brown, "EMA Urges Users to Adopt Policy on E-mail Privacy," *Network World* 7.44 (29 Oct. 1990): 2; Pamela Varley, "Electronic Democracy," *Technology Review* Nov./Dec. 1991: 40–43; Laurence H. Tribe, "The Constitution in Cyberspace," *The Humanist* 51.5 (Sept./Oct. 1991): 15–21; Willard Uncapher, "Trouble in Cyberspace," *The Humanist* 51.5 (Sept./Oct. 1991): 5–14.

Other studies of new modes of computer communication include: Magoroh Maruyama, "Information and Communication in Polyepistemological Systems," *The Myths of Information: Technology and Postindustrial Culture,* ed. Kathleen Woodward (Madison, Wis.: Coda, 1980) 28–40; Lee Sproull and Sara Kiesler, "Replacing Context Cues: Electronic Mail in Organizational Communication," *Management Science* 32 (1986): 1492–1512; R. E. Rice and G. Lover, "Electronic Emotion: Socioemotional Content in a Computer-Mediated Network," *Communication Research* 14 (1987): 85–108; James W. Chesebro and Donald G. Bonsall, *Computer-Mediated Communication: Human Relationships in a Computerized World* (Tuscaloosa: U of Alabama, 1989).

46   For a discussion of the gendered nature of communication technologies, see especially Lana Rakow, "Women and the Telephone: The Gendering of a Communications Technology," *Technology and Women's Voices: Keeping in Touch,* ed. Cheris Kramarea (Boston: Routledge, 1988). For other studies of the gendered nature of computer use, see Sara Kiesler, Lee Sproull, and Jacquelynne Eccles, "Poolhalls, Chips and War Games: Women in the Culture of Computing," *Psychology of Women Quarterly* 9.4 (Dec. 1985): 451–62; and Sherry Turkle and Seymour Papert, "Epistemological Pluralism: Styles and Voices within the Computer Culture." *SIGNS* 16.11 (1990): 128–57.

47   The Jargon File, version 2.0.10, July 1992. Available on-line from: ftp.uu.net. Also published as The Hacker's Dictionary.

48   See especially: Sherry Turkle and Seymour Papert, "Epistemological Pluralism"; and Dannielle Bernstein, "Comfort and Experience with Computing: Are They the Same for Women and Men?" *SIGCSE Bulletin* 23.3 (Sept. 1991): 57–60.

49 These discussions took place over several days in late 1992 and included a dozen participants, most of whom signed their postings with masculine handles.

50 Hoai-An Truong, "Gender Issues in Online Communication," CFP 93 (Version 4.1). Available on-line from: ftp.eff.org.

51 Carolyn Kay Steedman, *Landscape for a Good Woman: A Story of Two Lives* (New Brunswick, N.J.: Rutgers UP, 1987) 6.

52 Steedman, *Landscape* 6–7.

53 Steven Best and Douglas Kellner, *Postmodern Theory: Critical Interrogations* (New York: Guilford, 1991) 274.

54 In Raymond Kurzweil's account of the history of the computer, the identity of "the world's first programmer" is left out of the chapter title: "Charles Babbage and the World's First Programmer." We discover on the next page that "though Babbage was a lonely man obsessed with his vision of a programmable computer, he developed a liaison with the beautiful Ada Lovelace, the only legitimate child of Lord Byron, the poet. She became as obsessed as Babbage with the project and contributed many of the ideas for programming the machine, including the invention of the programming loop and the subroutine" (167). Apparently Lovelace translated a description of Babbage's machine, The Analytical Engine, and "included extensive discussion on programming techniques, sample programs, and the potential of this technology to emulate intelligent human activities" (167). Lovelace was honored by the U.S. Defense Department when it named its programming language after her: ADA. Lovelace and Captain Grace Murray Hooper (who is credited with developing the programming language COBOL) are usually the only two women who appear in histories of the computer. See Raymond Kurzweil, *In the Age of Intelligent Machines* (Cambridge: MIT P, 1990). For a brief biography of Ada Byron Lovelace (1815–1852), see Teri Perl, *Math Equals: Biographies of Women Mathematicians* (Menlo Park, Calif.: Addison-Wesley, 1978).

55 For their first assignment in my "Science, Technology, and Gender" course, students are required to write a basic biography/bibliography on any one of the 350 names listed in an appendix to Ogilivie's *Women in Science: Antiquity through the Nineteenth Century — A Biographical Dictionary with Annotated Bibliography* (Boston: MIT P, 1986). Students are instructed to document their research process, especially false leads or dead ends. I explain that discovering where women are *not* found is as interesting as discovering where they are found — especially if they aren't mentioned in sources that purport to be encyclopedias of "great men in science/mathematics/astronomy," etc.

56 Joan Rothschild, "Introduction," *Machina Ex Dea: Feminist Perspectives on Technology* (New York: Pergamon, 1983) xviii. In her 1982 review of women and the history of American technology, Judith McGaw identifies Ruth Schwartz Cowan's address to the 1976 meetings of the Society of the History of Technology as a significant founding moment for the feminist study of technology. It was also a *literal* founding moment for the organization of Women in Technological History (WITH). Judith A. McGaw, "Women and the History of American Technology," *Signs* 7.4 (1982): 798–828.

Other collections on the relationship between women and technological history include: Annie Nathan Meyer, *Woman's Work in America: Images and Realities* (New York: Henry Hold, 1891); Susan B. Anthony II, *Out of the Kitchen — Into the War: Women's Winning Role in the Nation's Drama* (New York: Stephen Daye, 1943);

Elizabeth Faulkner Baker, *Technology and Women's Work* (New York: Columbia UP, 1964); Martha Moore Trescott, ed., *Dynamos and Virgins Revisited: Women and Technological Change* (Metuchen, NJ: Scarecrow, 1979): Delores Hayden, *The Grand Domestic Revolution: A History of Feminist Designs for American Homes, Neighborhoods, and Cities* (Cambridge: MIT P, 1981); Marguerite Zientara, *Women, Technology and Power: Ten Stars and the History They Made* (New York: American Management Assoc., 1987); Barbara Drygulski Wright, ed., *Women, Work and Technology: Transformations* (Ann Arbor: U of Michigan P, 1987).

57   Autumn Stanley, "Women Hold Up Two-Thirds of the Sky: Notes for a Revised History of Technology," Rothschild, *Machina Ex Dea* 3–22. See also Judy Wajcman's discussion of how women are "hidden from histories of technology" in her book *Feminism Confronts Technology* (University Park: Pennsylvania State UP, 1991). A more popular treatment of the topic is Ethlie Ann Vare and Greg Ptacek, *Mothers of Invention: From the Bra to the Bomb, Forgotten Women and Their Unforgettable Ideas* (New York: Quill William Morrow, 1987).

58   See especially Cynthia Cockburn, *Machinery of Dominance: Women, Men and Technical Know-How* (London: Pluto, 1985); Wendy Faulkner and Erik Arnold, eds., *Smothered by Invention: Technology and Women's Lives* (London: Pluto, 1985); R. Arditti, R. Duelli-Klein, and Shelly Minden, eds., *Test-Tube Women: What Future for Motherhood?* (Boston: Pandora, 1984); Gina Corea, *The Mother Machine: Reproductive Technologies from Artificial Insemination to Artificial Wombs* (New York: Harper and Row, 1985); Michelle Stanworth, ed., *Reproductive Technologies: Gender, Motherhood, and Medicine* (Minneapolis: U of Minnesota P, 1987); H. Patricia Hynes, ed., *Reconstructing Babylon: Essays on Women and Technology* (Bloomington: Indiana UP, 1991): Ruth Schwartz Cowan, *More Work for Mother: The Ironies of Household Technology from the Open Hearth to the Microwave* (New York: Basic, 1983); Marion Roberts, *Living in a Man-Made World: Gender Assumptions in Modern Housing Design* (London: Routledge, 1991). Much of this work on technology is closely related to feminist studies of science, scientific knowledge, and the social arrangements supported by scientific evidence. I omit references to this material for space considerations.

59   See the chapter "Historical Patterns of Technological Change," in Heidi I. Hartmann, Robert E. Kraut, and Louise A. Tilly, eds., *Computer Chips and Paper Clips: Technology and Women's Employment* (Washington, D.C.: National Academy P, 1986) 40.

60   Other studies of women and workplace technology include: Margery Davis, *Woman's Place Is at the Typewriter: Office Work and Office Workers 1870–1930* (Philadelphia: Temple UP, 1982); Judith S. McIlwee and J. Gregg Robinson, *Women in Engineering: Gender, Power and Workplace Culture* (Albany: SUNY, 1992); and Uma Sekaran and Frederick T. L. Leong, eds., *WomanPower: Managing in Times of Demographic Turbulence* (Newbury Park, Calif.: Sage, 1992).

61   As a more recent contribution to the study of women's relationship to the technology of the workplace, Ruth Perry and Lisa Greber edited a special issue of *SIGNS*, published in 1990, on the topic of women and computers. The scholarship that they review considers the impact of the computer on women's employment and the structural forces that limit women's access to computer education. Ruth Perry and Lisa Greber, "Women and Computers: An Introduction," *SIGNS* 16.1 (1990): 74–101.

Other studies of the relationship between women, computing, and computer science education include: Diane Werneke, *Microelectronics and Office Jobs: The Impact of the Chip on Women's Employment* (London: International Labour Office, 1983); R. Deakin, *Women and Computing: The Golden Opportunity* (London: Macmillan, 1984); Agneta Olerup, Leslie Schneider, Elsbeth Monod, eds., *Women, Work and Computerization: Opportunities and Disadvantages* (North-Holland: Elsevier, 1985); Barbara Garson, *The Electronic Sweatshop: How Computers are Transforming the Office of the Future into the Factory of the Past* (New York: Simon and Schuster, 1988); Jill Lippitt, "The Feminist Face of Computer Technology," *Woman of Power: A Magazine of Feminism, Spirituality, and Politics* 11 (Fall 1988): 56–57; Sally Hacker, *Pleasure, Power and Technology: Some Tales of Gender, Engineering and the Cooperative Workplace* (London: Unwin Hyman, 1989); Karen A. Frenkel, "Women and Computing," *Communications of the ACM* 33.11 (Nov. 1990): 34–46; Pamela E. Kramer and Sheila Lehman, "Mismeasuring Women: A Critique of Research on Computer Ability and Avoidance." *SIGNS* 16.11 (1990): 158–72; J. Webster, *Office Automations: The Secretarial Labour Process and Women's Work in Britain* (Hemel Hempstead: Harvester Wheatsheaf, 1990); Gillian Lovegrove and Barbara Segal, eds., *Women into Computing: Selected Papers 1988–1990* (London: Springer-Verlag, 1991); Inger V. Eriksson, Barbara A. Kitchenham, and Kea G. Tijdens, eds., *Women, Work and Computerization: Understanding and Overcoming Bias in Work and Education* (North Holland: Elsevier, 1991); Dannielle Bernstein, "Comfort and Experience with Computing: Are They the Same for Women and Men?" *SIGCSE Bulletin* 23.3 (Sept. 1991): 57–60; Gill Kirkup and Laurie Smith Keller, eds., *Inventing Women: Science, Technology and Gender* (Cambridge, Eng.: Polity, 1992).

62 See chapter 5, "Conclusions and Recommendations," in Hartmann, Kraut, and Tilly, eds., *Computer Chips and Paper Clips: Technology and Women's Employment.*

63 Levidow explores the "price paid for cheap chips" in terms of the harassment and forms of control that Malaysian women endure. See Les Levidow, "Women Who Make the Chips," *Science as Culture* 2.10 (Part 1: 1991): 103–24. See also Aihwa Ong's ethnographic study *Spirits of Resistance and Capitalist Discipline: Factory Women in Malaysia* (Albany: SUNY UP, 1987).

64 Nancy Tosta (chief of the Branch of Geographic Data Coordination of the National Mapping Division, U.S. Geological Survey, Reston, Virginia), "Who's Got the Data?" *Geo Info Systems* Sept. 1992: 24–27. Tosta's prediction is supported by other statements about the U.S. government's efforts to build a Geographic Information System (GIS). A database system whereby "all public information can be referenced by location," the GIS is hailed as "an information integrator." The best use of GIS would be to support the coordination of local, regional, and national organizations — both governmental and private. See Lisa Warnecke, "Building the National GI/GIS Partnership," *Geo Info Systems* Apr. 1992: 16–23.

Managing data, acquiring new data, and guarding data integrity are issues of concern for GIS managers. Because of the costs of acquiring new data and guarding data integrity, GIS managers sometimes charge a fee for providing information. This process of charging "has thrown [them] into a morass of issues about public records and freedom of information; the value of data, privacy, copyrights, and liability and the roles of public and private sectors in disseminating information." Nancy Tosta, "Public Access: Right or Privilege?" *Geo Info Systems* Nov./Dec. 1991: 20–25+.

65 Kenneth B. Allen, "Access to Government Information," *Government Information Quarterly* 9.1 (1992): 68.

66 Teola P. Hunter, for one, argues that African American women must seek out potential political candidates who are already "appearing in city council seats, on county commissions, on school boards, in chambers of commerce and on many advisory boards at all levels of government" (49). The key for success that these women hold is their connection to "civil rights groups, education groups, and church groups." Hunter goes on to argue that when "minority women use these contacts and these bonds, they have a support base that is hard to match" (52). Teola P. Hunter, "A Different View of Progress — Minority Women in Politics," *Journal of State Government* Apr./June 1991: 48–52.

67 Council of State Governments, *Suggested State Legislation* 51 (1992): 17–19.

68 Jennifer Terry, "The Body Invaded: Medical Surveillance of Women as Reproducers," *Socialist Review* 39 (1989): 13–44.

69 An advertisement that appeared in *Essence* magazine in 1991 publicized Garrett Morgan's invention of the traffic light. The ad also illustrates the subtle appropriation of a black agent to support the ideological myth of technological progress, where a racist system can somehow be vanquished through a technological fix. The advertisement was sponsored by Amtrak, and includes a picture of a traffic light and the caption "How do you see the road in front of you?" The rest of the ad reads:

> The opportunity to get ahead isn't always a matter of red or green. Historically, it's often been a question of black and white. Luckily, Garrett A. Morgan didn't see color as an obstacle. Instead, this son of a former slave overcame tremendous prejudice to become one of the most important American inventors of this century. His creations ranged from a hair straightening cream to the gas mask which saved thousands of lives during WWI. But it was Mr. Morgan's development of the traffic signal which perhaps best symbolizes his life. In 1923, automobiles were increasing in number, and so, unfortunately were automobile accidents. After witnessing one down the street from his house, he developed and sold his patent for a traffic safety light to General Electric — the forerunner of the traffic light we see on practically every corner in the world. It typified his concern for the safety of people everywhere. His perseverance, and his refusal to let the color of his skin color anyone's perception of his ability. Which brings us the true lesson of Garrett A. Morgan. He may have invented the traffic signal. But he never saw a red light. *Essence* Feb. 1991: 95.

70 For a discussion of the technological takeover of higher education in Britain, one that offers insights into the shift away from the humanities and social sciences and toward technological and managerial fields that is going on right now in the U.S., see Kevin Robins and Frank Webster, "Higher Education, High Tech, High Rhetoric," *Compulsive Technology: Computers as Culture,* ed. Tony Solomenides and Les Levidow (London: Free Association, 1985) 36–57.

Epilogue

1 Elizabeth Grosz, "Notes towards a Corporeal Feminism," *Australian Feminist Studies* 5 (Summer 1987 special issue on "Feminism and the Body"; guest editors Judith Allen and Elizabeth Grosz): 1–16.

2   I review a wide range of body scholarship in an annotated bibliography and review essay on the body: "Reading the Gendered Body in Contemporary Culture: An Annotated Bibliography." *Women and Language* 13.1 (1990): 64–85.

3   Elizabeth Grosz, *Volatile Bodies: Toward a Corporeal Feminism* (Bloomington: Indiana UP, 1994) ix.

4   Here Grosz joins forces with other feminists such as Rosi Braidotti, Elspeth Probyn, Linda Singer, Moria Gatens, and Judith Butler, who in different ways have tried to reconceptualize the foundation of a specifically materialist corporeal feminism. See Rosi Braidotti, "Organs Without Bodies," *differences* 1.1 (Winter 1989): 147–61; Elspeth Probyn, "This Body Which Is Not One: Speaking an Embodied Self," *Hypatia* 6.3 (Fall 1991): 111–24; Linda Singer, *Erotic Welfare: Sexual Theory and Politics in the Age of Epidemic* (New York: Routledge, 1993); Moria Gatens, *Feminism and Philosophy: Perspectives on Difference and Equality* (Cambridge, Mass.: Polity, 1991); and, Judith Butler, *Gender Trouble: Feminism and the Subversion of Identity* (New York: Routledge, 1990).

5   Grosz, *Volatile Bodies* 189.

6   Grosz, *Volatile Bodies* 208.

INDEX

✳

Levidow, Les, 153
LIFE magazine, 1, 6, 7, 165n. 1
Liposuction Institute, 70, 73
Logli, Paul, 99
Lorde, Andre, 168–169n. 11
Lovelace, Ada, 207n. 54

Maher, Lisa, 103
Marvin, Carolyn, 139
Masculinity: cults of, 42; female, 47–54
Material body/ies: in cyborg conjunction,
   11–12, 32–33, 39; and epistemology,
   139; ontology of, 158–159; relation to
   discourse, 81, 83; as site of ideological
   struggle, 10; transformation of, 13, 56–
   79
Maternal body. *See* Reproductive body
Mauss, Marcel, 24, 171n. 9
Max Headroom, 17, 19
McLish, Rachel, 47, 48, 49–51, 53
McLuhan, Marshall, 12, 28–30, 118, 171–
   172n. 14, 173–174n. 20
Mead, Margaret, 93
Media: analysis of, 1, 4–5, 12, 13–14; rep-
   resentation of women, 12–13, 41, 43–
   55, 108
Medical discourse: the body in, 26–28, 42,
   166n. 5; in film, 57; gender identity in, 9,
   36–38
Metropolis (film), 17, 18
Military operations, U.S. *See* Gulf War
Miller, Frank, 17
Mondo 2000, 15, 117–120, 131–132,
   134–135, 203n. 10
Morgan, Kathryn Pauly, 66, 183n. 61
Mouffe, Chantal, 16, 170n. 20
Muscle and Fitness, 47, 49
Myth, 15, 35, 42, 53

Narratives: absence of, in virtual reality,
   127–128; as expressive resources, 161–
   162; family, 51, 54, 133, 150–151, 176n.
   14, 201n. 4; feminist, 155; of self, 150–151
National Aeronautics and Space Administration (NASA), 121

Nature, 15, 26–27, 33
Neuromancer (Gibson), 79, 117, 129
Neurotoxicology and Teratology, 106–107,
   108
New Edge, 15, 151, 203nn. 10–11

Other, 30, 32–33, 46–47, 55, 167n. 7

Pfeil, Fred, 127–129, 138, 144–145
Plackinger, Tina, 43–45
Plastic surgery. *See* Cosmetic surgery
Poovey, Mary, 26–27, 36
Postmodernism/postmodernity, 5, 18, 32,
   39, 41, 78, 145, 151, 159. *See also* Body
   scholarship: postmodern; Cultural crit-
   icism, feminist: of postmodernism;
   Cyberpunk science fiction: postmodern-
   ism in
Powell, Nelson, 59
Power. *See* Technology: power articulated
   through
Pregnancy: access to health care during,
   102–103; public, 13–14, 80, 154–155.
   See also Reproductive body; Reproduc-
   tive technology
Pregnancy Risk Assessment Monitoring
   System (PRAMS), 104
Prenatal Exposure to Controlled Substances
   Act, 154
Proportions of the Aesthetic Face, 59–62
Prosthetics, 1, 6–9, 168–169nn. 10–11,
   173n. 19
Provenzo, Eugene, 205n. 39
Public health: policies, 110–112; and
   women, 14, 102–112
Public Health Service, U.S., 102
Pumping Iron II: The Women (video), 12–
   13, 41, 47–55

Race, 53–55, 160, 176n. 14, 210n. 69; and
   cosmetic surgery, 60–63, 70; in cyberpunk science fiction, 144, 155; and female athletes, 45–47, 51–55; and
   pregnancy, 99–100, 102–103, 105–106.
   See also Body: race-marked

Anne Balsamo is Assistant Professor in the School of
Literature, Communication, and Culture at the Georgia
Institute of Technology.

Library of Congress Cataloging-in-Publication Data
Balsamo, Anne Marie, 1959–
Technologies of the gendered body : reading cyborg
women / Anne Balsamo.
Includes index.
ISBN 0-8223-1686-2 (cloth : alk. paper). — ISBN
0-8223-1698-6 (pbk. : alk. paper)
1. Feminist theory. 2. Cybernetics — Social aspects. 3. Body,
Human — Social aspects. 4. Gender identity. I. Title.
HQ1190.B35 1995
305.42'01 — dc20   95-22648 CIP